JOINT TRAINING PROGRAMS

A Union-Management Approach to Preparing Workers For the Future

Louis A. Ferman, Michele Hoyman,
Joel Cutcher-Gershenfeld,
and Ernest J. Savoie, Editors

ILR Press
Ithaca, New York

Library of Congress Cataloging-in-Publication Data

Joint training programs : a union-management approach to preparing
  workers for the future / Louis A. Ferman . . . [et al.], editors.
      p.   cm.
    Includes bibliographical references and index.
    ISBN 0–87546–177–8 (alk. paper). — ISBN 0–87546–178–6
  (pbk. : alk. paper).
      1. Employees—Training of—United States.   2. Occupational
  training—United States.   3. Occupational retraining—United States.
  4. Labor-management committees—United States.   I. Ferman, Louis A.
  HF5549.5.T7J53   1991
  331.25′92′0973—dc20   91–13215

Copies may be ordered through bookstores or directly from
ILR Press
School of Industrial and Labor Relations
Cornell University
Ithaca, NY 14853-3901

Printed on acid-free paper in the United States of America
5   4   3   2   1

To the next generation, especially Courteney, Gabriel, Jonathan, Daniel, Leigh, Harry, Ned, Courtney, Bill, Patrick, Colin, and Lauren

CONTENTS

ACKNOWLEDGMENTS

We would like to thank Frances Benson, the director of ILR Press, for helping to guide this venture from conceptualization through to publication. We would also like to thank Erica Fox, the managing editor of ILR Press, who assiduously and tirelessly edited the manuscript. She went beyond the usual tasks of editor and contributed considerably to the format and structure of the volume. We are also deeply indebted to Lana Vierdag, John Kalinowski, and Jan Frantzen for their many hours of work preparing the manuscript. They were cheerful to the end. Last but not least, we received many valuable suggestions from the editorial committee of ILR Press and the manuscript reviewers. We made every effort to incorporate their suggestions.

1 · INTRODUCTION

Louis A. Ferman, Michele Hoyman, Joel Cutcher-Gershenfeld, and Ernest J. Savoie

In workplaces across the country, dramatic innovations are occurring in the fields of training and personal development. One of these innovations—joint labor-management training programs—is the focus of this book.

As with any new development, joint labor-management training programs have distinctive characteristics: negotiated contract language by which they are established; a fund for their operation; jointness in all decisions and as an operating principle; and a range of services such as career counseling, vocational training, and relocation assistance that are offered to bargaining unit members.

This book examines a broad range of new training initiatives that are governed jointly by employers and unions. In many cases, state and local governments also join in, thereby forming a tripartite arrangement. In addition, secondary schools and institutions of higher education often participate. Thus this volume focuses not only on timely issues in labor-management relations but on concerns of government and education as well.

Not all joint training programs have been equally successful. But, likewise, some, such as the early programs in the automobile industry, have been so bold and imaginative as to suggest that joint training programs could irreversibly change the contours of industrial relations.

1

The broad purposes of this volume are to document the range of programs that are being established by employers and unions, to assess the functioning and results of these programs, and to offer some insights for practitioners, scholars, and policy makers. The task is a challenging one in that many joint training programs are still in a formative stage and there is a great deal of diversity across programs.

This introduction serves two functions: to provide a general framework for thinking about union-management training programs and to present an overview of the volume.

Joint Training Programs: A Conceptual Framework

We will begin by defining what we mean by union-management training programs. We will then consider some of the forces associated with their emergence, how joint training programs are structured, and, in a preliminary way, the benefits and costs associated with such programs.

What Is a Joint Training Program?

First and foremost, joint training programs are governed jointly by unions and employers. This is in sharp contrast to training programs that are governed unilaterally just by employers, just by unions, or just by government.

Second, the focus of the programs is on training and personal development.[1] Some programs offer classes in areas such as strategic planning skills and economic principles for hourly workers. Others offer such traditional services as training and assistance for displaced workers. All the programs described in this volume represent departures from preexisting training programs, however, in that they include personal development courses rather than just narrow, job-specific training.

Third, joint training programs involve populations of workers who are not usually reached by unilateral programs. Most unilateral

---

1. This is in contrast to joint programs focused on issues such as worker participation/quality circles, health and safety, employee assistance, and product quality. Typically, the emphasis in training programs, relatively speaking, is more on employee goals, whereas it is more on employer goals in worker participation/quality circle programs.

employer-sponsored training is aimed at professional, technical, and top-level managerial employees (Fossum 1990). Clerical and production workers tend to receive relatively little employer-sponsored training, and if they do, it tends to be focused on job-specific skills. In contrast, most unilateral union-sponsored training is either skills-oriented or applied training aimed at enhancing the functioning of union members and officials; apprenticeship training for skilled trades employees; or ad hoc initiatives for targeted populations such as displaced workers (Gray and Kornbluh 1990). Finally, most unilateral government-sponsored training is targeted at the disadvantaged—unemployed youth, displaced workers, the poor, or other groups that are subject to discrimination in the labor market (Levitan and Gallo 1990). By comparison, participants in joint training programs represent a broad range of active workers who do not traditionally have access to training.

Fourth, although there is often a great deal of collaboration and problem solving associated with joint programs, there also tends to be conflict. Both cooperation and conflict are part of the process.

Origins of Joint Training Programs

A number of economic and social conditions inspired the development of joint labor-management training programs. These include intensified global and local competition; industrial restructuring and geographical shifts in the location of industry (Bluestone and Harrison 1986); the relative decline of the goods-producing sector and the continuing growth of employment in the service sector; widespread technological change, especially in information processing and control; the deregulation of some industries; changes in the growth and composition of the work force; concern about the quality of education and of the new entrants to the labor force; and concern that better-educated, middle-aged workers face declining opportunities for upward mobility.

Each of these factors individually and in combination has affected unions and work forces in different ways and to different degrees. Many organizations suffered deep financial losses, significant reductions in union membership, a period of so-called concessionary bargaining, and a period of slow growth in worker income and benefits. In some cases, the stage was set for increasingly contentious relations. In others, companies and unions began working together in nontraditional ways, with the focus on increased employee participation and decision making and improved product quality and operating efficiency as necessary for job security and a return to profitability. As these efforts proceeded, industrial relations underwent what some scholars have termed a transformation (Kochan, Katz, and McKersie 1987).

Joint training initiatives are among the furthest reaching changes in industrial relations. Joint training promised to help address the realities of dislocation and permanent layoff, while assisting active workers in facing the changes caused by new technology, global competition, and new business practices. From a management perspective, joint training would help workers adjust to the shorter product cycles, shifts in the way production is organized, higher standards of quality, and increased pressures on cost.

Clearly, there were also advantages for unions and their members in initiating joint training programs. Some unions were beginning to recognize that workers' job responsibilities change many times in their lifetimes, even if their job titles do not change. Furthermore, there is an increasing likelihood that even production workers will have two or three distinct careers. With the compounding impact of corporate restructuring, takeovers, mergers, and corporate joint ventures, fundamental shifts in the structure of jobs are assured.

To the general public, the unionized sector of the economy is often seen as resistant to change. The breadth and scope of the programs reported in this volume are thus especially noteworthy. Compared to traditional unilateral programs, we find increased input, especially from workers, into the content of the training; powerful systems of checks and balances in program administration; a greater capacity to link with government and educational institutions; and, ultimately, a higher degree of legitimacy, stability, and success. Indeed, one of the key conclusions in this volume is that, although joint training programs are often complex to administer, they offer a range of advantages over traditional unilateral programs.

Scope and Structure of Joint Training Programs
Joint training programs depend on the existence of a relatively strong union-management relationship; an understanding by all parties of the potential value of new training initiatives; the commit-

ment of substantial resources; leadership; vision; and the capacity to administer a long-term and constantly evolving set of activities. Thus one would expect that joint initiatives would be rare. In fact, as discussed in chapter 2, they are quite common, especially in firms where other joint initiatives are in place. Programs have not emerged randomly, however; they are concentrated in the large manufacturing firms in the Midwest.

Union-management training programs are a new social phenomenon, so that describing and classifying them is challenging. There is great variation in the purposes driving the establishment of programs, in the structures that are created, in the scope of programs, and in the way programs and administrative structures evolve over time. Sometimes programs are established to address a highly specific training need, such as results after a plant closing. At other times, a broad institutional structure is established under union-management governance to address a wide range of training issues. Further, there is great variation in the degree of jointness embodied in the initiative and in the relation of the program to other joint or unilateral programs.

Needless to say, variations in the origins and purposes of joint training are reflected directly in the size, scope, and formality of the administrative structures. But even more important in determining their profile is the structure of the employer and the union, as well as the nature and stage of labor-management relations. Does more than one union represent the work force? Is industry collective bargaining highly centralized? Are there multiple work sites that are organized into divisions or other structures? What is the geographical spread, the industry composition, and the degree of centralization of power among the unions that are parties to these programs? These are just some of the issues that shape joint initiatives. As a result, there are a range of administrative structures, including national centers that work in tandem with work site joint initiatives; national centers that bring programming into the field; entirely local, work site–specific initiatives; joint programs that provide seed money and/or coordinate government training programs; and consortiums involving multiple employers and/or multiple unions.

The scope of training offered under joint programs also varies dramatically. We have observed programs that include training for displaced workers (e.g., job search assistance training to enhance existing skills and training for new careers); traditional training in job-specific skills; training associated with the introduction of new technology and new work systems; training aimed at improving organizational operations (e.g., quality control, health and safety, benefits administration, just-in-time delivery, employee involvement, or general business or union operations); basic skills training (e.g., literacy skills and high school equivalency); and training for personal development and career planning (e.g., public speaking, retirement planning, and college-degree programs). Changes in the range of topics that will be addressed may be made by any of the parties in response to changes in workers' needs and preferences, the competitive environment, company strategies or plans, and national union or local leadership. Frequently, the focus expands over time as changes in circumstances and new opportunities emerge.

Given the great variation and willingness to change endemic to joint training programs, there is a great potential for cross-site learning. Each program is a potential source of new ideas for others. There may not be a single "best" model, however. Thus the typical approach of pattern setting and imitation in collective bargaining may not be well suited to crafting and sustaining a joint training initiative.

Costs versus Benefits

A number of the benefits associated with union-management training programs derive at least in part from their joint structure. First, evidence suggests that the joint structure provides an important vehicle for high levels of participation by unions and employees in determining the programs to be offered at a given work site. High levels of program participation by workers tend to follow. Second, a system of checks and balances is built into the governance of the programs that seems to ensure that the needs of multiple constituencies are met. This system can have positive, reinforcing effects. Third, when a union and an employer jointly approach government and educational institutions, the resulting agreements tend to be stronger than those that occur when just an employer or just a union approaches these institutions. Fourth, because these programs are jointly operated, they tend to last longer than unilateral programs, which can be discontinued without the consent of the other party.

Setting up a joint training program is not cost-free. Virtually all are conducted in addition to unilateral programs. Also, because more parties are involved in decision making than in unilateral programs, a broader range, or at least a different mix, of training activities is likely to be offered. There may also be indirect costs. Union leaders may be charged with being "too close to management," for example. And managers may suffer indirect costs because they are associated with a decision-making process regarding matters that were previously subject to their unilateral control. Assessing these and other costs relative to the benefits of joint training programs is difficult, partly because the programs are still so new and measuring long-term results is still so difficult.

Many of the contributors to this volume expand on the above observations. Nonetheless, as the concluding chapter makes clear, we have only just begun to assess the impact of joint training programs.

Overview of the Volume

Each chapter in this book can stand on its own, but a number of important themes also span the volume. Chapter 2, on the scope and extent of joint labor-management training programs, by Michele Hoyman and Louis Ferman, offers data on the extent of such programs in the United States based on a 1988 survey of organizations in which there was some degree of labor-management cooperation. The next four chapters describe leading union-management initiatives. These are not case studies in the usual sense of the term, in that each was written by a practitioner who is directly involved in joint training activities. As such, the authors, especially of the first two case descriptions, have a strong bias in favor of their programs. The latter two cases were also written by individuals with direct ties to the programs, but their links are as third parties, affording them a more critical perspective.

The first case description, by Donald Treinen and Kenneth Ross, focuses on training programs being offered by the Communications Workers of America (CWA) and the International Brotherhood of Electrical Workers (IBEW) with the American Telephone and Telegraph Company (AT&T). Both technological change and divestiture in the telecommunications industry were major forces in establishing these programs. The parties face a unique set of dilemmas in that the work force is highly diverse and scattered over thousands of locations yet is represented by only two unions. In response, a structure is developing whereby a central joint operation (called the Alliance) brings "portable" joint programming into the field. The driving ideology behind this program is that of empowerment.

The second case description, by Elizabeth Tomasko and Kenneth Dickinson, presents a model that is typical of developments in the U.S. auto industry. Their focus is the UAW-Ford joint training program, which operates both a strong national center (the UAW-Ford National Development and Training Center) and a network of smaller programs in individual plants. The UAW-Ford case vividly illustrates the way joint programs may change over time insofar as joint training at Ford was initially aimed at addressing the needs of displaced workers (during the downturn of the early 1980s) but was later refocused on the needs of the existing work force. The UAW-Ford case appears to encompass the most robust range of programs under a joint structure to date.

The third case description, by Susan Schurman, Margrit Hugentobler, and Hal Stack, offers details on and a critical assessment of one of the most innovative programs that has emerged out of the range of joint programs offered by the UAW and General Motors. The Paid Educational Leave (PEL) program provides hundreds of local and regional union officials, as well as their management counterparts, four-week off-site sessions on topics ranging from the changing world economy, to principles of economics, to new developments in industrial relations, to the political context facing labor and management, to strategic planning skills. The program has recently been expanded to include dozens of local PEL programs in which the same topics are presented in condensed form to hourly workers during one week. The authors have direct experience as developers and trainers in the PEL program. They do more than just describe the joint initiatives, however; they also place them in the context of a broader theoretical framework for labor-management cooperation.

The fourth and final case description, by Lois Gray, Thomas Quimby, and Kathy Schrier, traces the ten-year history of union-management training programs in New York State. The authors provide the most complete documentation to date on the number and variety of such programs. As they discuss, some of the characteristics of the public sector in New York State, such as the extent and penetration of union membership and the tradition of "innovation," may be unique—or at least different—from the situation in other public sector settings. Thus, although Gray, Quimby, and Schrier are optimistic about the role of joint programs in transforming the workplace, they remain uncertain whether the conditions that led to their emergence could be replicated in other public sector settings.

Chapters 7 and 8 focus on training for dislocated workers. The former is written from the perspective of labor; the latter, from the perspective of state government. Chapter 7, by Michael McMillan, reviews a range of experiences with union-management initiatives (often involving government) and offers an unambiguous endorsement by the AFL-CIO of joint approaches to training dislocated workers. The chapter underscores that training and placement programs are more successful in a collective bargaining environment when a union is involved than in cases when one party alone is trying to do the job.

In chapter 8, Richard Baker discusses an innovative program in Michigan that the federal government has identified as a national model for programs aimed at dislocated workers and set up under the Job Training Partnership Act. Baker concludes, as McMillian does, that partnership arrangements are more effective than unilateral programs for addressing the training needs of the displaced.

Chapter 9, by Jeanne Gordus, Cheng Kuo, and Karen Yamakawa, describes a novel arrangement whereby outside professionals help facilitate lifetime education planning by workers in a union-management program. The authors present a highly detailed, quantitative model for assessing the impact of this innovative approach. The chapter represents a key contribution to a potentially rich new area for evaluation research.

The concluding three chapters examine broad themes that have emerged from field research on joint initiatives, much of which is described in this volume. Chapter 10, by Louis Ferman and Michele Hoyman, contrasts joint programs and traditional education and training programs. It then examines the principles and practices associated with service delivery under a joint structure. Practitioners should find the chapter valuable for its description of how joint programs become highly participant-driven, tightly integrated into workplace operations, and oriented around lifetime education planning.

Chapter 11, by Ernest Savoie and Joel Cutcher-Gershenfeld, offers a conceptual framework for understanding joint training programs as a special application of joint labor-management undertakings and an innovative form of workplace governance. Four elements of governance are highlighted: the interrelationship between conflict and cooperation; the process of shaping institutional arrangements; the importance of an emergent rather than a planned approach to strategy; and the central role of leadership. The authors suggest that it is possible to master both the art and the science of joint governance for worker training programs—even though they are different from the art and science of collective bargaining.

The final chapter, by Cutcher-Gershenfeld and Hoyman, focuses on key research and policy implications of the volume. In particular, they note the unique research challenges associated with the study of joint programs. The authors call for a national data base on joint initiatives. They also emphasize that although joint structures have many benefits, there are barriers limiting the degree to which joint innovations will be part of most unionized workplaces.

In deciding to produce this volume, we accepted at the outset that our task would be a difficult one in that union-management training programs are an evolving, dynamic phenomenon. It may thus be a decade or more before the contributors to this volume will be able to reach definite conclusions. So much is happening in the field, however, that we felt compelled to present preliminary descriptions, questions, evaluations, and theoretical frameworks.

Practitioners should find the case descriptions a useful source of encouragement and new ideas and the theoretical material helpful in understanding their experiences. We hope we have provided theorists with some valuable new information and, perhaps more important, that we inspire them to do further research. Finally, we hope policy makers find we have captured an innovation in U.S. labor-management relations that merits closer examination.

The 1980s have been a decade of experimentation in labor-management relations. Joint training initiatives may well strengthen collective bargaining relationships, contribute to the survival of American firms, and enhance the lives of workers. We hope they do.

2 · SCOPE AND EXTENT OF JOINT TRAINING PROGRAMS

Michele Hoyman and Louis A. Ferman

This chapter presents the results of the only survey of joint training programs. It addresses such important issues as the frequency of joint training programs and what is motivating labor and management to adopt them, as well as the character of the programs. It provides important background information for theorists and practitioners.

Joint training programs emerged as a result of several well-documented forces that are fundamentally changing the workplace: the transformation of industrial relations (Kochan, Katz, and McKersie 1987; Kochan, Cutcher-Gershenfeld, and MacDuffie 1989; Katz, Kochan, and Gobeille 1983; Cutcher-Gershenfeld, McKersie, and Wever 1988); deindustrialization (Bluestone 1984; Bluestone and Harrison 1986, 1988; Fedrau 1984; Hansen 1984a; Root 1984); the downward shift in the literacy levels of workers (Carnevale and Goldstein 1990; Sultan 1989); the increase in the literacy requirements for most jobs; the shift away from lifetime employment; and technological change (see chapter 3). All of these factors in combination have put substantial pressure on employers and unions to address the training needs of blue-collar workers. Whereas five or ten years ago, 90 percent of corporate training was designed for white-collar professionals, particularly executives, the emphasis has now clearly shifted, as the existence of joint training programs demonstrate.

As one of the major—and potentially one of the most far-reaching—innovations in industrial relations in the last ten to fifteen years, joint training programs raise many questions. Among them are, What gives rise to their development, and how prevalent are they? This chapter examines results from the first survey designed to address these questions.

The survey on which the findings in this chapter are based was conducted by telephone in August 1988. It is the only survey focused specifically on joint training. Essentially, the questions being asked were, Has joint training spread? If so, why? And what is driving labor and management to adopt this particular structure for delivering training?

Before discussing the research data, a few caveats are in order. Joint efforts unfold over time; they involve a longitudinal process. For this reason, they may evolve at different times and for different reasons. The process often begins with the development of apprenticeship programs and then progresses to the establishment of joint committees in areas such as health and safety and, in some cases, employee involvement or the problems of displaced workers. Joint labor-management training programs are adopted in the mature stages of this process. Programs may also emerge parallel to and under the rubric of employee involvement programs as firms and unions discover that they need training to implement their employee involvement goals. There is thus a fundamental problem of labeling. What are the criteria for labeling something a joint training program? Two suggest themselves: first, do the parties themselves identify the program as a joint training program, and, second, how does the program function? The functional characteristics thus would be more important than the structural characteristics in identifying a joint training program.

Since our survey provided only a "snapshot" of joint programs and the process of initiating them evolves, subtle information may have been lost about the different stages in the development of an individual case. The strength of the survey is its generalizability. The trade-off is the lack of a "process" examination.

Unlike the programs set up under the Comprehensive Employment and Training Act or the Job Training Partnership Act, joint training programs have not been set up long enough to conduct sound evaluations. With the exception of a study by Gary Hansen (1986) on the effect on workers in San Jose, California, of participating in the UAW-Ford program, little quantitative data are available. There are many reasons for this. First, some of the programs are so new—or their establishment in a particular locale so recent—that no data exist. Typically, the parties view their primary role as delivering programs, not collecting data. Second, the parties may not be eager to have outside researchers study their programs since the political costs of public criticism may be quite high. Thus access for objective outsiders is a problem. Third, even if data are kept and are accessible, the time frame is such that the measurement of effectiveness may not be valid. It may be too soon to assess whether the training "has taken," even for programs negotiated in 1979 or 1982.

Sample

There is no list of companies that have joint training programs, although there are lists that include union-management pairs (U.S. Department of Labor; see also Ichiniowski, Delaney, and Lewin 1989; Cooke 1990). The population we used for our survey was a 1978 list of 204 employers that had indicated to the Department of Labor that they were engaged in joint labor-management efforts. Most of these employers were large, national companies with multiple locations and thus multiple bargaining units.[1] Fifty-five, or 27 percent, were in the public sector.

On the one hand, because the sample contained primarily large, national firms, two characteristics associated with the establishment of joint training programs, our results may overstate somewhat the amount of joint training being conducted. On the other hand, given the number of years—a decade or so—that have passed since the survey list was compiled, perhaps more firms now have such programs.

---

1. There are other lists of firms that are involved in labor innovations, the subsets of which may contain union-management pairs conducting joint programming, but such programming may or may not involve training. Since a portion—even a majority of these firms—are not unionized, it was inefficient for the purpose of this study to use those lists instead of the list from the Department of Labor. For instance, see Ichiniowski, Delaney, and Lewin (1989) and Cooke (1990).

The approach taken was more like that used in a census than in a survey. Rather than drawing a sample, a census was taken of the 204 employers on the list to determine how many had joint training programs.

Initially, a letter was sent to all the employers to explain the purpose of the study. Subsequently, three phone contacts were attempted with each labor and management person. If contact was made, a ten-page survey was administered over the phone in which detailed information was solicited about the training program or, if there was no program, about the size of the bargaining unit and the industry. Interviews lasted between one and one-half and two hours if the company had a training program and a couple of minutes if it did not.

A total of thirty-seven labor-management pairs were eliminated from the survey. Eight of the companies had gone out of business, two had filed for Chapter 11 bankruptcy, and five were no longer unionized. Three had changed their names because of takeovers or mergers and could not be contacted, and one had changed ownership. Eighteen were eliminated because the cost of doing a phone survey would have been prohibitive. Of the remaining 167 pairs, phone contact was made with 109, for a response rate of 65 percent. Of these 109 pairs, only two refused to participate in the study. Thus the gross response rate was 107/204, or 52 percent.

Frequency of Joint Training

We hypothesized that the frequency of joint training programs would be low since we assumed that the conditions necessary for their establishment would not be easy to meet: the company had to be large and have many resources, a strong union, and a tradition of undertaking joint efforts with that union, as well as a particular combination of need and leadership.

Of the 107 labor-management pairs that were contacted, 45, or 42 percent, said they had joint training programs. This is a very significant result, indicating that programs clearly are not confined just to plants in a few industries.

Purposes of Training

Our findings demonstrate that companies and unions start joint training programs for several reasons. One reason is to meet staff-

Table 2.1   Purpose of Joint Training Programs

Purpose	Number
To improve employees' knowledge of safety and health	33
To upgrade employees' skills	26
To improve employees' communication skills	24
To assist displaced workers	17
To enhance employees' personal development	15
To increase employees' basic skills	13
To meet staffing (manpower) needs	13
To provide outplacement training	7
Other	4
Total[a]	152

[a]Many respondents mentioned more than one purpose, so that the total exceeds 45, the number that responded.

ing needs. Traditionally, apprenticeship programs fall in this category. Another reason is to upgrade individual employees' skills or to provide training or outplacement. Still other programs emphasize the need to enhance the security of the plant or the economy of the community. In such cases, training is linked to concerns about preserving the competitive status of the firm. Other programs emphasize basic skills or employees' personal development or personal enrichment. In many programs, the emphasis is on building communication skills either for their own sake or to improve employees' effectiveness on the job. Finally, training is offered for very specific or targeted purposes, such as to enhance health and safety, so as to maintain collective bargaining relationships. Obviously, many of these purposes are multifaceted. For instance, increasing employees' literacy in a basic skills program may aid both individual employees and the employer.

Table 2.1 indicates the reasons participants in our survey gave for having a joint training program. Data come from the forty-five labor-management pairs that indicated they had joint training programs.

Several results were somewhat surprising, especially the infrequency with which helping displaced workers was mentioned. One reason is obvious: programs for the displaced usually are instituted when a plant is closing. When the plant closes, the program disappears. Thus the data probably understate the number of displaced workers and the amount of activity directed at them. Helping the displaced may have been the primary purpose of a program when it was begun but no longer be the primary purpose today.

Table 2.2 Traditional versus Nontraditional Purposes for Having Joint
Training Programs

Traditional	Number	Nontraditional	Number
To improve knowledge of safety and health	33	To assist displaced workers	17
To upgrade skills	26	To improve communication skills	24
To meet staffing needs	13	To enhance personal development	15
To provide outplacement assistance	7	To provide basic skills training	13
Total	79	Total	69

Furthermore, programs are dynamic; parties may describe their
purpose differently at different times.

A high number of programs are started for the purpose of improving employees' communication skills (24) and enhancing personal development (15). These findings indicate a new emphasis on
training that is less specific and less vocational than in the past,
aimed more at developing "the whole person."

Basic skills are also more important than we expected. This is
particularly significant given the resistance of individual workers to
acknowledge deficiencies in this area. One reason for this increased
emphasis on literacy is that it has recently been put on the national
agenda. Basic skills take time to develop and usually form the foundation for entry into joint training programs.

To some extent, all programs have multiple purposes. For instance, if the purpose of a program is to upgrade workers' skills so
they can do a new job, literacy or basic skills may need to be honed,
as well as personal development skills.

The purposes listed in table 2.1 can be divided into those that are
traditional and those that are nontraditional. As shown in table 2.2,
there is almost as much nontraditional activity as there is traditional
activity. This is quite a dramatic finding in that many nontraditional
programs were started only recently. Thus these data, although incomplete, suggest that the existence of joint training programs may
be changing the character of training programs in general. It is now
hard to separate the effect of joint programs from the effect of other
changes on the content of training, employer-provided, union-

Table 2.3   Number of Programs for Active versus Displaced Workers

Active	37
Displaced	18
Both	13
Active only	16
Displaced only	5

provided, or joint. A fruitful area of research would be whether joint delivery systems are changing the content of training programs or whether all training efforts—joint and company-sponsored—are shifting more to an emphasis on personal development and basic education.

Character of the Programs

Who do the programs serve? What services are provided? How are the programs structured? Is there a special fund for their operation? Is there a nonprofit corporation? Is there language in the collective bargaining agreement guaranteeing them? How are the eligibility requirements set? How is selection determined? How are service delivery questions addressed? These are some of the questions we hoped to answer.

Audience for the Programs
One overriding question is whether joint training programs are established primarily to serve the needs of displaced workers or of active workers. This is a difficult question to answer since programs evolve and change over time. For instance, two or three of the pioneer programs in the automobile industry were initially targeted at displaced workers but were offered to active workers over time. In our study, these cases were coded as both. Table 2.3 indicates the relative number of programs for active workers only, displaced workers only, and for both active and displaced. As shown in the table, only five programs were for displaced workers only. This may seem like a small number since the threat of a plant closing is often the crisis that precipitates the establishment of a program. Unfortunately, there is usually too little time during a plant closing to institute any intervention, training or otherwise.

Table 2.4   Services for Active Workers

Service	Number
Upgrading skills	22
Vocational training/credit/ noncredit for degree	21
Career retooling	19
New technological skills	19
Personal skills	17
Apprenticeship skills	15
Basic skills	12
Career counseling	8
Other	6
Total	139[a]

[a]Total represents all programs, not only those administered jointly. Most of the 45 labor-management pairs that have programs offer more than one.

Services Offered

Table 2.4 lists the range of services available for active workers in joint training programs. Programs to upgrade workers' skills are gaining in importance in today's economy since most jobs require that workers keep acquiring new skills. Auto workers must now monitor robots, for example. They must therefore know something about robotics and computers. Similarly, secretaries must be familiar with computers and word processing packages to meet just the basic requirements of their jobs.

There is evidence in this volume that career counseling is one of the most critical aspects of lifelong learning and goal setting. Yet it is one of the least represented services listed in table 2.4. Most of the thirty-seven programs for active workers put a person immediately in programs without counseling.

Career retooling and the acquisition of new technological skills are offered in nineteen programs. Thus the four most popular services for active workers tend to be oriented toward meeting the new demands of a changed and changing economy.

As shown in table 2.5, programs for displaced workers frequently offer basic skills, more so than one would expect given the extraordinary time constraints under which jobless people operate. Relatively speaking, one would expect more emphasis on basic skills among active workers than among displaced since the development of basic skills is a long-term process. Nonetheless, twelve of the

Table 2.5   Services for Displaced Workers

Service	Number
Closing-related	18
Vocational	17
Career	16
Personal	14
Basic	12
Consortium	6
Other (job search, resumé writing)	5
Relocation	4
Total number of responses	92
Number of pairs with programs for the displaced	18

thirty-seven programs for active workers offered basic skills, as did twelve of the eighteen for displaced. There is a comparatively greater emphasis on basic skills among programs for the displaced than among programs for people who are working.

Structure of the Programs
Twenty-six or so respondents answered our questions about structure. Many others answered that these particular questions were not relevant. Given the small N, these data should therefore be viewed as illustrative rather than definitive.

Funding
Funds are usually earmarked for the program, sometimes in a separate fund. Of the twenty-six respondents who answered our question about funding, eight indicated that they had a fund and four indicated that they followed a funding formula. Apparently many programs have a high degree of informality in their funding arrangements.

Administration
Some of the first model programs, such as the UAW-Ford program and the GM-UAW program, were set up as elaborate nonprofit corporations that included centers. The parties in our survey were asked if they had created such separate organizational entities. Only six of the fifteen pairs who answered this question had such structures.

Relation to the Collective Bargaining Agreement

Nineteen of the thirty-two respondents who answered this question (59 percent) said that their collective bargaining agreements guaranteed the program. Again, this suggests that many programs are informally instituted, or at least differ from early cases in that they are not guaranteed.

Eligibility Requirements

Determining who is eligible to participate in joint training programs is not as simple as it would appear. Twenty-six programs in our survey limited eligibility to members of the bargaining unit. Seventeen allowed all employees to participate, including those not in the collective bargaining unit. (Open admission can be controversial, at least from the point of view of the union, since the program is a bargained benefit.) Only two of the programs had testing requirements; one had educational requirements; and one had a requirement other than those mentioned above. By and large, all active workers who are members of a bargaining unit are eligible. Obviously, eligibility for displaced worker programs is displaced status.

Union participation in joint training programs has probably made a great difference in determining the eligibility requirements. In general, unions and their members allow open admission for any bargaining unit member. If the program were employer-run, the process would most likely be more selective.

Selection

How participants are selected also raises some interesting issues. Self-selection may ensure that the person is sufficiently motivated to succeed and thus arguably raise success rates, but there are other ways of selecting participants, including using eligibility requirements. Using eligibility requirements ensures that participants are well suited to the program and thus results in a lower dropout rate.

Of the employers who answered the question, twelve out of twenty-seven had eligibility requirements, three out of twenty-six used seniority to select participants, twenty-one out of twenty-seven used self-selection by the participants, and eight out of twenty-six relied on management discretion.

In general, unions see self-selection by the participants as advantageous. At the same time, compared to an employer-provided program, this arrangement costs the employer considerable discretion in selection.

Location of Classes

Of the respondents who answered, eight said their programs were held in the plant, seven off-site, and fourteen both on-site and off-site. Classes are increasingly being offered in the plant for college credit or for the purpose of teaching basic skills, whereas in the past classes in the plant were more likely to be vocational.

One important constraint in determining whether classes can be taught off-site is whether special equipment or facilities are needed. Increasingly, even technical classes are being taught on-site, such as computer classes that used to be taught at community colleges or universities. Typically, a microcomputer lab is set up right in the plant or in a nearby trailer. Further research is needed to determine whether the decision to deliver the program on-site or off is functionally driven.

Scheduling of Classes

Whether classes are held during work time or not is a related issue. Of the employers who answered this question, eleven gave classes during work time, eleven at other times, and seven during both work times and other times. Joint training programs generally seem to be conducting classes during times that are convenient for workers.

Tuition Plan

Reimbursement upon completion of a class is the most common arrangement. This ensures that if the employee drops out, neither the union nor the employer has to pay tuition. It also motivates employees to stay in the class and complete it. Four of the programs prepaid tuition, ten paid upon completion, and three had arrangements for partial payment.

Marketing

Compared to employer-sponsored programs, marketing of joint programs happens in a myriad of ways. Methods range from news-

Table 2.6 Marketing Methods Used by Joint Training Programs

Method	Number
Newsletter	15
Direct mail	15
Union, bulletin board	12
Union meetings	10
Word of mouth	9
Other	7
Total	68[a]

[a]A total of 24 employers responded.

letters and direct mail to union bulletin boards and meetings, word of mouth, and in-plant videos.

As table 2.6 demonstrates, unions use bulletin boards, union meetings, and word of mouth almost as frequently as they use more traditional methods such as direct mail. Clearly, the jointness of the project changes the character of the marketing that is available to both management and the union. Further, a much broader choice and much more intimate and personalized marketing devices are available to the two parties than to government or other public agencies. Although the survey does not provide any direct data on this point, the evidence suggests that use of more personalized marketing leads to greater participation in joint programs than in others and to greater levels of participant success (see chapters 7 and 8).

Infrastructure

One of the issues in the development of joint training programs is how much organizational infrastructure is necessary, including committee structure or other personal and technical support. The conventional wisdom is that at the very least a labor-management committee is necessary. This committee is the basic building block of the program. Five of the forty-five companies we surveyed that had joint training programs had no committees, twelve had one committee, and twenty-eight had two or more. Thus it looks as though the existence of multiple committees may support the establishment of joint training programs. Of course, the direction of this relationship cannot yet be ascertained. Additional study is required to determine whether multiple committees lead to the establishment of joint training programs or whether the existence of a training program

Table 2.7   Forces Leading to the Establishment of Joint Training
Programs

Force	Number
Jointism	10
Competition	6
Leadership	5
Displaced workers	3
Schools/community colleges	2
Technology	2
Total number of responses	28[a]

[a]Twenty employers responded; many cited multiple forces.

leads to the establishment of multiple committees. Furthermore, an employee involvement committee may function as a training committee or at least initiate training programs.

Another concern is how best to train the members of a labor-management committee, particularly if there is turnover. Finally, does "osmosis" occur across locals in the same region and thereby build the momentum needed to form a joint committee? These issues require further research.

Reasons Programs Are Established

Respondents to our survey were asked, "What were the driving forces that helped to establish the programs?" Table 2.7 lists the responses of forty-five companies that had joint programs; 20 responded, or 44 percent.

The most frequently mentioned driving force was a desire for jointism, mentioned by ten respondents. This is not surprising in that we know from case studies of the earliest programs (Ferman and Hoyman 1987; chapters 4 and 11 in this volume) that one condition for establishing a program is the "unfreezing" of the traditional and adversarial labor-management relationship. Thus it stands to reason that a lengthy experience with jointism would lay the foundation for establishing joint labor-management training programs. Based on the experiences of the early and "model" programs, programs seem to emerge in highly unionized industries. Generally, joint training programs do not arise in industries with little or no unionization. Nor are weak unions likely to embrace such programs.

The second and most important force in establishing joint train-ing programs is competition, cited by six of the respondents. Cer-tainly the notion here is that necessity is the mother of invention. When faced with an external threat, individual employers, unions, and indeed whole industries will embrace joint experiments, includ-ing labor-management training programs.

Another driving force is the plight of displaced workers. Given that the data may underplay their problems and the threat of plant closings, more programs may be established for this reason than the table suggests. The motivating force may initially be competition or changes in technology, causing the parties to respond accordingly.

Location of Programs

Our results indicate that just as joint programs are not randomly distributed across industries, neither are they randomly distributed across regions. The Midwest or Rustbelt has much experience with jointism, much more than the Northeast, West, or South. We thus hypothesized that because the Midwest has industries with strong unions and a high rate of unionization (i.e., auto, steel), it would have more joint training programs than other regions. Although the Northeast has a fairly strong manufacturing base, the labor-management environment is not as conducive to jointism. Thus we did not expect the area to have many joint training programs. Like-wise, we expected the South and West to have very few programs, the former because it has a low rate of unionization, the latter be-cause the tradition of jointism is not well established and the indus-tries in the region are not generally of the sort that spawn joint efforts.

As illustrated in figure 2.1, the results of our survey support the hypothesis that there is a regional bias toward jointism. This leads to another question: does the Midwest have more joint training pro-grams than other regions, relatively speaking? In fact, there are more training programs in the Midwest (58 percent) than in the sample as a whole (50 percent). By comparison, the Northeast rep-resented 28 percent of the sample as a whole.

Industry Distribution

According to our survey, industries in heavy manufacturing or those that are increasingly at a competitive disadvantage are the most

Figure 2.1   Regional Distribution of Joint Training Programs

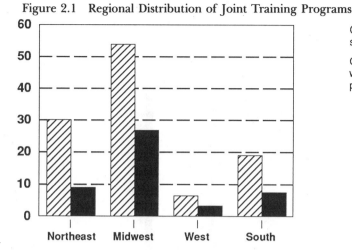

likely to establish joint training programs: specialty chemicals, oil refinery, rubber, steel, brass, nickel and aluminum, auto body, manufacturing, writing instruments, transportation services, and cement. Industries that are proportionately less well represented are canning, confectionery, flour, and grain products; air transportation; and public service and highway maintenance. Industries that are represented in the same proportion (or nearly the same) among active programs and the sample as a whole are textiles; lumber; machine tools and elevators; electric power and telephone; public utilities; and public services and health (fig. 2.2).

Although these data were useful, we were interested in determining more regarding which industries tended to support the growth of joint training programs. We thus developed two more hypotheses: the decline hypothesis and the change hypothesis. To begin, all the industries were coded as to whether they were in decline: 54 percent of the 107 cases were in such industries.

Decline hypothesis. The decline hypothesis stated that companies in decline are more likely to adopt joint training programs than companies in industries that are doing well. Our data supported this hypothesis: of the companies with joint training programs, 50 percent were in industries in decline and 33 percent were in industries that were not in decline.

Figure 2.2   Distribution of Programs by Industry

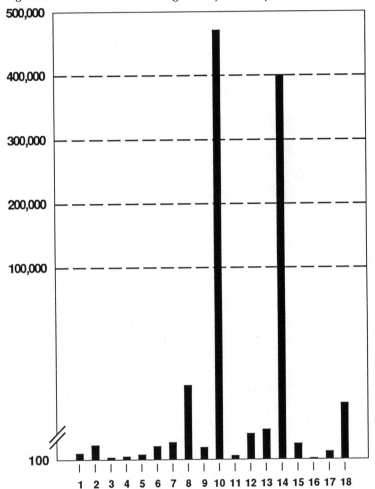

1 = canning, confectionery, flour, and grain, SIC = 30; 2 = textile, SIC = 22; 3 = lumber, SIC = 24; 4 = paper, SIC = 26; 5 = chemical, SIC = 35; 6 = oil, SIC = 29; 7 = rubber, SIC = 30; 8 = steel, brass, nickel wire, and aluminum, SIC = 33; 9 = machine tools and elevator, SIC = 35; 10 = auto body, SIC = 37; 11 = manufacturing writing instruments, SIC = 39; 12 = transportation services, SIC = 40; 13 = air transportation, SIC = 45; 14 = electric power and telephone, SIC = 48; 15 = public utilities, SIC = 49; 16 = cement, SIC = 52; 17 = public services and health, SIC = 80; 18 = public service/highway maintenances, SIC = 91.

Change hypothesis. A related hypothesis stated that companies in industries experiencing a great deal of change would be more likely to adopt a joint training program than those in industries not experiencing change. Of 107 companies in different industries, 40 percent were experiencing change, and of the companies in these industries, 53 percent had programs. Only 34 percent of the companies in industries experiencing no change had programs.

It thus seems that change and not just decline spurs the establishment of joint training programs. The change can be internal or external in nature, related to technology or competition, and either threatening or empowering. In that we are in an era marked by change, one would expect the external environment to create more and more pressure to establish these programs.

Inside the firm, pressure to change is also building. Firms are involved in increasing numbers of dramatic experiments in areas such as self-management and shared management through employee involvement. One would expect that these changes will inspire joint training programs.

Size

Another factor thought to correlate with whether a company would have a joint training program was the size of the employer. Our findings indicated that there is a tendency for programs to be started in large firms. Of those with more than six hundred employees, 57 percent had programs and 43 percent did not. Among those with fewer than six hundred employees, only 34 percent had programs and 66 percent did not. This is probably because the amount of resources required is substantial. Also, large firms have training departments.

Our original assumption was that necessity was driving joint training programs; firms and industries in trouble would be more likely to adopt such programs. Based on the data on industry and indirectly regional distribution, it appears that this is certainly the case, but it tells only part of the story. It appears that not just decline but any change can cause a firm to launch a program. In other words, firms and unions become more innovative in a changing environment. We were not able to test whether joint programs are technologically driven, but it is worthy of note that the two industries characterized by high change, the telephone and communications

Figure 2.3   Number of Employees Covered under Joint Training Program*

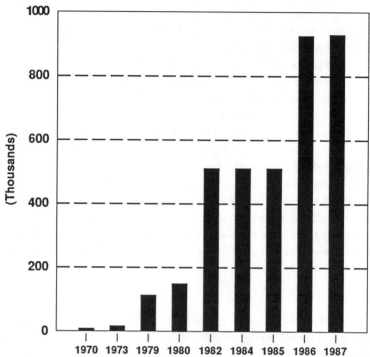

*Out of 43 joint training programs, 24 answered the question of how long they had been in effect. Of these, 16 were formal joint training programs and 8 were informal joint training programs. These figures are cumulative.

industries, both had joint training programs. Further support for the notion that technology drives these programs is found in Treinen and Ross's insightful case description on the AT&T-CWA-IBEW Alliance (see chapter 3). Finally, labor-management pairs in our study mentioned that technology was one of the forces driving their programs. Determining how technology-driven these programs are would be a fruitful area for future research.

Diffusion

Figure 2.3 shows the number of employees covered under training programs over time. Note that the data are displayed this way instead of by the number of programs over time since one program may have fifty employees in a bargaining unit and another may have

Table 2.8   Accomplishments of Joint Training Programs

Accomplishment	Number
Increased employees' personal development	12
Increased worker effectiveness	9
Increased employees' job satisfaction	8
Increased workers' job security	7
Aided displaced workers	7
Helped workers retool	6
Retained plant size/industry security/ lowered costs	3
Other	2
Total nonunique responses	54
Unique programs responding	24

two hundred thousand employees. The graph provides a measure of the extent of coverage.

As can be seen from the graph, the number of employees covered by joint training programs in their collective bargaining agreements increased each year. There was a dramatic increase in 1979, in 1982, and again in 1986. Based on our sample, 904,502 employees are currently covered under these programs. An important question is how the instigation of these programs is linked to micro and macro political factors.

Accomplishments

Any discussion of joint training programs would not be complete without examining their accomplishments. Table 2.8 lists the answers given by the forty-five employers who said they had joint training programs.

In that the leading accomplishment cited was that programs increased workers' personal development, it seems that joint training programs generally have innovative purposes and are focused on active workers. The idea that programs can help firms retain their size and industry security and lower costs is gaining currency as training and upgrading are becoming increasingly linked to economic development and the ability to compete.

Summary and Implications

To a certain extent, our survey raised more questions than it answered. There are, however, a few questions for which the data provided definite answers. Is the innovation spreading? Definitely yes.

Forty-two percent of the respondents indicated that they had joint training programs. Is there a standard model? No. Each management and union pair seems to be fashioning its own program. Not many are emulating the leading examples in the auto industry in scope, range, or structure, let alone ambitiousness.

Several research questions arise from the data. First, is the variation in the structural arrangements of programs functionally driven or is it undertaken by choice? Second, are differences in eligibility requirements a function of the particular program or of some overall philosophical difference between one labor-management pair and another? It is impossible to answer these questions.

To some extent, this survey shows that having a joint delivery system may make a difference in the effectiveness of a training program. Chapters 7 and 8 also discuss this issue. Chapter 5 on the Paid Educational Leave program and chapter 9 on life education advisors discuss two specific examples of innovative structures.

Training programs have multiple purposes. Some are being used for such traditional reasons as to upgrade employees' skills and meet staffing needs or to provide lifetime job security for union members in firms in technological or economic transition. Others have more nontraditional purposes, such as basic skills education or personal development. These findings raise the question of whether joint delivery is changing the content of programming from traditional to nontraditional or whether the overall content of all training (employer-provided and jointly provided) is changing.

Programs are concentrated in industries in decline or in a state of change, particularly in the Midwest, where there is a long tradition of jointism and where most of the industries are in decline or changing. Finally, larger firms tend to adopt joint training programs more than smaller firms. All of these issues are explored throughout the volume.

3 · THE ALLIANCE FOR EMPLOYEE GROWTH AND DEVELOPMENT, INC.

Donald Treinen and Kenneth Ross

The Alliance for Employee Growth and Development is a joint training program run by AT&T, the Communications Workers of America, and the International Brotherhood of Electrical Workers. This case description, which was written by the Alliance's co-executive directors, explores the conditions leading to its development; its philosophy and underlying assumptions; the adaptations the Alliance has made to meet the needs of the company and the work force; and the forces, both human and technological, that have shaped it. The chapter should be of particular interest to practitioners, in that it describes a prototype for planning, and for researchers seeking background material.

The Alliance for Employee Growth and Development, Inc., is a cooperative venture between AT&T, the Communications Workers of America, and the International Brotherhood of Electrical Workers whose aim is to enhance the human resource potential of active and displaced unionized workers. The effort is supported by and draws on the resources of both management and labor and functions as an independently chartered corporation.

The purpose of this chapter is to describe the assumptions, strategies, and activities that underpin the joint training efforts of the Alliance. Specifically, the chapter will address the conditions leading to its development; the collective bargaining agreements of 1983 and 1986 that gave substance and structure to the Alliance concept; its philosophy and underlying assumptions; how the Alliance has adapted to the needs of the company and work force; and the forces, both human and technological, that shape and move Alliance programmatic activities.

The Alliance has several unique features. The first is that its union-management agreement covers more than twenty-five hundred work sites, which vary in size and are in every region of the country. To reach all the union-represented workers at these locations, diverse and variable organizational structures had to be developed, each with considerable discretionary authority and empowerment.

The second unique feature is that AT&T divested itself of its regional operating companies in 1984 and the divested companies began to change the joint training structures that had existed before then. Thus joint training by AT&T, the CWA, and the IBEW was of one kind before the divestiture and another kind after it. After divestiture, the unions and former Bell operating companies began to move toward establishing separate agreements and away from using the national bargaining agreement.

Third, and very important, since 1988, AT&T and the two unions have been covered under one unified training agreement. The current administration of the Alliance thus represents a co-determination in decision making between AT&T and the CWA and the IBEW.

Joint training in the Alliance can be understood only in the context of the increasing competition and changing technology occurring in the communications industry and the effect of these changes on the unionized work force. Thus the Alliance was formed not just to meet the training needs of the unionized work force but to increase their employment security, their human resource potential, and their personal development.

Background

Over the past several years, employees at AT&T and the former Bell System in general have been more and more subject to the effects of increasing competition in the telecommunications industry. The advent of customer-owned Bell System equipment in the mid-1960s, changes in regulations regarding the integrity of the telephone network, and the dramatic entry of numerous other companies in the long-distance market all affected the work lives of AT&T employees. In some cases, new skills were required, and sometimes the result was a reduced labor force. In other cases, the AT&T market share was reduced or working conditions changed based on the new federal regulations.

Technological change has always been a fact of life in the telecommunications industry, but the pace of such change has never been faster. In the past, the Bell System, through its research organization, Bell Laboratories, and its manufacturing and installation organization, Western Electric, had been able to introduce technology at a controlled pace. With this planned approach, Bell System employees were insulated and largely immune from the vagaries of a competitive, market-driven work environment in which there is continuous pressure for technological and operational changes.

In the hundred years of its existence, the Bell System had waged long-term and expensive struggles with its competitors to gain its status as a regulated monopoly. The loss of this status after the divestiture agreement was signed affected all aspects of the company's operation: rate setting, manufacturing, research, labor relations, and expansion.

With the easing of domestic regulatory pressures, other nations began to compete with AT&T for a share of the U.S. market. Thus, as the postdivestiture era was launched, it was clear to the company, unions, and employees that new ways had to be found to remain competitive as a company, relevant as a union, and gainfully employed as a work force. Instead of the slow pace of change that had characterized the company's history, AT&T was now being driven by global competition. No longer was it possible to rely on regulatory agencies to set the total corporate budget and direction for the future. Survival depended on working together.

Thus the stage was set for the negotiation in 1986 of an agreement to establish the Alliance for Employee Growth and Development. As we shall see, however, the stage was already being set years earlier.

Leading up to the 1983 national negotiations between AT&T and the CWA, many employees and local union leaders had been clamoring to find a way to address the training needs of AT&T workers.

Apprehension surrounded the issue because of the impending divestiture and its many unknowns for AT&T's work force. Further, in recent years, AT&T had reduced the amount of attention, time, and money it devoted to developing and updating employees' skills.

The Training-Retraining Agreement negotiated in 1983 was designed to respond to employee needs and concerns by establishing jointly staffed Training Advisory Boards at the corporate level of AT&T, in the other Bell companies, and at the bargaining agent level of the union. In AT&T, the advisory board was staffed by three AT&T and three CWA representatives.

From 1983 to 1986, the AT&T-CWA Training Advisory Board met a number of times and developed a program for self-study at home which eventually offered employees about two dozen courses. These courses were done by correspondence, and the costs were paid by AT&T. Courses ranged from basic mathematics to business writing and basic electricity to Job Control Language training for computer center work. The average cost per course for materials and processing was about twenty dollars.

During its three years of operation, the AT&T-CWA Training Advisory Board enrolled about thirty-two thousand employees. Of these, only about 15 percent completed courses. It is generally believed that a lack of course management contributed greatly to this low completion rate. For instance, there was no process for students to call for assistance or for project administrators to track student activity and offer assistance. In 1986, bargaining effectively eliminated the advisory board, and the self-study program was closed down.

The only other project the advisory board attempted to institute was an education and training program through the New Jersey community college system. This effort entered the discussion stage about a year before bargaining in 1986, but AT&T elected not to consider it. Thus, as the company and union went into bargaining in 1986, the Training Advisory Board was keenly aware that it would need to control funding if future efforts were to be successful.

By the 1986 bargaining negotiations, divestiture was a reality and the regional operating companies were independent of AT&T. The focus was on reaching agreement between AT&T, the CWA, and the IBEW and, equally important, on finding ways to make AT&T more competitive in the domestic and world markets, on upgrading the skills of the work force, and on preparing displaced workers for other employment either inside or outside the company.

The establishment of the Alliance was one result of these negotiations. Provision was made for it to be governed by a board of trustees (three union, three company), for it to have a national center in Somerset, New Jersey, and for it to be co-directed by union and management personnel. Provision was also made for a staff to be recruited and established in the national center. Such a central facility had not existed under the Training Advisory Board structure. An ongoing fund was to be established under the control of a joint governing board with a monthly company commitment of $3.75 for each union-represented worker who was employed. Finally, provision was made to establish a network of local union-management committees that would be empowered to organize and deliver program services. Emphasis was placed on providing services to both active and displaced workers.

Philosophy

The premise behind the Alliance is that people locally know their situation best, how to change it, and how to catalyze other people. In contrast, attempts by centralized national staff to control activities carried out locally will inevitably fail because of a lack of commitment. In short, for people to develop themselves, they must "own" the process that is structuring their development. This is more than a philosophical belief in local control. Because of the geographic dispersion of AT&T employees, it would never be practical to carry out employee development activities from a national center or other central location. AT&T operates in all states and at thousands of work locations, where the number of employees range from a handful to thousands. These employees are represented by five hundred union locals. The two major international unions—the CWA and the IBEW—represent about 131,000 AT&T employees, who can be found in virtually every AT&T business unit and have a wide array of job titles and levels of skills. Thus the realities of life both within the company and within the unions is so diverse as to make it impossible to create one model or optimal way to carry out personalized human resource ventures.

The most compelling reason for not attempting to centralize, however, lies in the nature of the Alliance itself. Services are offered on an individual employee basis and must be available at the local level, at "any time, any place." Thus employees are not constrained from taking advantage of Alliance services by a schedule or their personal situations.

Local empowerment increases because Alliance programming is at the local level. For example, members of an Alliance local committee, typically made up of shop stewards, supervisors, and a number of represented employees, may work on Alliance activities as part of their normal business routine. The committee may also identify potential training providers and has the final say in their selection. Finally, the committee may develop its own strategy for awareness, marketing, scheduling, and analysis of program results. These and other measures of committee autonomy bear witness to the effects of local empowerment.

Alliance activities cannot be carried out unless the CWA, the IBEW, and the management of AT&T find a way to cooperate. This is the chief implication of the Alliance vis-à-vis labor-management relations. Relations at the local level are also enhanced in that Alliance programs are undertaken only in response to employee needs.

Goals

The central goals of the Alliance are fourfold: (1) to develop employment security among union-represented employees; (2) to develop a human resource development program that is driven by program participants (i.e., the content and administration of the program are derived from the expressed needs and wants of the participants); (3) to develop opportunities for union-represented employees to advance both in the internal and external labor market; and (4) to develop a measure of empowerment among local union-management committees of the Alliance and union-represented employees.

Several years ago, AT&T, the CWA, and the IBEW realized that traditional job security within the company would most likely be impossible to attain and sustain over time. Even the best and most creative attempts of skilled and visionary negotiators on both sides of the table could do little to diminish the impact on workers of global competition and rapid turnover in technology. In this traditional context, job security was defined as security in one's job from date of hire until retirement. In contrast, employment security allows for the possibility of adapting to new skill requirements and learning new ways of working as some jobs become obsolete and others emerge. In addition, employment security suggests that one must be flexible enough to learn new skills but also that such tools must be portable to other positions either within the company or with a different company.

Traditional job security dictates that the bulk of the skills training has to be tailored to the specific tasks and equipment used by the employer. Such training, therefore, is usually provided by the employer rather than in the open market. When the goal is employment security, however, skill sets have to be portable and applicable to a wide range of occupations and normally are delivered through other than internal company channels. To deliver such training, a new way had to be found to identify skill deficiencies among employees, skill sets needed in a wide range of occupations, occupational opportunities for workers with these skill sets, and providers of the training. Clearly, no company would be willing to train its work force for other employers' use. Furthermore, the company would still have job-specific training needs and would continue to carry out such training.

AT&T and union bargainers also recognized that to concentrate on AT&T's own future, own growth, and own internal employee development needs, it would have to be freed from the full-time task of carrying out a true employment security approach to work force preparedness. Furthermore, if the employment security of the work force was to be realized, the unions had to be full partners in the development and implementation of any strategy designed to provide such security. The Alliance was created to serve this broader purpose.

Partners in the Program

The best way to understand the Alliance is from the perspective of its three parent organizations, AT&T, the CWA, and the IBEW.

AT&T has assets of about $39.3 billion (third quarter 1988 report). It operates throughout the United States, including Hawaii and Alaska, in well over eight thousand cities and towns, and has partnerships with firms in a number of foreign markets. Even after the divestiture of the Bell System, AT&T controlled nearly 70 percent of the long-distance telecommunications markets, and it is moving into computer markets with its own line of computer hardware and software. Before the divestiture, AT&T had about forty-five thousand employees (AT&T was the financial holding company of the Bell System and had a small operating company known as Long Lines). AT&T then became a full-service company for both small and large businesses, as well as an equipment and service provider for residential markets. After the breakup, it grew to about 371,000 employees. It then began a drive toward reduction and consolidation that left it with well under 300,000 employees. The core demand for Alliance services has been from the 100,000 displaced workers.

The CWA represents 700,000 employees at a wide range of employers and industries in the United States and Canada, in private industry as well as the public sector. Its membership is assigned to more than one thousand union locals and is organized into eight geographic districts in North America. Collectively, AT&T bargaining units represent the single largest bloc of CWA members in the union.

The IBEW is the largest of the three partners that own the Alliance. An international union with over 1 million members, it is found in thousands of communities in North America. Its members are in almost twenty-four hundred union locals, which are assigned to twelve geographic districts. Its telephone segment within AT&T is quite small, however, numbering about thirty thousand employees. Of these, about seven thousand are covered by Alliance services.

As discussed earlier, telecommunications technology has had a significant impact on AT&T workers, who either must use that technology or be replaced by it. Current estimates are that the number of operator services offices will be reduced from about 250 to perhaps under 100 by 1992. This means that the number of telephone operators will be reduced by an estimated six to ten thousand in the same period. What happens to these people will also be a function of technology.

AT&T's Network Services Division (NSD) is another example of a group being driven by technology. Among other things, this organization provides the long-distance voice and data telecommunications services of AT&T nationwide. Because of the explosion of fiberoptic technology and the digitization of the transmission systems possible as a result, AT&T has found that it must rapidly replace its old technology in order to stay up with, and surpass, its major competition. Its goal is to do so by 1995.

Again, such a decision has a significant impact on workers. Over the next five years, NSD is expected to reduce its current work force of almost forty thousand by 25 percent. This reduction will be realized either through normal attrition, layoff, or rotation to other jobs (inside and outside of AT&T) because of training and placement activities. In all likelihood, a combination of the three strategies will be used and the level of layoffs will be a function of how effectively the Alliance is able to train workers to do other work.

The above examples are but two of a host of technology-related reductions in work force either already being undertaken or expected in the next few years. These projections do not address ongoing, technologically driven changes in work processes, however, which will require constant updating of skills and abilities on the part of workers who remain with AT&T. In fact, these workers and the skill sets they will need will determine AT&T's success or failure in years to come. It may also determine the ability of organized labor to remain relevant to future generations.

Early Leadership

The supportive structure of the Alliance can best be described as "one company—two unions." Given that both unions were sought out to organize workers in the same industry, it is not surprising that the history of the CWA and IBEW is one of less than complete harmony. In recent years, however, the national leaderships of both organizations have taken it upon themselves to ensure that counterproductive activities are kept to a minimum. The success of this effort has more to do with the work of two individuals than with any other single factor.

Jack Barry, international president of the IBEW, and Morton Bahr, international president of the CWA, both became presidents precisely at the moment when conditions were ripe for a cooperative union-union venture—perhaps more so than at any time in the histories of their respective organizations. The Bell System had been broken up, and both had been thrust into a new world of global competition, domestic competition, technological explosion, and political realities that meant that organized labor had to develop innovative ways to stay alive, grow, and remain relevant. For the CWA and the IBEW, this meant recognizing that the immense amount of time and money spent in competitive dealings with each other had to be refocused on a common adversary. Both men have spoken to this issue and have talked to each other's members about the need for cooperation rather than confrontation.

The realization that a new view was in order occurred at the time of the 1986 national negotiations with AT&T. Because of their histories of simultaneous but not coordinated bargaining, the two unions came to the table with different agendas. The result was that the CWA went on strike and the IBEW settled. The effect was traumatic wherever CWA- and IBEW-represented employees worked in common surroundings. Both unions heard a hue and cry from local constituencies that such perceived "whipsawing" should never happen again. Fortunately, both Morton Bahr and Jack Barry had recently taken over the leadership of their unions.

Almost immediately after negotiations in 1986, both unions, along with AT&T, began to explore ways to deal with the issues vital to a successful relationship. The leadership of both unions at various levels began to work with each other in common interest groups and to hold joint sessions with AT&T. Of course, AT&T also had to have visionary leadership to see the wisdom of such cooperative ventures and to see how they would help position AT&T for growth and development in broader global markets in the future. Raymond Williams, AT&T's former corporate labor relations vice-president, was just such a leader. His relationship with both unions and his strong leadership during this period made AT&T's commitment to jointism possible.

The common interest groups are an excellent example of efforts by all three organizations to develop cooperation. Through these groups, labor and management come together to identify problems, explore possible solutions, and carry out those solutions together. The problems deal with issues ranging from product and service quality to employee skills to placement of surplus employees either inside or outside AT&T. Meetings regularly involve AT&T, CWA, and IBEW representatives, and their agendas deal with issues relevant to all three groups.

By the conclusion of 1986 negotiations, AT&T had developed the Alliance with the CWA and two employee development programs—the Partnership, for its nonfactory workers, and the Enhanced Training Opportunities Program (ETOP), for its factory-based work force—with the IBEW. In January 1987, less than six months after ratification, the CWA, the IBEW, and AT&T agreed to merge the Partnership program and the Alliance and to serve nonfactory IBEW-represented employees through the Alliance. (ETOP continues as originally constituted.)

About twenty-one local unions of the IBEW represent those members of AT&T who used to be covered by the Partnership Agreement: telephone operators, material handlers, marketing representatives, technicians, and clerical staff. Virtually every IBEW local is involved with an Alliance local committee, and in several cases these efforts involve CWA locals as well. In Chicago, outstate Illinois, New Jersey, and New England, cooperative ventures between the unions have enabled the Alliance to institute programs for employees who work in one union's jurisdiction but who will eventually work within the jurisdiction of the other. In addition, another effort is under way in California which involves the CWA and the Order of Repeater and Toll Technicians, a subunit of the IBEW. In the past, many local union relationships were strained by jurisdictional disputes. Today's cooperative agenda is a credit to the local leadership.

Also noteworthy is work done by a local committee on behalf of employees after a closing in Springfield, Massachusetts. The CWA local in that case was able to work out an arrangement with the IBEW to allow CWA members to take jobs in IBEW-represented operator services offices. Without this understanding, many employees might not have been placed.

It may be a long time before Morton Bahr, Jack Barry, and Ray Williams are recognized for their efforts in making the relationship between AT&T, the CWA, and the IBEW more harmonious. There is already recognition, however, of the benefits to AT&T, as well as the two unions, of working together. Perhaps their efforts could serve as a model for other companies and unions that are facing an uncertain and dubious future.

Organization

As with any organization, the Alliance is a combination of formal arrangements supported by informal processes that have evolved over time. We can define these arrangements in terms of the Alliance's internal structure, staff relationships, programmatic activities, and relationship to the parent organizations.

Internal Structure

The Alliance is driven by a cooperative, team-oriented approach whereby local committees are served directly and participants are served indirectly. Regional managers work in teams with associate directors, who work in teams with support staff. These team relationships cross organizational boundaries, so that team members may come from any geographic part of the organization. The Alliance has tried to create a relatively flat structure (not hierarchical). The Alliance recognizes, however, that a career path with the Alliance is the best way to ensure ongoing skill and continuity from within. To that end, all positions and work within the Alliance must continually be justified as a function of serving the mission of the Alliance, which is as follows:

> AT&T, the CWA and the IBEW share a vision that the growth and development of the individual is the key to success in a competitive worldwide marketplace. The ALLIANCE for Employee Growth and Development was born out of this shared vision to serve as a resource to individual employees who want to take charge of managing change in their own lives. The ALLIANCE mission is to support individual efforts to develop career and personal growth and enhance employability through continuation learning experiences. The success of these individual efforts will be assured by the cooperative activities of the ALLIANCE, CWA, IBEW and AT&T.

Staff Relationships

The Alliance views its staff as colleagues. Their daily work lives are expected to be driven by the mission. Staff are encouraged to continue their education, and the Alliance financially supports their efforts to do so. It also provides support by offering creative work schedules within the parameters of local committee needs.

Within the Alliance, it is believed that the success of employees is a function of their personal goals and how they work to realize those goals. In effect, the Alliance tries to serve as a local committee in supporting staff members as they pursue their own work-related goals.

The Alliance strives to hire "the best of the best" and to use a combination of "buy and make" in staffing. For the most part, employees are hired who already possess the skills necessary to carry out the Alliance mission. The technology surrounding our work is forever changing, however, so staff must stay current with new methodologies through educational opportunity, research, and experimentation. Nor can staff be expected to understand completely the political realities of dealing with a cooperative union-management structure such as the Alliance. Thus there is necessarily an ongoing process of educating and reeducating staff in the nuances of working with organizational representatives who, for the most part, got where they are because of their adversarial abilities.

Programmatic Activities

The Alliance develops its activities mainly through informal constructs, which are driven largely by local needs and perceptions. Once Alliance guidelines and policies have been developed and promulgated, great care must be taken to ensure that its programs are not restricted by these policies or guidelines but that programs serve the needs of individual employees. For this reason, there are few guidelines and even fewer policies, and both are constantly subject to review, modification, or rejection based solely on the needs of employees and how best to serve those needs.

Such an approach is certainly countercultural, and working for the Alliance is difficult at times. The Alliance is convinced, however, that this approach makes more options possible for both staff and members working with local committees and program participants themselves. Furthermore, there is the belief that tight policies and guidelines shut off alternatives, which can be explored only if there is freedom to do so.

Relationship to the Parent Organizations

The relationship of the Alliance to AT&T, the CWA, and the IBEW is potentially the most sensitive area of all. All three organizations are politically driven. With their democratic method of leadership selection, the two unions require that Alliance leadership stay in touch and in tune with their needs. Selection of the leadership at AT&T can also be politically driven. It is thus incumbent upon Alliance leadership to stay sensitive to the relationships of different units to the corporation and to how those units interrelate with one another.

Administration

The Alliance is currently headed by a six-person board of trustees that includes John Barry; Morton Bahr; Bill Ketchum, corporate vice-president of labor relations for AT&T; Jim Irvine, vice-president of the CWA; John O'Neill, executive vice-president of AT&T; and Paul Wondrasch, president of AT&T General Business Systems.

Two co-executive directors, Kenneth Ross, from AT&T, and Donald Treinen, from the CWA, report directly to the trustees and are charged with running the daily operations of the Alliance and managing its fiscal goals. The director of the Alliance, Marshall Goldberg, is responsible for all Alliance programming. He reports to the co-executive directors and works closely with them in formulating policy, practice, and program activity. His staff includes three regional managers, employment and training professionals, and support personnel.

The backbone of the Alliance organization is the local committees. These committees are usually made up of about six persons, three each from the company and unions. It is their job to raise the awareness of the Alliance in the eyes of their work force; to survey the work force to identify training needs; to identify potential vendors of services within the local community; to work with Alliance staff to negotiate contracts with vendors; to monitor training activities for quality and relevant outcomes; and to perform posttraining analysis to ensure that programming is ongoing and fits the needs of the workers themselves.

Alliance local committees are found at the local work force level, wherever a need arises. In some cases, the need is an impending layoff or surplus labor situation in which employees need services to stay employed within AT&T or to be reemployable in the outside labor market. In other cases, activists within the union and company start committees to serve the needs of workers whose jobs are relatively secure but whose skills need updating.

The work of Alliance local committees is generally carried out during regular work hours, but members quite often contribute their own time as well. AT&T has made a commitment that Alliance local committee work is a regular part of an employee's job. The committee members make a committment to spend whatever time is necessary to bring services to their people—even if it requires personal time to do so.

Service Delivery

The client base is made up of AT&T employees represented by the CWA or the IBEW (except the IBEW factories), whether they are actively employed or on layoff. It has been said that the only difference between an active worker and a laid-off worker is a job. The Alliance approach to service delivery can be defined as a slightly different version of that premise: services must be relevant both to workers who are currently without work and to those who may be without work unless they undertake preparatory activities to stay employed.

Meeting Diverse Needs

Global competition, technology, the methods by which technology is introduced, decisions governing pricing arrangements, and the national and international political climates governing how corporations do business are largely outside the scope of an individual worker's influence. Nonetheless, these forces affect both employed and unemployed workers. The difference is in the immediate impact. Those who are laid off obviously feel the effect immediately, whereas those who remain employed wonder just how long it will be before the "other shoe falls."

AT&T functions within a fairly well-defined industry with its own unique set of cultural circumstances but widely shared global realities. It must seek its share of a marketplace which while global is still discreet. It must maintain a reasonable rate of return to its shareholders. It must stay current with the latest in technology. It must attract capital for growth and expansion. And it must develop and maintain workers who are committed to ensuring the success of their employer. The company must do all of these things within the constructs of a range of political systems with varying views of the world and the ability to affect it.

In contrast, the sole purpose of unions is to better the lives of working people and their families. Unions have found many avenues for achieving this goal. Some of these avenues involve methods adversarial to the interest of employers. Other methods call for cooperation among various coalitions of unions, community groups, special-interest groups, government units, corporations, and corporate interest groups. The underlying premise of all of these efforts, however, is to serve the membership.

It has been the goal of the Alliance to develop programs that serve the needs of both current and separating employees. The approach with displaced workers is to implement Alliance awareness, a work force survey, career assessment, personal growth programming, skills assessment and training, educational opportunity training, job development, and ultimately job placement. The approach with active workers is very much the same; placement *within* the corporation is the ultimate goal for every employee to whom that decision makes personal and good sense.

In a very real sense, outplacement is part of the internal staffing strategy. How it is done, how it is received, and how effective it is have a great deal to do with how successful the organizations carrying out such activities will be.

Importance of Timing
It is difficult to measure directly the impact of short notice versus advance notice of a change in employee status such as layoff, downsizing, or transfer, but the Alliance has found, in general, that the more time employees are given, the more preparation can be undertaken. In Merrimack Valley, Massachusetts, for example, there were two layoffs of about seven hundred AT&T employees each. The Alliance was contacted before the second layoff. Our data suggest that, in spite of valiant efforts to reach those involved in the first layoff, most of the almost eight hundred employees who went through Alliance programming were from the second group.

Timing was also vital in Houston, Texas, and Springfield, Massachusetts, projects. In Houston, technicians knew that their work had been reduced to a point where layoffs would occur and had been given information about other locations where work was available. The Alliance was asked to help during this period, which it did by holding a relocation planning session. According to personal interviews with the participants after the project was completed, many technicians found the relocation service helped them not only to move but to do so intelligently.

In Springfield, a full year's notice was given. The local committee was thus able to find jobs within AT&T for the vast majority of the nearly two hundred employees affected. Many of these placements involved physical moves, and again the local committee was able not only to find jobs but to gather data about the locations, which was very useful to the participants.

When no notice or little notice of layoffs is given, the participation rate in Alliance activities is much lower. In late 1986, we were called in to serve a group of employees in the Minneapolis area who were faced with job loss at the end of the year. The Alliance representative reported that the initial orientation session was so disruptive that it was impossible to launch any meaningful preparation effort. Employees had just been notified of their layoff and their anger level was such that they could not think rationally about their future. As a postscript to this story, a significant number of these people were apparently supported through career counseling and placement activities, but the Alliance was unable to ascertain placement rates because it lost touch with them shortly after layoff and had to rely on the service provider for data on how many were served. Clearly, this experience was not optimal, but it supports the notion that local committees should be able to work with service providers to ensure that the product serves the needs of the employees. It also placed the Alliance in the uncomfortable position of having to rely on a vendor report because it was unable to monitor or verify the level of service given.

The most current example of what can be done with advance notice of displacement concerns the operator services project, which is aimed at the several thousand telephone operators who are being laid off because of changes in technology. In this case, the Alliance received notice ranging from several months to several years, which was enough time to negotiate a sound working arrangement with AT&T, the CWA, the IBEW, and the U.S. Department of Labor to implement strategy; plan and carry out regional planning conferences so as to get Alliance local committees launched; identify nationwide providers of services; and develop long-term processes for identifying jobs both within AT&T and in the labor market at large, as well as the skills needed to secure those jobs. Because this is a nationwide effort affecting employees in about 250 work locations, the necessary coordination and networking of people and organizations simply could not have happened with short notice.

To summarize, the most successful Alliance efforts have been the ones in which there was the most advance notice. At the very least, individuals must have enough notice to work through the "death and dying" process that is inevitable when employees are being laid off. If meaningful and useful support is to be given, this process must take place while employees are still at work, since support mechanisms are delivered best in familiar surroundings.

Services Provided

Any measure of the success of the Alliance should be solely a function of how well it served individuals. Nonetheless, there is at least some value in examining organizational activity. Such a view provides a yardstick by which the Alliance can be measured by those who are unable to get qualitative and ongoing opinions of Alliance-sponsored services from thousands of individuals.

The Alliance was formally chartered in October 7, 1986, and it launched its first project in late December of that year. Since then, the organization has grown as follows:

January 1987—opened national headquarters in New Jersey and hired first two employees.

Second quarter 1987—staff level at six.

Third quarter 1987—staff level at nine.

Fourth quarter 1987—staff level at eleven.

First quarter 1988—staff level at sixteen.

April 1, 1988—opened regional office in Texas.

Second quarter 1988—staff level at thirty-one.

Third quarter 1988—staff level at forty-one.

August 1, 1988—opened regional office in Georgia.

August 23, 1988—opened regional office in New Jersey.

Fourth quarter 1988—staff level at forty-six.

First quarter 1989—staff level at fifty-five.

Current staff level—fifty.

The Alliance co-executive directors are not part of this count since they are part of their parent organization's staff. In addition, from time to time, college interns work for the Alliance as part of an Alliance-college partnership.

Ongoing Programs (as of mid-1990)

Established 450 Alliance local committees.

Committee presence in forty-nine states.

Committee presence in all represented AT&T business units.

Committee presence in 300 CWA locals.

Committee presence in twenty-one IBEW locals.

Surveyed over 45,000 employees.

About 30,000 professionally developed career plans are on file.

Over 5,700 employees are in prepaid college credit tuition programs.

Tuition payments have been paid to over 325 colleges and universities, totaling in excess of $3 million.

Displacement projects have served over 10,000 workers.

Over 48,000 employees have been in program activities.

Over 600 vendor contracts have provided group-sized training services.

Over $3 million in federal and state grants have been obtained for displaced worker programs.

Educational assistance ranges from basic skills upgrades through specific skills education to high school equivalency and a full range of college degree programs.

Have trained workers in over 300 different occupational categories.

Over 1,500 persons have been placed in work as a result of displacement in Alabama, Illinois, Massachusetts, Michigan, Minnesota, New Jersey, Ohio, South Dakota, Texas, and Washington.

Established employee resource centers in sites where there is significant AT&T employee presence, staffed with professional counselors and run by Alliance local committees.

Developed a relocation assistance workshop.

Developed a career assessment package for on-site and remote delivery.

Developed a databased tracking system for worker participant tracking, for prepaid tuition payment tracking, for career counseling, and for financial control tracking.

Developed a databased tracking and retrieval system for survey documentation.

Established an Alliance local committee training process complete with documentation.

Established an institute for training the technician for tomorrow in cooperation with the community college system.

Negotiated master contract arrangements with community college networks to serve as an umbrella administrative organization with a number of colleges to deliver services in a high-quality and cost-effective manner.

Established on-site computer-based training classrooms in six AT&T factories.

These efforts would not be in effect today were it not for an effective Alliance local committee structure served by professional Alliance staff and supported by AT&T, the CWA, and the IBEW.

Issues of Service Implementation

The initiation of Alliance-sponsored services starts at the local level with individual employees, their employer, and the union local. The Alliance operates within a framework of local-level cooperation. One of its basic premises is that Alliance programs may be initiated only at the request of a worker or committee.

The assumption of the Alliance is that employees will initiate individualized programs. The culture in which employees operate, however, suggests that someone a level or more above them will decide what is best, how programs are to be constructed, and how to measure results. At the same time, employees do not believe such a process works well for them. One of the assumptions, therefore, is that the Alliance must be countercultural. Furthermore, there are not enough Alliance employees to carry out Alliance activities in AT&T's thousands of work locations nationwide. Finally, Alliance staff assume that any program designed and carried out by some central bureaucracy will never be fully supported and owned at the level where the program is implemented.

Based on these realities, the Alliance works as a partner with local committees in training members how to plan and implement basic human resource services. Assistance is provided in surveying workers, raising the awareness of the workers about the Alliance and its services, assessing needs of the work force, and identifying providers of services. The Alliance assists local committees in selecting vendors and analyzing vendor activities over time. The Alliance also signs and holds service delivery contracts and assists local committees in monitoring those contracts. Finally, the Alliance works with local committees to find other work and assist employees in placement, both internally and externally.

From time to time, committees are unable to get started or to sustain themselves. Sometimes it is because of problems in the labor-management climate, but quite often it is because there is a lack of knowledge about the Alliance at higher organizational levels of the company. In such cases, the Alliance is called upon to raise consciousness so that local activities can get started or resume.

One of the most vital parts of implementation is the visible, action-oriented support of both union and management, and the very highest levels of both organizations are looked to for such support. Those at the local level who actually carry out Alliance programming cannot do so if they have no support from above. Between local-level people and top leadership exist mid-level union and company officials. This group tends to be left out of the Alliance program support equation. To alleviate this problem, AT&T, the CWA, and the IBEW have established regional-level committees whose job it is to support local-level Alliance activities in whatever manner is indicated. These committees are informally constructed and involve representatives from AT&T labor relations, AT&T human resources, and the CWA and/or IBEW international staff. It is their responsibility to perform damage control when necessary and, more proactively, to help local people get started.

In certain cases, AT&T and the unions have created a process to involve higher-level people in providing visible and action-oriented support by establishing national working committees and policy committees and by having high-level representatives present at Alliance training and planning conferences. This combination of formal and informal efforts has created a smooth process for empowering union and company people at the local level.

A basic premise of the Alliance is that service delivery must conform to the needs of employees, when they need it and where they can use it. Any effort to provide training and educational or placement services without regard to this premise will fail.

The Alliance cannot be relevant to employees who are laid off or scheduled to be unless it is willing and able to respond rapidly, coherently, and within the time frame that is most desirable to the affected employees. (We also consider this to be true without the compressed time frame for career-track employees.) The greatest ally for workers faced with layoff is time. There must be adequate time for employees to experience anger, betrayal, frustration, bitterness, resignation, and denial and finally to act toward planning a future. The next greatest ally is support. Our experience shows that it is unwise to try to compress unnaturally the time needed to go through the inevitable "death and dying" syndrome. We believe that the first intervention for such employees must be professional counseling. Usually, this must include at the very least stress management, an analysis of the current situation both at work and at home, and the opportunity to develop and preserve feelings of self-worth. These components are vital if workers are to progress to the next step: undertaking a thoughtful process of self-evaluation and preparing for future work.

Early intervention will not succeed unless the service delivery organization has a high level of credibility. Critical to this effort are local-level union and company program planners—the members of the Alliance local committee. We have found that before any professional intervention can take place, workers must believe the local committee is truly committed to their well-being. Given that most laid-off workers feel the union and company have somehow let them down, this is very hard to do. If the union-management relationship has been emotionally charged and highly adversarial, it sometimes takes months to start effective programming and sometimes programming never happens. We have also found, however, that where a long-standing mature union-management relationship exists, the time required to move through the death and dying stage can be reduced because workers believe in the source of help and will reach out.

Once the conditions are right for professionally developed service delivery, the Alliance is prepared to move in quickly. We currently have a cadre of professional counselors under contract with the Alliance who are mobilized—literally—to go to the location of individual employees and work with them. The Alliance is responsible for the expenses incurred by the counselors, and the counselors are responsible for concentrating on the work of assisting employees. Individual employees involved with this program are responsible for concentrating on assessing where they are, where they want to go, and how to get there. Several hundred employees have been involved with this effort, and early indications are that the process works because the workers believe in the service, the counselors are well trained and committed, and the Alliance is seen as value added to these employees' lives.

Our data show that employees' needs are bottom-line oriented. They need meaningful work, and they need options to find and keep such work. This idea of options is strongly embedded in the Alliance culture because we have consistently found that where options do not exist, people who are laid off, even those with marketable skills, are paralyzed and find it difficult to take the necessary steps to get on with their lives. Thus the next step after counseling is to move people quickly through career assessment, skills assessment, aptitudes assessment, job market analysis, skills training, and preparation for placement in other work. Only after other meaningful employment is found and people are placed is the effort considered successful. Only when workers feel successful do we consider our efforts to have met their goals.

Long-Term Initiatives

The Alliance was founded on the notion that employment security has more to do with meeting individuals' long-term needs than with meeting short-term needs of the employer at any given moment. For the employer to "buy in" to this outlook, there must be both immediate and long-term payoffs, however. The same is true for a union.

For the company, the payoff is the prospect of having an employee body that has a host of general skills: keyboarding, data manipulation, problem solving, and decision making; an understanding of technology systems, resource management, the economics of work, human relations, math and science; and career planning and development skills. Virtually every work setting of the future will require skills in these areas. In addition, it is in the best interest of the company to have employees leave for other work with a good feeling toward their former employer. In the case of AT&T, such people will most likely continue to utilize services provided by the telecommunications industry—either from AT&T or from one of its competitors. Who they choose as their supplier may be a function of how they were treated as employees.

For the CWA and the IBEW, future success is tied to their ability to serve their memberships in ways that are seen as value added by the members themselves. Being partners in helping people develop strong employment security is perhaps the greatest service any union can provide. As workers leave AT&T, there is a greater than even chance they will find work in nonunion settings. Having these "goodwill ambassadors" of organized labor moving into other work cannot help but enhance the image of labor to a broader audience.

Conclusion

The Alliance continues to better people's lives by providing education that enhances life at work and at home. We are a catalyst organization, a tool of AT&T, the CWA, and the IBEW, to help people become better, more productive members of society. Most of our efforts are internal to AT&T. We help those transitioning out do so with dignity and success. And we help those staying keep their skills current and take on new work.

There is a great deal of interest in the education of America. The Alliance is reaching out with industries, labor organizations, government agencies, academic institutions, and other groups to those who are economically and educationally disenfranchised. We see this effort as directly supporting our mission. If we can develop a better system of planning and delivering meaningful education to all Americans, we will serve the needs of our constituents—those employees of AT&T represented by the CWA and the IBEW.

The Alliance believes it is at the forefront of a great experiment. Within the larger context of the global marketplace, organizations such as the Alliance can—and should—be seen as "living labs" for research into ways cooperative efforts can benefit all the stakeholders involved.

4 · THE UAW-FORD EDUCATION, DEVELOPMENT AND TRAINING PROGRAM

Elizabeth S. Tomasko and Kenneth K. Dickinson

This chapter provides a detailed overview of the UAW-Ford Education, Development and Training Program, one of the most advanced programs of its kind. Written by co-directors of the program, it describes the activities available rather than providing evaluation or analysis. (Since the chapter was written, Bill Stevenson has replaced Elizabeth Tomasko as co-director of the program.) The chapter will be particularly valuable to practitioners and program planners who want a model for joint training and development.

Throughout most of the history of labor-management relations in the United States, training and employee development played at best a minor role in collective bargaining. Except for some pure on-the-job training programs or apprentice training, unions and companies tended to focus on traditional bargaining subjects, notably wages, benefits, job security, and working conditions.

As the 1970s came to a close, however, it became increasingly evident that powerful new forces were altering the essential nature of American industry. These forces included global competition, the relative decline of the manufacturing sector of the economy, sweeping technological advances, changes in the growth and composition of the work force, and, in some instances, a crushing recession.

Unions and companies came to realize that they were facing a serious common peril and that meeting this peril required a trained and productive work force. They also recognized that worker dislocation had to be handled responsibly and humanely. Logic urged that the parties turn their attention to human growth—to helping workers achieve their full personal potential. During the 1980s, a number of unions and companies thus addressed training and employee development concerns in their collective bargaining agreements.

The UAW-Ford Education, Development and Training Program (EDTP), negotiated in 1982, was among the first such efforts, and it pioneered many of the features that are now appearing in other collective bargaining agreements. Hailed as "a prototype of the kind of cooperatively run institutions . . . desperately needed in America" (Hansen 1987:553), this fully joint program offers personal growth, education, and development opportunities for both active and laid-off UAW-represented hourly Ford employees.

Overall, the EDTP has been remarkably successful, and both the UAW and Ford are justifiably proud of its accomplishments. One of the most extensive joint efforts undertaken by the UAW and Ford, the program demonstrates what is possible when adversaries join forces to meet mutual goals.

The EDTP gives UAW-represented hourly Ford employees the opportunity to upgrade their skills and undertake a wide variety of personal development courses of their own choosing. In addition, the effort has contributed to improving product quality, operating styles, communication between the UAW and Ford, and the working environment in Ford plants. Numerous articles in national periodicals have documented how these changes have contributed to Ford's competitive resurgence.[1]

The EDTP is built on participative principles and has many of the ingredients basic to other UAW-Ford joint efforts: local committees; voluntary participation by workers; local program flexibility; and national support, including personnel, resources, and encouragement. The program is funded under the collective bargaining agree-

---

1. See, for example, *Time*, June 13, 1988, p. 46; *Motor Trend*, special 1988 issue; *Fortune*, January 4, 1988; *Barron's*, June 15, 1987, p. 8.

ment by company contributions based on the number of hours worked by UAW-represented hourly employees.

The policy-making unit of the EDTP is a joint governing body composed of equal numbers of UAW and company representatives. The co-chairs of this body are Ernest Lofton, vice-president of the UAW and director of the union's National Ford Department, and Peter J. Pestillo, vice-president of corporate relations and diversified businesses for Ford. The joint governing body establishes program policy, provides overall guidance, authorizes expenditures of funds, and directs program administration through the UAW-Ford National Education, Development and Training Center.

A nonprofit corporation, the center is located on the campus of the Henry Ford Community College in Dearborn, Michigan. Opened in 1983 as a ten-thousand-square-foot facility and expanded to sixty thousand square feet in early 1988, the new center now houses nine UAW-Ford joint initiatives: the Education, Development and Training Program; the Employee Assistance Plan; the Health and Safety Program; the Employee Involvement Process; the "Best-in-Class" Quality Program; Mutual Growth Forums; the Labor-Management Studies Program; the Child Care Resource and Referral Service; and the Apprenticeship Program.

The center's staff, who are employees of the nonprofit corporation, has grown from eight to more than ninety. The staff includes both union and company representatives, who play a key role in implementing the center's programs, as well as professionals with backgrounds in education, counseling, training, placement, and information processing. The center concentrates on planning, design, and coordinative functions and provides on-site assistance to local committees in implementing national programs and, as appropriate, in designing and implementing local programs. It functions principally as a broker of services and limits on-site training to local committee members and certain program coordinators. The center also assists in identifying outside funding sources when appropriate and integrating them with the negotiated joint UAW-Ford EDTP fund. The center is action-oriented. Its main function is to make things happen and to evaluate their effectiveness.

The EDTP implements its activities through local EDTP committees at eighty Ford facilities throughout the country and in their surrounding communities. The EDTP works closely with local government, social, and educational resources. This is a conscious choice, both philosophically and practically. The local committees and the national center, for the most part, do not provide educational or training services directly. Rather, they arrange for existing institutions and organizations to provide such services. Thus the EDTP has access to a broad delivery network whose components can be assembled and reassembled to match specific needs.

The program's principal objectives are to provide education, training, retraining, and development opportunities for both active and displaced employees; to support other local and national UAW-Ford joint activities; and to provide opportunities for Ford, the UAW, and other employers and educational institutions to exchange ideas regarding employee education, development, and training needs.

When the program was established, no attempt was made to set out all the details of what was to be done or how to do it. Rather, the union and the company formulated a general charter and broad guidelines. Given employees' ever-changing training needs, there is probably no other way to administer such a training program.

From the outset, the EDTP recognized that planning and administration of the program required professional support. Yet they also wanted to encourage local union and plant management autonomy and local ownership of the program so that program users would be intimately involved. Finally, they wanted to identify and serve the needs and desires of individual workers and not impose preconceived notions. The national center was established with these goals in mind.

Although assistance to displaced workers was one of the principal reasons the EDTP was established, relatively few workers are now on lay-off with seniority recall rights. Consequently, we will begin by reviewing programs for active workers and then discuss programs for the displaced.

Programs for Active Workers

The key EDTP programs for the approximately 105,000 Ford Motor Company and Rouge Steel Company U.S. active employees represented by the UAW are usually presented internally under the general heading of "Avenues for Employee Growth" (see fig. 4.1).[2] The emphasis is on the broad personal development and growth of individual workers. Within these "avenues," UAW-represented Ford employees can select programs suited to their backgrounds, interests, and goals.

In contrast to traditional concepts of employee training and education, which are usually focused only on specific job-related skills, these programs are designed to meet individual needs. The general components of this effort are the Life/Education Planning Program; the Education and Training Assistance Plan; the Skills Enhancement Program; the College and University Options Program; the Targeted Education, Training, or Counseling Projects; the Successful Retirement Planning Program; and the Financial Education Program. Some of these are umbrella programs that embrace other related elements. Individual programs are available to active workers through participation in nationwide programs administered by the national center; others are designed by local EDTP committees assisted by the center.

The hope is that these "avenues" will help UAW-represented Ford employees prepare for a changing workplace. Specifically, the EDTP aims to provide workers with the basic foundation necessary to get, keep, and progress on a job, including the attitude, behavior, and ability to work with others. In addition to the education, development, and training programs, Ford workers also receive considerable company training so they can perform their assigned jobs.

Life/Education Planning Program

Typically, participating in the Life/Education Planning Program (L/EPP) is the first step a worker takes toward planning future educational and personal goals. Through workshops and related exercises, this program helps workers assess various aspects of their lives, identify methods and resources available to them, and, finally, use the EDTP and community resources to help achieve their personal and career goals. By focusing on the workers' needs and interests, the program provides an incentive to all workers to participate.

---

2. Rouge Steel Company is an independent steel company located in the Rouge complex. All of its hourly employees are represented by the UAW.

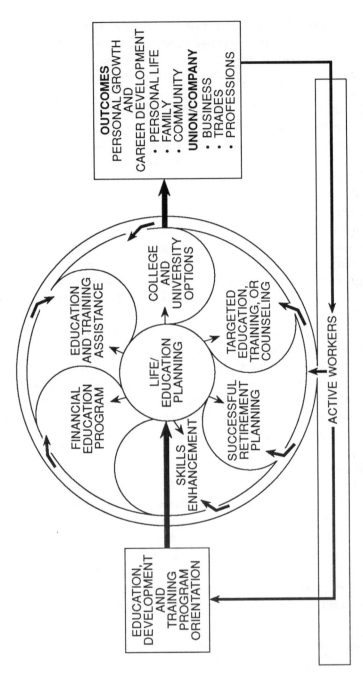

Figure 4.1   UAW-Ford Education, Development and Training Program Avenues for Employee Growth

Under the guidance of the local EDTP committee, a full-time on-site professional life education advisor (LEA) provides workers at each major facility with advice, information, referral, and support regarding education and training. LEAs are employees of the University of Michigan but are under contract with the national center. They receive support, guidance, and professional development from the university. The relationship of the L/EPP with other EDTP programs and with UAW-represented Ford employees is shown in figure 4.1.

Since the Life/Education Planning Program was launched in July 1985, sixty-seven locations have formally implemented the program, utilizing the services of approximately sixty LEAs. These on-site LEAs have provided individual advising and information sessions for over twenty thousand workers and have conducted over one hundred L/EPP workshops involving over seven hundred workers. Evaluations of the Life/Education Planning Program have indicated that the on-site LEAs have significantly increased worker participation in programs implemented by the national center.

Education and Training Assistance Plan

The Education and Training Assistance Plan (ETAP) is designed to enable workers to return to school on their own. It provides for prepayment of tuition and other compulsory fees, up to a maximum of $2,550 per calendar year, for approved, self-selected credit and degree courses at approved colleges and universities. Such assistance covers most formal courses that workers may wish to pursue.

Included in ETAP is a special personal development assistance feature that enables workers to take courses not generally covered by the plan's basic provisions. Under this provision, workers may take noncredit and nondegree courses and activities for personal development in areas such as communication skills, success and motivational training, and time management. Tuition and compulsory fees are paid, up to a maximum of $1,800 per calendar year, as part of the annual $2,550 ETAP allocation.

The Education and Training Assistance Plan, including its personal development assistance feature, has grown dramatically since 1984, the first year of the plan, when the number of participants totaled 4,100.[3] It reached 7,700 in 1986 and 15,000 in 1988. This increase is even more significant given that during the twenty years when the company unilaterally administered an hourly employee tuition refund program (1964–83), no more than 2 percent of the work force participated in any year. The 1988 figure of 15,000 participants represents 14 percent of the work force.

A 1986 case study of the Education and Training Assistance Plan by Abt Associates, Inc., of Cambridge, Massachusetts, noted that there was an 80 percent increase in the number of approved applications between 1983 (the last year when the hourly tuition refund program was in force) and 1984, when ETAP was initiated. Furthermore, this growth occurred in a population whose average age is forty-four years.

In general, the key reasons for the success of ETAP and its personal development assistance feature, in addition to the LEAs, have been the scheduling of registration, the availability of counseling, and the fact that classes are given at the plant and union leadership and company management actively promote the program.

Skills Enhancement Program

The Skills Enhancement Program (SEP) invites workers to pursue their education and includes learning and counseling with respect to adult basic education, high school completion, general educational development, English as a second language, educational enrichment, and academic advising. The program is delivered on-site in conjunction with local school systems and includes features such as open entry, open exit; computer-aided instruction; private tutorials; low teacher-student ratios; self-paced learning; and peer support.

Since the first Skills Enhancement Program was started in 1983, the program has been established at most major locations, and 10,700 workers have participated. There are varying emphases: remediation, updating, and college or technical preparation. Because the program instills self-esteem and self-confidence in its participants and materially improves their quality of life, the objective by year-end 1990 is to have a Skills Enhancement Program at every ma-

---

3. If a worker participated in both ETAP and in the personal development assistance feature, he or she would have been counted only once for that year.

jor Ford location where there are UAW-represented employees. Experience has shown that the key to the success of any plant's SEP is the involvement and support of the local union-management committee, union leadership, and company management.

College and University Options Program
This program is designed to make both degree and nondegree college and technical training more accessible to workers. Key elements of this program include workshops for workers, the involvement of partner educational institutions, the transfer of credits among partner institutions, on-site course registration and classes at times that are convenient to workers, individual couseling by academic advisors, and credits for college-level knowledge and skills gained outside the college classroom.

The College and University Options Program was piloted in 1985 and made substantial progress in 1986 and 1987. As of the fall of 1988, more than 120 colleges and universities had joined the UAW-Ford National Education, Development and Training Center as partners in striving to achieve program objectives. All major company locations are now sponsoring on-site classes either at their plants or at local union halls. The first groups of degree-earning students are now beginning to graduate from two- and four-year institutions.

Targeted Education, Training, or Counseling Projects
The Targeted Education, Training, or Counseling Projects (TETCP) include carefully selected pilot projects that are responsive to specific educational training or counseling needs of a particular location or segment of the work force. TETCP is the most specialized of the UAW-Ford EDTP "Avenues of Growth." To ensure consistent high-quality program content and delivery, these projects are initially conducted on a one-time basis as a pilot to allow for proper analysis and evaluation before they are made available under ETAP.

There is a lot of variation in the content of these programs. Programs in 1984 through 1986 included computer awareness, electronics training, small-engine repair, roofing assistants training, and time management. Technology literacy was among the offerings in 1988.

Successful Retirement Planning Program

The Successful Retirement Planning Program (SRPP) provides pre-retirement planning to workers and their spouses. The program's objectives are to aid workers in making the transition to retirement by providing information that enables them to undertake comprehensive planning and enhance their understanding of UAW-Ford benefits applicable to retirees. SRPP emphasizes early planning for retirement. Attendance is open to workers of all ages, and spouses are encouraged to attend. The program typically consists of eight two- to three-hour on-site workshops at either the Ford facility or the local union hall. Selected resource persons—experts in the subjects—provide information on such topics as Social Security, pension benefits, health awareness, medications (including prescription drugs), legal and financial matters, and leisure time planning.

Since SRPP was established in the fall of 1984, more than four hundred programs have been conducted at all major Ford locations. More than ten thousand workers and spouses have attended the workshop sessions.

In May 1987, this program received a certificate of appreciation from the Social Security Administration for advising UAW-represented Ford workers and their spouses about Social Security benefits.

The key to the success of the program is identifying hourly and salaried employees who will participate in the training necessary to facilitate the workshops.

Financial Education Program

During 1987 negotiations, the UAW and Ford agreed to establish a personal financial education program as a new feature of the EDTP. This decision resulted from a "grass-roots" push for such a program, which had surfaced at numerous locations. The program, which was started in July 1988, covers such subjects as personal financial planning and goal setting; investments and insurance; wills, trusts, and titling property; loans and consumer hints; Ford's financial fringe benefits for UAW-represented employees; and implementation of a financial planning checklist. The program is delivered by providers certified by the national center. Local committees evaluate and select a provider of their choice, and, as with the Retirement Planning Program, spouses are encouraged to attend.

Response to the Financial Education Program has exceeded the EDTP's expectations. By the end of 1989, four thousand workers and spouses had attended programs. The program is attracting not only large members of workers but also many who have never participated in center programs before.

Activities to Promote the Program

The EDTP depends for its success on making UAW-represented employees aware of the programs. Extensive national and local promotional materials on video and in print are regularly prepared and updated. In addition, the national center conducts in-depth training for members of joint local EDTP committees and, in conjunction with the University of Michigan, for the life education advisors. The center is also committed to improving its staff in order to ensure the best in class planning, delivery, and administration.

One way active workers are reached is through education fairs. These fairs are typically conducted at work locations and are scheduled to accommodate workers on all shifts. They have been very successful in familiarizing large numbers of workers in many plants with EDTP activities. Representatives from local education and training institutions assist the workers by providing information about how they might pursue their personal education, training, and development goals and often allow workers to register for classes immediately.

In 1986 and 1987, EDTP programs were also promoted through a traveling exhibit. The exhibit consisted of a custom-designed CL 9000 Ford highway tractor and trailer that contained a thousand-square-foot theater and displays explaining center programs. The exhibit visited over sixty locations, traveled over thirty-three thousand miles, and was viewed by an estimated sixty thousand workers and guests.

In 1987 negotiations, Ford and the UAW agreed to develop a satellite communications system, including a broadcast studio, for use by EDTP programs. The first nationwide teleconference emanating from the center was broadcast in July 1988 to introduce the Financial Education Program. Compared to traditional methods, the communications system has added greatly to the center's ability to reach workers quickly and in a manner that is clearly understood by union leadership and company management. The system's success was borne out by the rapid response from local joint committees to implementing the Financial Education Program. The satellite broadcast facility is the first such jointly owned facility. The system should both increase services available to workers and reinforce joint programs. The national center offers the satellite system to all the joint programs housed at the center.

A grants-for-plants initiative was developed in 1986 to assist local plants in delivering more uniform education and training opportunities and to ensure that facilities and equipment are comparable at all locations. Under this initiative, larger Ford Motor Company plants may apply for a one-time grant of up to $30,000 and small locations for a one-time grant of up to $15,000 for the purpose of securing items needed for training, such as tables, chairs, desks, and audiovisual equipment, and to make temporary modifications in the plants to provide classroom space. The program has increased significantly the capability of local facilities to establish on-site classes. The equipment is owned by the national center.

Programs for Displaced Workers

At the time the EDTP was negotiated in 1982, the auto industry was in the depths of a terrible recession. U.S. hourly employment at Ford had peaked in 1978 at just over 200,000. By 1982, the hourly work force was a little more than 100,000. As a result, the national center's first efforts were focused on providing assistance to employees affected by plant closings or major layoffs.

One of the reasons for establishing the EDTP was to provide those workers who had little likelihood of returning to Ford or to the industry with assistance in finding new jobs. Both the company and the union recognized that traditional income support during layoff had to be supplemented so as to address the problems of permanent structural dislocation.

National Vocational Retraining Assistance Plan

The National Vocational Retraining Assistance Plan (NVRAP) was the first program lauched by the national center and the first tuition assistance effort for laid-off employees in a major collective bargaining setting. The plan, which became operational in August 1982, makes it possible for eligible laid-off workers to return to school to take courses of their choosing. Depending on their years of seniority at the time of layoff, workers have up to $6,000 in prepaid tuition. As in the Education and Training Assistance Plan, workers are expected to take classes at accredited colleges, universities, or other recognized educational providers.

As a result of the decline in the number of laid-off workers with recall rights since 1982, the utilization of NVRAP has dropped from a peak of 2,100 participants in 1983 to fewer than 400 in 1987 to fewer than 250 in 1988. For the most part, workers have selected technical courses in areas with good employment prospects.

Career Services and Reemployment Assistance Centers

Assistance to laid-off workers is provided primarily through "one-stop, full-service" centers referred to as UAW-Ford Career Services and Reemployment Assistance Centers (CS/RACs). The centers provide a variety of services.

Career counseling. Professional staff help laid-off workers determine their interests, skills, and marketable experience and how to achieve their personal career goals.

Supportive counseling. Workers are referred to community service resources for assistance in dealing with concerns related to being unemployed.

Skills enhancement courses. Workers are given refresher instruction in mathematics and communication skills.

Classroom training. Workers are given prepaid tuition and specialized intensive vocational retraining for occupations in demand in the local labor market.

On-the-job training. Participants are hired by an employer and trained on the job with a limited subsidy (when available) through applicable federal displaced worker assistance funds.

Job clubs and job search workshops. Trained staff assist workers in preparing resumés, developing effective interviewing techniques, and learning the skills necessary to find a job.

Job placement assistance. Professional job developers assist laid-off workers in locating employment.

Government funding is used if appropriate and available to provide these services.

Through the end of 1990, more than ten thousand UAW-represented Ford hourly employees had taken advantage of one or more of the services provided by the centers. Such centers are established when and where they are needed and are phased out when their services are no longer required.

As of year-end 1990, centers served workers affected by the closing of the Canton, Ohio, and Green Island, New York, plants. (Figure 4.2 shows the services available from the centers.)

Relocation Assistance Program

The Relocation Assistance Program was developed in 1984 to help both active and dislocated hourly workers who are transferring to a Ford facility that is at least fifty miles from their former work site. A family relocation assistance center provides a broad range of services including individual and family counseling, assistance with locating temporary housing, information on housing sales and purchases, job placement assistance for family members, tax information, discounts on moving, truck rentals, community profiles, and a relocation planning guide. The relocation center also has a nationwide toll-free telephone number. Relocation assistance loans are also available ranging from five hundred to one thousand dollars. Finally, relocation coordinators are assigned to plants that are adding large numbers of workers from other Ford facilities. These coordinators provide counseling and assistance.

Conclusions

Since the inception of the UAW-Ford EDTP in 1982 and its expansion as a result of 1984, 1987, and 1990 negotiations, overall utilization has steadily increased. To date, approximately fifty-three thousand active and laid-off workers have taken part in some part of the program. Based on evaluation and monitoring projects, studies, and surveys of both active and laid-off workers and the opinions of center staff, the program has been successful primarily because it offers fields of study workers want. Furthermore, classes are available at each location and are focused on the interests of workers at that location. Both plant management and local union leadership actively encourage workers to participate, and workers may participate without any financial commitment on their part. Classes are scheduled to accommodate all shifts and, where appropriate, are self-paced. Thus classes are structured for the adult learner. The value of the life/education advisors is also important in providing counseling and assistance.

PERSONAL DEVELOPMENT AND SERVICES COMPONENT

TRAINING AND PLACEMENT COMPONENT

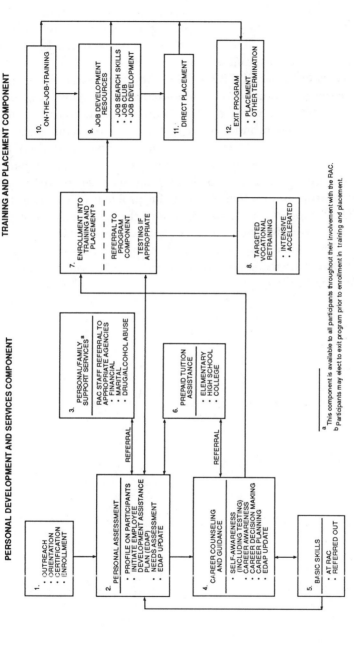

1.
• OUTREACH
• ORIENTATION
• CERTIFICATION
• ENROLLMENT

2. PERSONAL ASSESSMENT
• PROFILE ON PARTICIPANTS
• INITIATE EMPLOYEE DEVELOPMENT ASSISTANCE PLAN (EDAP)
• NEEDS ASSESSMENT
• EDAP UPDATE

3. PERSONAL/FAMILY a SUPPORT SERVICES
RAC STAFF REFERRAL TO APPROPRIATE AGENCIES
• FINANCIAL
• MARITAL
• DRUG/ALCOHOL ABUSE

4. CAREER COUNSELING AND GUIDANCE
• SELF-AWARENESS (INCLUDING TESTING)
• CAREER AWARENESS
• CAREER DECISION MAKING
• CAREER PLANNING
• EDAP UPDATE

5. BASIC SKILLS
• AT RAC
• REFERRED OUT

6. PREPAID TUITION ASSISTANCE
• ELEMENTARY
• HIGH SCHOOL
• COLLEGE

REFERRAL

REFERRAL

7. ENROLLMENT INTO TRAINING AND PLACEMENT b
• REFERRAL TO PROGRAM COMPONENT
• TESTING IF APPROPRIATE

8. TARGETED VOCATIONAL RETRAINING
• INTENSIVE
• ACCELERATED

9. JOB DEVELOPMENT RESOURCES
• JOB SEARCH SKILLS
• JOB CLUB
• JOB DEVELOPMENT

10. ON-THE-JOB-TRAINING

11. DIRECT PLACEMENT

12. EXIT PROGRAM
• PLACEMENT
• OTHER TERMINATION

a This component is available to all participants throughout their involvement with the RAC.
b Participants may elect to exit program prior to enrollment in training and placement.

Figure 4.2 Services Provided by UAW-Ford Career Services and Reemployment Assistance Centers (RACs)

Our experience indicates that if workers have the opportunity to participate in interesting and positive learning experiences, they will come back to education. "Returning to Education," focusing on the individual worker's interests and needs, is one of the key principles on which the program is built.

As successful as the EDTP has been, however, certain issues have required the attention of the union-management governing body and center staff (see Ferman, Hoyman, and Cutcher-Gernshenfeld 1988). These issues include the need for frequent training because of turnover among local EDTP committee members and UAW and company representatives assigned to the center; the need for control by the joint governing body of local programs; the need for program follow-up and evaluation; and the problem of ensuring that local EDTP committees are able to absorb the wide diversity of programs developed by the center. But, as Ferman, Hoyman, and Cutcher-Gershenfeld also point out, although jointness in all aspects of the EDTP can create some administrative problems, the benefits outweigh the burden.

5·LESSONS FROM THE UAW-GM PAID EDUCATIONAL LEAVE PROGRAM

Susan J. Schurman, Margrit K. Hugentobler, and Hal Stack

Chapter 5 provides an in-depth look at the paid educational leave provision of the 1984 labor agreement negotiated by General Motors and the United Automobile Workers. The authors were involved in planning the program and are currently instructors. The chapter examines the target groups, program goals, curriculum, and instructional strategies and concludes with a discussion of lessons for further program development. The UAW-GM PEL program represents a promising model for company, union, and educational institutions seeking to work together to increase business viability while improving the quality of life for American workers. The essay should be especially useful to practitioners, researchers, policy developers, and educators.

The severe economic consequences of global competition for American core industries have focused attention on relations between organized labor and management. As this volume reveals, the pressures on labor and management to cooperate have already had a major impact on corporate and union human resource policies and

The authors wish to thank the editors for their helpful comments on an earlier version of this chapter. In addition, thanks are expressed to Donald F. Ephlin, former international vice-president of the UAW, and to Alfred S. Warren, former vice-president of industrial relations, General Motors Corporation, for their encouragement and comments.

practices. The shifting nature of labor-management relations also has significant consequences for American postsecondary education. For example, the prospect of union leaders becoming involved in major strategic business decisions raises the issue of whether they are prepared to assume such responsibility, which has not been part of their traditional role. Similarly, if workers are to have more input into managing business at the point of production, their ability to take on this function successfully must be addressed. Likewise, demands that management personnel adopt a different approach to leadership that emphasizes teamwork, the sharing of power, and worker participation in decision making instead of the traditional authoritarian style suggests the need for managers to learn the skills required for success in this new role. The result of all of these changes in roles has been an increasing demand on postsecondary educational institutions for programs and assistance aimed at equipping employees in all functions with the knowledge, skills, and abilities to perform effectively in work activities characterized by broader participation in decision making.

Calls for collaboration among educational institutions, business, labor, and government in periods of social or economic crisis are not new; indeed, American adult education was born largely of socioeconomic upheaval (see, for example, Kornbluh 1987 for a historical perspective). Yet, despite their promise and record of accomplishments, these educational partnerships have seldom been achieved without difficulty. Each party to the effort brings different institutional goals, values, and preferred methods that are often contradictory (see, for example, Denker 1981).

This chapter describes an innovative collaborative effort by a major corporation and union, General Motors and the UAW, and a loose consortium of postsecondary education providers, both public and private, that designed and implements a program aimed at involving both local union leaders and plant management personnel in intensive study and discussion of the issues facing the union and the corporation. This project, the UAW-GM Paid Educational Leave Program (PEL), has received outstanding evaluations from participants and has begun to receive national attention as an important element in an overall strategy by General Motors and the UAW to create the more informed, responsive, and productive work culture many argue is necessary to compete in today's challenging global business environment. Since its inception in 1985, more than one thousand local UAW leaders and GM plant management staff have attended the intensive four-week program, and more than ten thousand employees, both hourly and salaried, have attended a week-long abbreviated version.

As might be expected, the success of this program was not achieved without some difficulties. First, there were conflicting institutional goals and values that required negotiation and compromise. Second, few of the key actors from any of the parties were experienced in this type of collaboration. Thus, in the process of designing and implementing the program, important lessons were learned about engaging in educational partnerships. Our purpose in this chapter is to describe our experience in the hope of helping educators, employers, and unions create effective educational partnerships that will contribute to the shared goals of improving the performance of American companies and the quality of life of American workers.

Before describing PEL, we place the program in the context of the changes occurring in labor-management relations in the United States and between GM and the UAW in particular. This is followed by a description of the design process, curriculum, and implementation of the basic PEL program, as well as a discussion of the impact of the program on the parties (company, union, and participants). The final section presents a summary of some key lessons learned.

The Context for Change

The emergence of widespread efforts by American companies and unions to engage in some form of collaborative power (win-win) as opposed to—or, more typically, along with—traditional relative power (win-lose) labor relations strategies has occurred in the context of a number of broad environmental changes that crystallized in the early 1980s (Cooke 1990). These changes have been well documented (see Katz and Sable 1985; Monat and Sarfati 1986; Kochan, Katz, and McKersie 1987) and can be summarized in terms of short-term and longer-term forces (Cooke 1990). The short-term forces include recession, high interest rates, unfavorable exchange rates, and energy price shocks. The longer-term forces include rising domestic (nonunion) competition, increasing international competition, sluggish growth in productivity, government regulation and deregulation, technological advances, changes in the characteristics and values of the work force, and a shift toward an increasingly specialized world market.

The available empirical evidence suggests that companies and unions respond to such forces either by altering their labor-management relationship or maintaining the status quo based on a cost-benefit analysis of the likely outcomes of collaboration versus relative power tactics (see, among others, Cooke 1989). This cost-benefit analysis is mediated by the companies' and unions' respective "cultural" characteristics (values, beliefs, and rules) and their historic relationships and strategies (Cooke and Meyer 1990; Kochan, Katz, and McKersie 1987). Such a scenario suggests that it is unlikely that a particular company and/or union would immediately abandon traditional relative power tactics in favor of collaborative power options. Indeed, in some cases the parties may be unable to assess the change in their environment and to modify their relationship accordingly (Schuster 1984). The more common scenario involves the juxtaposition of relative power and collaborative power tactics in a broad company or union strategy. Empirical attempts to uncover such strategic responses and their impact on both company and union outcomes have identified the following major corporate tactics to address environmental pressures: capital substitution and worker displacement, increased subcontracting (outsourcing) and transfer of work to nonunion facilities, massive layoffs and plant closings, widespread concession bargaining, and widespread experimentation in employee involvement as well as union-management collaboration (for a review of this literature, see Cooke 1989).

These are not either-or propositions; many firms have adopted more than one—if not all—of these tactics as part of an overall response to changing environmental conditions and pressures. Thus attempts to initiate cooperative ventures with unions often coincide with capital displacement, outsourcing, concessionary bargaining, plant closings, and so forth. This scenario complicates and often undermines the implementation of cooperative efforts since unions and employees generally view these other tactics as counter to the premises of cooperation and as evidence that management is not really committed to cooperation but is trying to co-opt the union and the work force. A number of unions have attempted to counter this trend in management strategy by introducing quid pro quo demands that exchange various concessions of status quo contractual provisions (e.g., wages and/or work rules) for job security provisions and structural influence in managing the firm.

Thus the general picture of changing labor-management relations in the United States is far from clear-cut. Companies and unions are tentatively experimenting with cooperative efforts to improve company performance and enhance job security while continuing to engage in traditional adversarial tactics. It is within this context that General Motors and the UAW elected to engage in one of the most far-reaching experiments with joint decision making.

The 1984 Negotiations and the Commitment to Joint Decision Making

General Motors' difficulties in the changing marketplace of the 1980s has been well documented (Reilly 1987; Brown 1988). As recently as 1984, GM was the industry leader, capturing 44.5 percent of the U.S. car market. By 1988, it had dropped to 36 percent. No longer the low-cost producer in the U.S. market, GM is now confronted by intensifying competition from a resurgent Ford and Chrysler; imports, which have captured 28 percent of the market; and the growing threat of "transplants." GM's overall responses to these competitive pressures have included all of the major tactics listed above—both adversarial and cooperative. But perhaps most important in terms of labor-management relations was GM's decision to decentralize operating decisions and incorporate "employee involvement" (Keller 1989).

The historic relationship between GM and the UAW has been analyzed extensively (see Serrin 1973; Brody 1980). Though reflecting the "archetypal" (Kantor 1984) professionalized adversarial labor-management relations found in core American unionized manufacturing firms, the UAW and GM were also one of the first companies and unions to experiment with the use of collaborative approaches to common problems (Kochan, Katz, and Mower 1984). This willingness to cooperate reflects both the UAW's long-standing commitment to workplace democracy and General Motors' experimental approach to improving managerial practice (Warren 1986; Ephlin 1986; Branst and Dubberly 1988).

During the difficult reopened 1982 concessionary negotiations and the 1984 regular negotiations, GM and the UAW fashioned a deal that exchanged wage and work rules "concessions" for income security provisions. Also included in the deal was a commitment to joint union-management decision making on a wide variety of issues that had formerly been management's prerogative.

Though the contract was ratified by UAW members, the deal was by no means universally popular. The perceived link between jointness and concessions created a widespread distrust among UAW-GM workers that joint decision making meant management co-optation of the union. Jointness became a political issue in local union elections, and a number of local leaders who had supported the international's deal during the 1982 negotiations were defeated in 1984 local elections. At that time, most GM workers believed that American automobile companies, especially GM, were vastly overstating their competitive problems as a means to extract concessions. Likewise, skepticism was widespread in management quarters; many salaried employees privately expressed doubt about the union's or the workers' willingness or ability to assume a new role in the business.

A New Kind of Employee Education

Against this background, Donald F. Ephlin, international vice-president of the UAW and director of the UAW's General Motors Department, recognized that there was a major need for local UAW leaders to acquire a greater understanding of the environmental forces in the automobile industry that were driving the international union's bargaining strategy with GM, where joint decision making fit in with these changes, and the implications of these changes for their roles as leaders. The 1984 national agreement between GM and the UAW thus contained the following memorandum of understanding concerning joint activities (page 239):

> The concept of "jointness" is understood to mean that the decisions for these activities be jointly conceived, implemented, monitored, and evaluated. Furthermore, decisions must be arrived at in a setting which is characterized by the parties working together in an atmosphere of trust; making mutual decisions at all levels which respect the concerns and interest of the parties in-

volved; sharing responsibility for the problem-solving process; and sharing the rewards of achieving common goals.

The paid educational leave provision included in the 1984 labor agreement became the vehicle for providing a new kind of union and employee education aimed at implementing this agreement and thereby providing employees with full-time "selected training to enhance their skills" (page 348). Unlike previous training programs aimed primarily at narrow job training, the aim of the new training was to familiarize union representatives with the complexities of the automobile business.

At the newly formed UAW-GM Human Resource Center, company and union officials were appointed to implement the PEL agreement. Educators from Wayne State University, the University of Michigan, Harvard, MIT, Boston College, and the National Institute for Work and Learning were asked to advise PEL administrators on program development and to help design various modules of the curriculum.

Target Group
Though administered through the UAW-GM Human Resource Center, the PEL program was initially intended to be a union-only program. The initial target group was to be top-ranking leaders of local unions, especially presidents and chairs of bargaining committees. The terms of the 1984 agreement had greatly increased the responsibility and authority of these leaders in making critical local plant decisions. Their active support and involvement during the three-year life of the contract would be crucial if the GM-UAW experiment in joint decision making was to be successful.

We and a number of the other designers of the initial program believed there was a need for union officials to engage separately—without the presence of management representatives—in study and discussion of the many controversial issues surrounding their industry, joint decision making, and so forth. We believed this would encourage more open discussion and debate among the union leaders. A number of the educators involved also assumed that management personnel were probably already exposed to the subject matter of the program and accepting of jointness and therefore less in need of such a curriculum. This assumption turned out to be false on all

three counts. Beginning with PEL I, the pilot group (each participant group is assigned a number), union participants argued that
their management counterparts needed to be exposed to the same
information at the same time, so that they could begin the process
of dialogue and debate that would lead to joint decision making.
The target audience was subsequently broadened to include management personnel.

Basic Program Goals

PEL's original goals were to involve local UAW officials from GM
locations (later amended to include management staff) in a process
of study and discussion of the fundamental changes taking place in
the automobile industry; the problems facing both the corporation
and the union; the strategic directions GM was pursuing; and the
implications of these changes for the UAW's strategy. The purpose
was to expose participants to the same information top-level corporate and international union officials were using to make decisions
and to help prepare participants to meet the demands of a rapidly
changing environment and play a more active and effective leadership role in the decision-making process, which was becoming increasingly decentralized on operational matters.

Curriculum

Designing program content and a process to meet PEL's goals posed
a number of unique challenges. The problems facing the industry
were wide ranging, complex, and often controversial. Both the company and the union had agreed that the only way to begin to solve
their problems was to face the issues squarely, in an atmosphere of
open discussion, without soft-pedaling problems or solutions, and to
locate top experts in different content areas and allow them to
present their views. In short, this was to be an *education* program,
not a *training* program; the emphasis was to be on helping participants formulate their own views based on the best information available rather than on convincing them to adopt a particular company
or union line of reasoning (for a distinction between education,
training, and indoctrination, see Green 1969). The only condition
imposed was that the overall program had to maintain a balance
between presenting union-oriented and company-oriented perspectives. A key underlying assumption was that the program would

model the process of joint decision making. By fostering a climate in which there could be open discussion of problems and solutions, based on facts, to the largest extent possible, participants would be exposed to a new form of problem solving that the designers hoped would be transferred into "back-home" behavior.

Such a strong commitment to academic freedom is relatively rare in American company- or union-sponsored continuing education programs. The past cultures of both companies and unions have often led them to try to exert strong control over curricula and to rely heavily on training rather than educational approaches to workplace learning (see, for example, Schurman 1989). Participative problem-solving work cultures depend for their success on broadly distributed intelligence (Cherns 1971) and on workers in all functions having "learned how to learn" (Kornbluh, Pipan, and Schurman 1987).

Virtually everyone connected with the PEL program attributes its success in large measure to the willingness of GM and the UAW to foster open, critical discussion of controversial issues. Yet it has not always been easy to achieve or maintain this openness. Each part of the curriculum was the subject of intense disagreement and debate among the design group. The design process was thus an invaluable learning experience for the design group and laid the foundation for extending the process to the implementation of the program.

After months of preparation, the original design group agreed on a five-week course of study that was subsequently shortened to four weeks based on PEL I evaluations. With minor modifications based on changing environmental conditions and instructor availability, the content of the four one-week modules has remained essentially the same during the four years of the program. Table 5.1 shows the major content areas of the modules along with the principal instructional strategies employed in delivery.

The overall curriculum is organized around the concept of strategy, strategic planning, and strategic thinking. Participants learn a systems model of strategic planning that links a clear definition of the mission, values, and goals of an organization to opportunities and external threats to its mission and its internal resources for responding to these challenges. In the first three modules, top outside experts describe major environmental trends and analyze GM's strengths and weaknesses as a corporation. In the fourth module,

Table 5.1 UAW-GM National PEL Curriculum

Topic	Presented by	Instructional strategies
Module 1: "The Changing Auto Industry," University of Michigan, Ann Arbor (40 hours)		
Changing Corporate and Union Strategies in the Development of the U.S. Auto Industry (8 hours)	Hal Stack Wayne State University Labor Studies Center	Lecture, small-group activity, tour of Henry Ford Museum exhibit "Evolution of the Automobile in America"
Restructuring of the U.S. and Global Auto Industry (6 hours)	David Cole University of Michigan Transportation Research Institute Dan Luria Industrial Technology Institute	Lecture, discussion
The Evolution of Manufacturing and the Factory of the Future (2 hours)	Walton Hancock University of Michigan Center for Research on Integrated Manufacturing	Lecture, discussion
The New Competitors: Japan and the Newly Industrialized Countries (8 hours)	John Campbell Vladimir Pucik Robert Cole University of Michigan Center for Japanese Studies	Lecture, discussion
Product and Process Innovations at GM (8 hours)	GM Tech Center	Tour of GM Tech Center
Technology and New Forms of Work Organization (4 hours)	Peter Unterwegger UAW Research Dept. Susan Schurman University of Michigan Labor Studies Center	Lecture, small-group activity, participant panel

Module 2: "The Changing Economy, Technology, and Industrial Relations in Transition," University of Massachusetts, Boston (40 hours)

Understanding a Changing Economy: —Corporate Strategies in a Competitive Economy —Trade and Industrial Policies (16 hours)	Barry Bluestone University of Massachusetts	Lecture, small-group activity
New Technology and Work Organization (4 hours)	Charles Sable MIT	Lecture
The Evolution of Industrial Relations in the U.S. Auto Industry (8 hours)	Harry Katz Cornell University	Lecture, small-group activity
Change and Continuity in the U.S. Industrial Relations System (8 hours)	Thomas Kochan MIT	Lecture, small-group activity
Case Study in Labor-Management Cooperation (4 hours)	Charles Heckscher Harvard Business School	Small-group activity
Evaluation of Module 2		

Module 3: "Public Policy and the Auto Industry," Washington, D.C. (National Institute for Work and Learning, NIWL) (40 hours)

Public Policy and the U.S. Auto Industry	NIWL	Meeting with variety of public officials
Understanding the Legislative and Regulatory Processes	NIWL	Films; meeting with public officials; visits to agencies, UAW and GM lobbyists, NLRB, etc.
Corporate Average Fuel Economy (AFE) Legislation: A Case Study	NIWL	Small-group activity
The Role of Government Agencies	NIWL	Visits to agencies; meetings; and discussions with officials
Evaluation of Module 3		

Table 5.1 UAW-GM National PEL Curriculum (continued)

Topic	Presented by	Instructional strategies
Module 4: "Strategic Management of Change," Detroit (40 hours)		
Strategic Planning and Managing Change (6 hours)	Hal Stack Wayne State University Susan Schurman University of Michigan	Lecture, film, small-group activity
Leadership and Strategic Change (4 hours)	Susan Schurman University of Michigan	Lecture, small-group activity
The GM Strategic Planning Process (4 hours)	GM Strategic Planning Dept.	Lecture, discussion
UAW Strategic Options (8 hours)	Hal Stack Wayne State University Susan Schurman University of Michigan	Small-group activity
Impact of Joint Labor-Management Activity on Company and Union Goals: Results of a National Sample in Manufacturing (4 hours)	William Cooke University of Michigan School of Business Administration	Lecture, small-group activity
Saturn as a Joint Strategic Response (4 hours)	Mike Bennett UAW manufacturing advisor—Saturn	Lecture, discussion
Discussion with top GM and UAW leaders (2 hours)		
Applied Strategic Planning (4 hours)	Hal Stack Wayne State University	Individual planning, small-group activity
Evaluation of Module 4		
Evaluation of PEL		

participants analyze the applicability of this information to local plant and union strategy.

Participants attend module 1, which lasts a week, then return to their plants for a week. Modules 2 and 3 are presented in two consecutive weeks, followed by a week back home before module 4.

Instructional Strategies

While the curriculum has been relatively stable, the same is not true for the instructional strategies. It is in this area that many of the educators were forced to make adjustments. Because a number of the PEL faculty were accustomed to teaching undergraduate and graduate courses at major universities, the original program had a graduate school orientation. Traditional lecture methods were employed, and little time was built in for other learning transactions, such as group discussions, experiential learning, and so forth. This approach reflected the absence of a strong focus on the principles of adult learning (e.g., Brookfield 1986).

Beginning with PEL I, the participants objected to the format of instruction. The most frequent criticism was that too much material was presented without adequate time for participants to digest the information and engage in discussion among themselves. This criticism reflects the strong bias of professional educators, especially those accustomed to university instruction, toward highly didactic modes of instruction that leave little room for participant involvement. At the same time, other instructors tended to rely too heavily on poorly designed group discussions or experiential methods that left participants unclear about the point of the presentation and insulted by the instructors' lack of preparation.

Another problem in the original design was that it did not account for the strong affective reactions participants would have to the content. As has been emphasized in literature on educational practice and learning (e.g., Novak 1977; Goldstein 1981), most theories of teaching and learning are heavily cognitive in nature and ignore the affective dimension that is likely to be present when the subject matter is threatening, violates strongly held beliefs, or otherwise creates stress for the learner. The reactions of PEL participants to the content were often strongly emotional, ranging from depression to anger or outright hostility toward the instructors. With experience, instructors have learned to anticipate these responses, to prepare participants better for their reactions to the content, and to allow participants to "debrief" by ventilating their feelings and separating their emotional reactions from their strategic responses.

All of these methodological problems seemed to occur because many of the instructors, like most higher education professionals, had neither experience in interacting with an audience of mostly local union leaders nor practice in teaching "emotionally hot" topics (see Sutton and Schurman 1985). Their instructional methods revealed that they had made incorrect assumptions about their audience. One of the major challenges of the PEL program has been to encourage educators unaccustomed to adult union and worker audiences in noncredit settings to incorporate more participative methods in their presentations and to be more sensitive to the affective dimension of their topics.

The Growth of the "PEL Process"

From its inception, the PEL program was highly controversial among local union leaders. Participants in PEL I (fall of 1985) arrived highly skeptical, assuming that the program was, in the words of one local union president, "a brainwashing program designed to prepare us and our members for concession bargaining in 1987." This remained the dominant view of new PEL groups through approximately PEL IX in the fall of 1986. By that time, nearly three hundred leaders from a wide cross section of local GM facilities and unions had participated in the program and word of its unique and innovative approach had started to spread. Though the brainwashing issue has never totally disappeared, the program has acquired a reputation for providing an honest presentation of information by qualified experts external to both the company and the union and for encouraging open and critical discussion of the issues among the participants without fear of reprisal by either the union or the corporation.

PEL relied from the beginning on volunteers from local unions, whose participation is approved by their respective UAW regional officers and, in the case of managers, GM staff. As a result of the controversial nature of the program, some of the early groups were quite small (twenty to twenty-five participants) while many in the target group adopted a "wait-and-see" attitude. As the program's reputation spread, however, more people requested to participate and group size increased to thirty-five to forty.

PEL-related language has been retained in the 1990 agreement between GM and the UAW with a commitment to expand the program further. Approximately one thousand local union leaders and managers (about 80 percent of participants have been union officials) have attended the program.

Local PEL

Once participants concluded that the program was not a brainwashing session and that the issues raised were important, a major reaction was "How am I going to share this information with my members and not be accused of selling out?" The controversial nature of the material, as well as its complexity, in the context of volatile local union politics led many of the first union participants to fear that their political survival depended on whether they became the messengers of disconcerting news. Many also believed that the credibility of the program was due in large part to the involvement of outside educators, and they wanted to preserve this aspect of the process. Consequently, as part of its final program evaluation, PEL I recommended creating a "mini-PEL"—a one-week distillation of the four-week "national PEL"—to be delivered in local GM facilities to all UAW-GM workers. They even designed a preliminary curriculum.

The first local PEL was piloted in one GM division in the fall of 1986. Since then, more than ten thousand employees from different GM divisions have attended the week-long program. Of the initial groups who attended, close to 60 percent of the participants were hourly, and only about one-third held an elected or appointed union office; the other two-thirds were shop-floor skilled trades and production workers. Most of the salaried participants were first-line supervisors and salaried coordinators of joint programs at the plant level, and many attended together with their hourly counterparts. Additional local PEL programs have been conducted at the UAW regional level, bringing union and management staff together from a variety of divisions, for the entire work force of the plant.

GM and the UAW have stated that they intend to expose the majority of the GM work force to the "PEL process," as it is now termed in the official UAW-GM *Local PEL Administrators Guide.* The terminology itself reflects an awareness that the process of study and discussion is as important as the subject matter.

There are presently more requests for programs than PEL administrators and faculty can handle. A major difficulty is finding qualified instructors who are experts in the content areas, acceptable to both the company and union, and competent in adult learning methods. Two instructor training programs have been held for potential instructors from a variety of postsecondary institutions.

Assessing the Program's Impact

Assessing the impact of a program like PEL presents major conceptual, methodological, and political problems in organizational contexts like the UAW and GM. The sheer size of the organizations and the magnitude of experimentation and change occurring within them make it difficult to determine where the PEL program fits in. One auto executive summed up the problems: "Evaluation is a great idea in principle, but some of these programs are too controversial to evaluate. We want to give them time to grow without the pressure of evaluation." For these and other reasons, PEL has not been evaluated "scientifically." We have, however, collected systematic data on participants' reactions to the program, experimented with an approach to assessing changes in participants' perspectives on key issues as a result of the program, and collected a variety of anecdotal data about program outcomes in terms of participants' actions and changes in behavior back home.

Participant Reactions

Participants are asked to fill out daily evaluation forms and a final evaluation at the end of each module. These were initially used to improve the program but are now used primarily for quality control purposes. With few exceptions, the program receives consistently high evaluations. A GM production superintendent stated two of the core themes echoed by the majority of participants, both union and management: "This is by far the best educational program GM has ever sent me to. The exposure to the outside experts is crucial—we've learned not to believe either the corporation or the union. For me, though, it was maybe even more important to spend this time with UAW guys. I feel I understand where they're coming from a lot better, and I was really impressed with their knowledge of the business."

Changes in Perspective

In a series of divisional local PEL programs, we conducted a structured assessment of the effects of PEL on participants' perspectives (Hugentobler and Schurman 1988). Of the six hundred people who completed the assessment, 60 percent were hourly workers; only about one-third of these held elected or appointed union office, and the other two-thirds were production or skilled trades workers. Most salaried participants were first-line supervisors and coordinators of joint programs. These data indicate that 90 percent of the participants consider the program to be either somewhat (30 percent) or very helpful (60 percent) in their jobs. Asked to explain the most helpful aspects of the program, participants emphasized awareness and knowledge of key issues confronting the industry, which they believed would enable them to do a better job and to explain decisions and share information better with other employees.

At the beginning and end of the program, participants were asked to fill out questionnaires in which they were given an extensive list of the major problems and possible solutions facing GM and the UAW (derived from discussions with initial participants) and asked to rank what they believed to be the top five problems and solutions. Preliminary findings indicate that at the start of the weeklong program product quality, employee attitudes, and product design were considered the top three problems in this order and that participants thought they should be addressed by improving quality and design and increasing employee involvement. While product quality and design were still listed as the two top problems at the end of the week, corporate strategy had replaced employee attitudes as problem number three. Similarly, after the program, solutions focused on the improvement of product quality and design, followed by the need for better corporate strategy. These findings suggest, first, that participants enter the course with a rather sophisticated understanding of the key issues to be addressed by GM and the UAW and, second, that the program fosters a shift in focus from a tendency to blame individuals (employee attitudes and management competence) to an emphasis on strategy.

The data also indicate that word about the program spreads to the local plants. Of the first two local groups that filled out the evaluation questionnaire (groups 12 and 13), 70 percent of the participants attended the program because they were sent by the union or management, whereas the percentage was 49 percent in groups 20 and 21, and over half the participants said they asked to attend the program because someone had told them about it.

Behavioral Outcomes

The obvious question is "So what?" Is anything happening as a result of this effort? A reasonable operating assumption is that all the parties to PEL expend resources and effort to achieve certain outcomes. While no systematic data are available on the impact of the program on the company, the union, employees, or the education providers, the following examples illustrate the kinds of results that seem to be occurring.

A local union-appointed quality of work life (QWL) coordinator attended a local PEL program sponsored by his division. Based on the emphasis on strategy and the need for strategic planning at all levels of the company and union, he decided he would more actively elicit the involvement and advice of local union leaders in getting the floundering employee problem-solving program back on track. He claims that prior to his PEL experience, he had been inclined to bypass the union but has come to realize that without its active influence and involvement, his efforts were probably unlikely to succeed. His initiative has led to a local union strategic planning process centered on union goals for QWL.

One local union has been particularly active in formulating strategy on how to achieve union goals through joint decision making. A large number of elected and appointed officials have attended either national or local PEL programs. Using access to business information gained through the joint process and applying it strategically, the shop chairman was able to convince plant management to avert a major temporary layoff. By calculating hidden costs associated with turnover in terms of, for example, scrap and quality control problems, he was able to show that it was less costly to keep people working than to lay them off. He states flatly that he would not have been able to formulate this strategy before he had access to information available through the joint programs and knowledge gained through PEL and other educational efforts on business strategy.

These examples illustrate the variety of direct and indirect ways in which the PEL program is contributing to change in General Motors. On a more "macro" level, one of the important outcomes of the PEL process in our view is the "cross-pollination" that results when men and women come together from a variety of locations with different roles and perspectives—across a large corporation and union—for intensive study and discussion. In addition to the rich exchange of local experience fostered by this "maximum-mix" design, participants typically achieve a better and more realistic understanding of the difficulties inherent in making change happen in a large organization with such a strong culture. As one manager told his PEL colleagues, "Look at the trouble we've had coming to agreement on what to do during these four weeks, and there's only thirty-five of us. Multiply that by 400,000 and it's not hard to figure out why change is slow in GM. What's amazing is how far we've come in ten years."

Recently, GM's vice-president for industrial relations, Alfred S. Warren, listed changes related to the PEL program as one of three factors responsible for GM's decision to consider keeping production for substantially more component parts in-house rather than outsourcing it (*Detroit Free Press*, Sept. 14, 1988).

Lessons and Issues Raised

The growth of the UAW-GM PEL process suggests a number of lessons and raises a number of issues important to educators and company and union officials contemplating similar educational ventures.

Employees Want Knowledge

The most overwhelming and gratifying lesson is the range and scope of demand by GM employees in all job classifications for "objective" knowledge and information. From the beginning, there was widespread agreement among the PEL design team that local union officials and managers would be interested in the program content, but there was considerably less agreement about whether shop-floor employees would react favorably. Skepticism was voiced about whether the rank-and-file (in both hourly and salaried jobs) "could handle" the information. The debate centered on two distinct issues: whether the material was "too academic" and perhaps too "advanced" in its format for hourly workers and whether the program content was too politically "hot," that is, whether people, once exposed to the information, would use it politically against their local leaders.

The answer to the first question is clear. Educational level was not a significant factor in local PEL participants' reactions to the program or in their changes in perspective, even though close to 25 percent had no more than a high school education.

The significance of this finding cannot be overstated. First, in contrast to many other countries, the United States has little precedent for large-scale education of hourly workers in the principles of strategic planning, economics, organizational change, and other issues. Second, the emergence of a perceived need for such education is evidence of the delicate role local union officials can play in the present economic era and underscores the role education can play in helping union leaders prepare their members for difficult changes. Third, and finally, the willingness of employers to join in support of such education and training is evidence of a growing awareness among management of the contribution an educated work force can make in today's economy.

Positive employee reactions to PEL also lend support to the vast literature on occupational stress, suggesting that in periods of crisis people have a high need for credible information so as to predict, understand, and exercise control over the events in their lives (House 1981). This literature further shows that providing employees with information and opportunities to become involved not only contributes to improved business outcomes but also helps protect them against deleterious health effects resulting from job stress (Israel, Schurman, and House 1989).

The answer to the second question is less clear; no systematic data currently address the important issue of how programs such as PEL affect union politics at national or local levels. The effect of joint labor-management education programs is both an important area for research and an important issue for educators to consider as they become involved in joint offerings. We contend that these programs can be successful in the longer term only if they contribute to positive outcomes for all parties. Because unions are democratic institutions in which leaders must regularly stand for election, local union leaders are faced with a very different set of issues than are managers. Educators unaccustomed to dealing with unions need to be ever mindful of the political process and avoid becoming involved either directly or indirectly. One of the local PEL instructors likes to tell how, as a young labor educator, he once asked a union education director to send some people to one of his labor studies classes. "No," replied the education director, "I tried that once, but when the folks came back, they voted me out of office."

Information Begets Information
A second lesson, stemming from the first, is that the process of sharing information, once initiated, is likely to grow exponentially. It now seems inevitable, though it was not anticipated, that national PEL would spawn local PEL or that national PEL may yet spawn "advanced" PEL. It is nearly axiomatic in literature on organizational effectiveness that the open exchange of information, in a forum that fosters confidence in the credibility of the information, must form the cornerstone of a strategy intended to produce a more knowledgeable, competent, and committed work force. The only question has been how. The PEL model appears to offer great potential for forming the kind of partnerships suggested by the Initiative on Education and a Changing Economy put forth by the U.S. Department of Education's Office of Post-Secondary Education (1988:13). (We assume the writers meant to include unions.)

> In structural terms, one promising way to promote economic objectives and the goals of liberal education at once is through partnerships between corporations and colleges. An educational institution may be able to draw on its experience, trained faculty, and specialized facilities to provide occupation-specific training more efficiently than a corporation, for example, while also nurturing and serving the interest in liberal study that adult workers frequently bring with them. This development presupposes, however, that educational institutions can in fact retool for teaching new subject matter to a student population increasingly heterogeneous in age, needs, and educational background and can do so while retaining the strengths of traditional colleges.

Critics have argued that the PEL design is unrealistic in companies and unions without the vast resources of the UAW and GM. We have been experimenting with a similar approach in much more modest contexts, and our experience thus far is that the model works in a variety of settings. We are currently assisting the state of Michigan in preparing a similar program aimed at small Michigan companies and unions.

The key is the quality, process, and credibility of the instruction. This, in turn, depends on the willingness of the company and the union to allow the instructors academic freedom and to encourage a climate of open debate among participants and on the willingness of the educators to accept the realities of organizational and union politics, which may preclude some topics from discussion. To achieve such a partnership requires a strong commitment by all parties, especially during the design phase but also during program delivery, to engage in discussion about each other's institutional goals and values so that a clear understanding is reached about the program. Such dialogue will not eliminate conflict, but it has the potential to turn disagreement into creative educational design. Several of the core pieces of the PEL program are the result of such conflict.

The Process Is Fragile

Lesson three is less optimistic. Despite its success thus far, the PEL process represents a fragile innovation in an essentially hostile environment. The atmosphere of open discussion, so crucial to the program's success, was almost certainly the result of the "unfreezing" of traditional company and union behavioral patterns caused by GM's business crisis. It remains to be seen whether this openness can be sustained either during the diffusion process or in the event that GM's business position takes a marked turn for the better or worse. There are already indications of difficulties ahead.

Like most human resource innovations, PEL is ultimately subject to the severe pressures of the line-manufacturing environment. As is well known, managers in manufacturing have a different agenda from that of human resource staff. Despite GM's progress in reorienting management in manufacturing to the importance of "people processes" or improved human resource management, there is still a clear cultural lag between human resource theory and manufacturing practice. Herein lies a classic double bind for educators. Managers want to know how programs like PEL can help them meet their goals. If business improves sharply, managers wonder why they need to send valuable human resources, in a system with continually decreasing slack, to broad educational programs. "Obviously, we're doing better without it, and the pressure is on me to get the numbers out—nothing's changed," one manager remarked recently. Conversely, if business worsens, managers, under tremendous pressure to cut costs, want to know the short-term payoffs. At the same time, UAW-GM Human Resource Center officials have been reluctant to evaluate the impact of PEL beyond participants' reactions. "After all," said one official, "not everyone in either the union or management is enthusiastic about a more actively involved work force." There are still strong factions on both sides that advocate a return to traditional labor relations practice. In the absence of evaluation, it may become increasingly difficult to demonstrate the value of PEL, yet it is unlikely that such evaluation will be conducted.

Apart from the business and political pressures PEL faces, issues are also arising surrounding the diffusion process. It is unclear how or whether the dynamic educational quality of the program can be "packaged" for diffusion. There have already been instances in which local plant or union officials have attempted to modify the program to reflect a narrower "business awareness" training orientation. In some cases, new union and management appointees in charge of PEL implementation at the regional or local level lack the broader orientation of the initial design group as a result of having missed the experience of the design phase. As one new appointee asked, "Why do we want to educate all those people?"

Even more important to the quality of the program are the educational providers. The diffusion of local PEL will probably involve a number of postsecondary institutions with little experience in adult noncredit education. Instructors from business schools at private universities, for example, tend to provide a business or managerial perspective, creating complaints of management bias. Likewise, instructors from university labor studies centers are more likely to emphasize a union-related perspective, causing management participants to object. Furthermore, instructors who are unfamiliar with adult education techniques have had difficulty making the content interesting and have requested more detailed "scripts" in the instructor's manual. Conversely, experienced educators have complained that the curriculum has a cookbook feel to it and stifles their creativity as teachers. The age-old debate between content people and process people is likely to continue.

These issues suggest that unless preventive steps are taken, the PEL program will experience "infidelity" during the diffusion process as each location modifies the content and delivery to suit its own style. Whether this issue is important and how modification affects the program remains to be seen. We believe that the process of discussion and mutual learning is as important to the program as the content of the courses. Whether this process can survive the pressures of diffusion remains to be answered.

Summary

The UAW-GM PEL program represents a promising opportunity for companies, unions, and educators to work together to restore business viability and job security while contributing significantly to improving the quality of life for American workers. Both Ford and Chrysler, in partnership with the UAW, have initiated similar programs. In addition, the state of Michigan is sponsoring a "Strategic Education Program" for Michigan firms and unions, and Massachusetts is considering a similar program. These developments suggest a growing awareness of the importance of an educated work force to our national well-being and of the role educators can play in helping to achieve this goal.

6 · UNION-MANAGEMENT TRAINING PROGRAMS IN THE PUBLIC SECTOR: THE NEW YORK EXPERIENCE

Lois Gray, Thomas B. Quimby, and Kathy Schrier

New York State has a long history of union-management education and training programs, making it unique in public sector employment. This chapter examines the programs undertaken at both state and city levels, as well as the applicability of the New York experience to other public sector jurisdictions. Although the profile of the New York state and city work force differs from that of the rest of the nation, there is much of value here for educators, union leaders, and others involved in public sector employment.

The public sector, with its emphasis on credentialing for employment, could well become a major player in employee training and, with growing unionization, ripe for union-management cooperation in the delivery of its education and training services. To date, however, only New York has undertaken this seemingly natural partnership on a comprehensive scale.[1] Why is the Empire State

---

1. In 1987, the U.S. Department of Labor, Office of Labor-Management Cooperation, conducted a survey of state and local government labor-management committees in which it asked for information about program features. Only two jurisdictions

unique in this initiative? What led to the evolution of its union-management training programs at state and city levels? Does the New York experience suggest possibilities for other public sector jurisdictions?

This chapter, which draws primarily on printed reports and interviews with key officials, examines the New York experience with respect to funding, governance, administration, scope of coverage, and services offered, highlighting patterns of structure and administration that have evolved within New York State and New York City. Attention is focused on the applicability of these experiences to other public sector jurisdictions.

Characteristics of the State and City Work Force

New York State currently employs almost two hundred thousand workers in seven thousand job titles, ranging from unskilled to professional. The profile of this work force differs from that of the nation as a whole in its relatively higher percentage of minorities and females. In New York State government, for example, women constitute half of the total and minorities constitute 23 percent; the comparable figures for the U.S. work force are 44.6 and 13.3 percent. New York also differs in the extent and penetration of union membership. The vast majority of state workers (93 percent), including most supervisors, belong to one of six unions that negotiate contracts with the state. These include two affiliates of the American Federation of State, County and Municipal Employees (AFSCME)—the Civil Service Employees Association (CSEA), a general union of nonsupervisory employees; and Council 82, which represents corrections facility officers. Together, these unions represent 63 percent of all state employees. The Public Employees Federation (PEF), which is affiliated with both the Service Employees International Union (SEIU) and the American Federation of Teachers (AFT), represents technical, professional, and supervisory employees, constituting 28.5 percent of the total (Task Force on the New York State Public Workforce 1989). Labor relations in state govern-

---

outside New York State reported that their committees dealt with training issues. An interview with Al Bilik, president, AFL-CIO Department of Public Employees, confirmed the unique experience of New York in developing training programs sponsored by both union and management.

ment is regulated by the Taylor Law, which is administered by the Public Employment Relations Board (PERB).

Forces leading to an emphasis on employee training in New York State government stem in part from trends common to private sector employees: changes in technology that require restructuring of jobs; labor shortages caused by slow growth in the working-age population; and the need to train workers in basic reading, writing, and computational and reasoning skills to meet the demands of the new workplace. Further pressures for employee training have occurred as a result of a trend toward deinstitutionalization in the mental health field, explosive growth in the number of incarcerated criminals, massive efforts to rebuild the state's roads and bridges, and a downsizing of labor services as a result of cutbacks in federal funding.

Although New York City employs an even larger labor force than the state—320,000, including the Board of Education—the percentage of unionized workers is approximately the same.[2] New York City has a higher percentage of minorities, and more than half its work force is female. As in state government, the leading organization of city employees is affiliated with AFSCME. District Council 37 represents 34.6 percent of all unionized city workers; the United Federation of Teachers (AFT), 24.8 percent; and the unions of uniformed services (a total of eleven), 26.2 percent. Other major unions are Local 237 of the International Brotherhood of Teamsters (IBT), 6.3 percent; the Communications Workers of America (CWA), 3.5 percent; skilled trades unions (eleven crafts), 3.1 percent; and sanitation workers (IBT), 2.8 percent. Overall, the city negotiates with more than fifty unions ranging in size from 40 members to 111,000.

Labor relations in New York City is extraordinarily complex. Most city agencies are regulated by a law separate and distinct from the state law of public sector collective bargaining and are administered by a separate agency, the Office of Collective Bargaining (OCB).[3]

2. These figures do not include state-chartered authorities in New York City such as the Metropolitan Transit Authority. Figures are from the Office of Municipal Labor Relations.

3. The Board of Education and state-chartered authorities, including the Metropolitan Transit Authority, are covered by PERB.

Evolution of Union-Management Training

New York State was the birthplace of the civil service system. Inspired by the 1881 assassination of President James Garfield by a disappointed job seeker in Buffalo, the federal government replaced "the spoils system" with civil service, which aimed to staff government with people whose talents were assessed by fair examinations. Shortly thereafter, Assemblyman Theodore Roosevelt promoted a similar statute in New York State. Thus testing and training became the province of the New York State Civil Service Commission.[4]

This long-established system came under challenge with the unionization of public employees and the establishment of the Governor's Office of Employee Relations (OER). Sandy Frucher, director of OER under Governor Hugh Carey in the early 1970s, says that one of the things he did was "consciously blow up the training unit of Civil Service" because he thought it was antiquated (Benjamin and Heard 1985 and personal interview). Frucher put training and development on the bargaining table in negotiations with public employee unions because he recognized the need for high-quality training targeted to specific goals and saw a way to get it funded. Experience showed that the budget process gave training expenditures short shrift, but the collective bargaining process gave training a constituency. Unions were given a piece of the action through a voice in the training to be funded and the choice of staff positions to oversee the training funds. The first state contracts with funds for training programs sponsored jointly by union and management were negotiated in 1971. Current contracts with CSEA, PEF, and Council 82 allocate approximately $14 million a year to this purpose, an annual expenditure of $85.50 per employee.

In contrast to the history of state labor-management training programs, which were initiated by management, the first city program was initiated by one of the unions. In the 1960s, District Council 37, which represents members ranging from some with minimal education and skill requirements (e.g., custodians, hospital orderlies, and park attendants) to others who must have professional degrees (e.g., accountants and engineers), became a major force through its suc-

---

4. Burstein 1986 describes the historical mission of the commission and its conflict and overlap with the Governor's Office of Employee Relations.

cessful drive to organize the city's Department of Hospitals. One of its major campaign issues was the development of a career ladder for hospital workers at the bottom of the wage scale. Initially, city officials did not respond positively to this demand. As one city official expressed it, "The City government did not see training as a long term investment" (Bellush and Bellush 1984:307). Influenced by a civil service orientation, the city expected to fill its staffing needs through individual employee efforts to acquire skills and education in traditional educational institutions.

Faced with city indifference to an organizational imperative, District Council 37 established an education department within the union that negotiated federal grants for career ladder training programs and offered a variety of educational services to members. In 1971, the union negotiated a benefit package that included city support for the expenses of training and education. During the fiscal crisis of the 1970s, increases in benefits became a trade-off for wage restraint (Bellush and Bellush 1984, chap. 14, and interviews with Al Viani). Set at $10 per covered member, the package has been increased in subsequent contract negotiations to its current level of approximately $60 per member, for a total of $7 million. Additional educational initiatives have been undertaken by Local 237 of the IBT, with the help of city grants, and joint programs have been inaugurated in public education through agreements between the New York City Board of Education and the United Federation of Teachers, affiliated with the AFT, and in higher education through contracts negotiated by the State University of New York (SUNY) with United University Professions (UUP), also affiliated with the AFT.

The push for innovative training programs in the Board of Education, as in the rest of New York City, came from the union, whereas the UUP-SUNY program followed the pattern of state government initiative that had emerged in negotiations with the other unions of state employees.

Services Provided

A multiplicity of programs serve the wide range of educational and training needs of the state and city work force. Major categories, classified by purpose, are basic and remedial education, training for occupational advancement, skills and knowledge enhancement, and personal growth.

Implicit in administering these programs are choices concerning the distribution of resources and the delivery of services. The rest of this chapter explores some of these choices and examines the decisions the parties have made in designing and administering programs funded under their collective bargaining agreements.

Basic and Remedial Education

Despite the civil service testing process, the changing workplace has created a continual need for city workers to improve their basic reading, writing, and math skills. Municipal unions have initiated efforts to provide these skills to all their members. The experience of District Council 37 illustrates the potential contribution of union involvement in overcoming barriers to basic and remedial education for adults.

The District Council 37 program is designed to provide basic education for workers who lack the credentials to pursue the career in which they are interested. The union's approach to the design, implementation, and evaluation of its basic and remedial education program is a response to the fact that many members have been victims of an education system that, as a result of gender, ethnic, and racial stereotyping, did not give them support to pursue academic studies. Besides working full time and attending classes on a part-time basis, the "DC 37 student" is often a single head of household and union activist. The students' many roles often come in to conflict, and the DC 37 program is designed to be both sensitive and responsive to this dilemma. Curriculum, course structure, administrative procedures, counseling services, and even recruitment methods are designed to develop confidence in an effort to guarantee academic success.

The confidence the DC 37 basic skills program inspires in union members is the key to its success. The union knows that its role is to defend its members, to be nonjudgmental in evaluating their concerns, and to be their advocate. In turn, members view the union as the vehicle to helping them when they have a problem at the workplace, the means by which they receive pay increases, and the institution that provides them and their families with health care and other services. Likewise, the membership trusts that the union will help them pursue their educations. Members know that union-sponsored education programs will be designed to meet their needs and that due process mechanisms exist to resolve problems. Not surprisingly, many members turn to union education programs after failing or being disappointed in more traditional academic settings.

DC 37's basic skills program begins with recruitment. In addition to such traditional means as newspaper articles and direct mailings, recruitment includes personal appearances by staff of the DC 37 education department at work locations, union meetings, and union-sponsored conferences and seminars.

District Council 37 supplements the printed materials and oral presentations by union staff with a videotape in which students describe their experiences in union-sponsored education programs. Thus union members viewing the video hear fellow workers tell their success stories.

In some cases, the recruitment campaign points out the connection between the basic skills program and a specific career. For example, literature is distributed to hospital workers who applied for nursing degree programs and failed the college assessment examination. These letters congratulate the person for his or her desire to enter the field of nursing and describe how the basic skills program could help prepare the union member to take the entrance examination for the nursing program.

The basic skills program utilizes the members' educational goals as a recruitment tactic. Since many members considering enrollment in a high school equivalency or college preparatory program do not want to admit that they lack education credentials, the union's promotional materials stress the skills needed to receive a high school diploma, pass a civil service test, or enter college. Materials state that classes are designed to help students in reading, writing, and math. This approach is especially important because students are placed in classes to meet their particular educational needs rather than in groups in which everyone is preparing for the same examination or studying for the same purpose.

Before beginning their course of study, all students attend a multipurpose orientation and testing session (diagnostic tools are not called entrance examinations but rather placement tests, indicating that all prospective students are guaranteed a seat in class) at which a counselor provides the students with information designed to help them make the transition back to school. Counseling is an integral part of the union members' endeavors. Every student is assigned a counselor who calls the student when he or she has missed a class, is available to discuss problems or difficulties, and is clearly a key supporter of the student's desire to be successful in school. Counselors also sponsor group sessions on time management, study skills, and resumé writing.

All union members are eligible to enroll in basic skills classes. Classes are currently offered in the five boroughs of New York City and at union headquarters and are given during the day, in the evenings, and on Saturdays, so that all members, regardless of their work shifts, can attend.

Enrollment is continuous, although there are three semesters per year. Students can enroll at any time, and students who need to withdraw from a class can return at any time. This flexibility is imperative to the success of adult education programs since personal and family problems and responsibilities often require a union member to interrupt study. In addition, it is difficult for adults to make the commitment to return to school. It is therefore important that administrators not require potential students to wait until the beginning of the next semester to start their education.

To make it easier for members to attend classes, the union offers activities for their children on Saturdays in guitar playing, photography, and ballet. In addition, younger children may be left at an activities center, staffed by union members who work for the New York City Board of Education, while their parents and/or grandparents attend classes.

The District Council 37 basic skills program is structured so that students can study at their own pace. At union headquarters, where students are placed in a class by grade level, a learning lab is available for students who need tutoring in a particular subject, as a supplement to the classroom experience. At the union's off-site programs, each student has an individual learning plan and is assisted by an instructor in meeting his or her educational goals. Individualized study is complemented by weekly lectures and group discussions.

Another approach to basic education for city employees is the citywide Worker Literacy Consortium spearheaded by Local 237 of the

IBT. The unusual features of this program, which is targeted at workers who lack even the most basic reading skills, are its emphasis on reading required in the workplace—a stimulus to motivation—and its utilization of co-workers as recruiters and instructors.

The District Council 37 training fund is directed by a board of trustees that consists of representatives of local unions affiliated with the district council and council officers and is administered by staff appointed by the trustees. While the city personnel office has the power and responsibility to review and approve expenditures related to program content, it has rarely if ever vetoed union-initiated programs. The Worker Literacy Consortium, funded by state and city grants, is also administered by union-appointed staff and is governed by a policy board of union representatives.

Training for Occupational Advancement

Many training programs cater to union members in state and city government who want to get ahead within the civil service system. Classes are offered to prepare these workers for specific civil service examinations and for state and national licensing tests.

New York has pioneered two programs that prepare employees for upgrading; one is a traditional apprenticeship program, a concept borrowed from the private sector but adapted to the special needs of state government employees, and the other is a new form of apprenticeship that upgrades school personnel to professional positions as teachers and guidance counselors.

In 1982, New York State and CSEA established an apprenticeship program that is unique for the public sector. Unlike apprenticeship programs in other states, New York's is collectively bargained and based on the private sector model. Inspired by a shortage in skilled personnel to operate the state's physical plants, the first pilot apprenticeship program, for stationary engineers, was incorporated into the 1985–88 collective bargaining agreement between the state of New York and CSEA and thereby established a statewide Joint Apprenticeship Committee (JAC). This concept has been applied to other trades and now has an enrollment of eighty-nine apprentices and annual funding of $900,000. At its inception, the program encountered conflict with the traditional promotional system of civil service, but these barriers were resolved through negotiations (Burstein 1986:40). The program is now rated as highly successful by representatives of both the union and state agencies, who note that its high retention rate, high-quality training, and relatively low cost are the result of the active involvement of union and management in all phases of the program from recruitment and selection of apprentices to curriculum design to the monitoring of results by regional labor-management committees.

The JAC also provides continuing education for journey-level personnel through periodic seminars designed to enhance their technical knowledge. A further step toward skills enhancement and occupational mobility has been forged by linking apprenticeship and college degree programs through agreements negotiated by the state JAC with Empire State College, a unit of SUNY that grants credit for knowledge acquired through experience.

Another approach to preparation for upgrading is a program sponsored jointly by the UFT and the New York City Board of Education in which paraprofessionals are prepared to become fully qualified teachers. This program, initiated by the UFT in a period of tense community relations, is tailored to community activists, most of whom are minority group members, who work as paraprofessionals in neighborhood schools. The program provides counseling as well as tuition support for courses required to attain a bachelor's degree.

The UFT and Board of Education initiated another apprenticeship program in response to an acute shortage of vocational teachers with the skills needed to train today's labor force. It combines classroom training under the supervision of licensed instructors with on-the-job training in the trade in private sector employment. At the end of five years, the apprentice "substitute vocational assistant" becomes a vocational high school teacher.

Yet another program sponsored by the UFT and Board of Education enables teachers to become guidance counselors through an internship supervised by a licensed guidance counselor. The teachers are given release time and tuition assistance to acquire graduate-level education.

Job-Related Knowledge and Skills Enhancement
Improving performance on the job, normally the major focus of private sector employer-sponsored training programs, is also an important theme of joint training programs in New York. A number of

training initiatives deal with specific job titles. State collective bargaining agreements set aside approximately $1.5 million each year, for example, for grants for which state agencies and unions may apply. Small projects are reviewed by administrators of a program (union and management designate one administrator each). Larger grants are reviewed by top union and agency officials and must be approved by both. This somewhat unorthodox structure appears to have several positive attributes. First, it encourages labor-management cooperation at the local level by requiring the parties to interact on issues such as need, subject matter, scope, and vendor selection. Second, it gives the parties a great deal of flexibility and room to be creative. Third, the modest administrative structure and workshop orientation suggest low per unit training costs. Fourth, by being clearly bilateral and operating on an agreement rather than a meet-and-confer basis, the structure obviates issues of control and ownership at high levels and requires key decisions to be addressed at lower levels.

Supervisory Training
Another example of job-related education for state employees is the supervisory training funded under their contracts. Except for building construction and printing, unions in the private sector rarely include supervisors among their members, much less as participants in their training. In contrast, only 7 percent of the New York State work force is classified as managerial/confidential, which means that most supervisory employees are members of a union. Under contracts with CSEA and PEF, training for supervisors is an ongoing activity, most of which is provided through contracts with colleges and universities.

Teaching Skills
Toward the same objective, the UFT and the New York City Board of Education sponsor a variety of programs to increase the effectiveness of classroom teaching. Teacher centers offer graduate-credit courses taught by experienced teachers, and skills-oriented classes with such titles as "Critical Thinking," "Creative Conflict," "Learning Channels," and "Techniques for Working with Exceptional Students" are offered by area colleges for participants nominated by district organizations of their union. On-the-job training for teach-

ers is provided, through mentor interns, as is intervention for experienced teachers who are in trouble. These programs are co-sponsored by the union and Board of Education and are staffed by union members.

Handling of Grievances

Performance as union-management representatives in the collective bargaining and grievance resolution process is also a subject of state-funded training programs under PEF and CSEA contracts. PEF has contracted with Cornell University's School of Industrial and Labor Relations for a labor studies credit and certificate course funded under its contract, while CSEA's contract funds a Labor-Management Institute that offers a variety of workshops, including "Using the Grievance Procedure Effectively," "Counseling and Disciplinary Procedures," and "Conducting Effective Labor/Management Meetings." Although formal control of the institute is exercised by two high-level appointees, one union, one management, in practice the parties have delegated administrative responsibilities to the director, who works with union locals and state agencies to determine the content, timing, and format of the workshops. Local union and agency representatives are allocated seats that they fill with their own nominees.

Professional Development

PEF's contract aims to provide employees with a wide variety of professional training and development opportunities ranging from graduate credit and degree programs to workshops, conferences, and independent study and research. In addition, major programs of professional development are sponsored jointly by the United University Professions, which represents the faculties and other professional employees of SUNY, and the Governor's Office of Employee Relations.

The PEF contract, funded at $13.6 million a year and covering fifty-seven thousand professional, scientific, and technical workers, is administered through Rockefeller College, a unit of the state university, and includes the largest university-based professional development program in the United States.[5] In consultation with a

---

5. Foerman, Quinn, and Thompson 1987, pp. 310–19, describes the program in detail and analyzes its implications for other public sector jurisdictions.

higher education advisory committee, composed of representatives of PEF and state agencies as well as educational institutions throughout New York State, the program is overseen by two management and two labor representatives. Much of the curriculum and course development is subcontracted to other universities, which also deliver the classroom instruction. Educational services available to PEF members include graduate and undergraduate courses specifically developed for public administrators; professional noncredit workshops of one to five days duration; and a variety of graduate and undergraduate courses generally for professional development.

The parties have adopted meet and confer as their method of operation on issues involving graduate and undergraduate public administration courses as well as workshops. On issues involving professional development courses, the parties must agree. In practice, it appears that management seeks agreement on most issues. The parties have delegated substantial authority to the contractor, Rockefeller College, on a wide range of matters, including the selection of subcontractors and instructors, delivery sites, and class size. When the number of applicants exceeds available seats, local management and union representatives are responsible for selecting students.

Representatives of both the union and management seem proud of this program and cite its stability; graduate-level, custom-designed offerings; cooperative, bilateral nature; size; and positive impact on New York's higher education system. The parties' selection of a public university as the third-party administrator appears to have had several positive outcomes. First, it appears to have mitigated most issues concerning program control. Indeed, with its several committees and jointly employed staff representatives, the program appears largely insulated from disruptive political influence by either labor or management constituents. Second, Rockefeller College appears to have given the program a prestige that pleases both parties and contributes to the stability of the program. Third, the subcontractors—the colleges in the SUNY system that design and offer the courses—are responsive to Rockefeller College, which is a member of their same system. On the down side, there is the possibility of higher costs per training unit given the program's third-party, contractor-subcontractor structure coupled with the cost of custom-designing undergraduate and graduate-level courses.

The UUP-SUNY program is directed by the Professional Development and Quality of Work Life Committee (PDQWL), consisting of a total of six representatives, three from the UUP and three from the state (including SUNY and OER), and is managed by a full-time staff that is responsible to the committee. Policy decisions and staff appointments are made by mutual agreement. Currently, the UUP's collective bargaining contract allocates $1.8 million a year for professional development, which has been defined, in practice, to include individual awards of study leave for library and professional employees; research grants and travel funds for faculty members; and special campus programs for professionals to increase their skills and enhance their performance. In the latter category, projects generated and conducted by local campus groups deal with such wide-ranging subjects as teaching students with learning disabilities, AIDS education, time management, computer training, and new faculty orientation.

Another joint venture of the UUP and SUNY is focused on retraining retrenched or high-risk professionals. Under this program (Continuity of Employment), which spends some $300,000 a year, individual grants enable UUP members to undertake education leading to the acquisition of new skills and knowledge so that they may change occupations.

Personal Growth

One of the unusual features of New York's jointly sponsored educational programs is the attention given to personal growth and development. Both the state and the city, as well as the unions, are committed to the concept of lifelong learning and personal growth. The unions see the results of these programs in their employees' job security and mobility, and the employers support the investment in a more productive and stable work force. Therefore, most of the union contracts do not restrict tuition reimbursement to college courses in job-related subjects. District Council 37 of AFSCME and 237 of the Teamsters have established liberal arts college-degree programs under the auspices of colleges and universities in New York City and encourage their members to attend.

CSEA's Labor Education Action Program (LEAP) is a massive college enrollment effort funded at approximately $4.5 million per year. LEAP contracts statewide with public and private colleges and universities for seats in their classes for the membership of the bargaining units CSEA represents. The program is overseen by the training arm of OER and is administered by union-employed staff who negotiate with educational institutions; publicize, accept, and prioritize applications; and enroll students in classes.

Although program administrators have the authority to act on routine matters, they must get approval from OER to make personnel changes in the administrative staff and large expenditures, initiate new programs, and the like. Thus LEAP is organizationally and politically responsible to its client population—the union members—and empowered to act on day-to-day matters, but its authority on critical issues, especially financial matters, is limited by the need for management approval. If approval is not forthcoming on a particular issue, LEAP must be prepared with an alternative plan. This structure suggests that LEAP must be responsive to members, since it must get their support in dealing with management, and, at the same time, be cost-conscious, since its program is subject not only to management's scrutiny but to the scrutiny of the union membership. Indeed, LEAP's principals cite responsiveness and cost effectiveness as among the strong points of the program.

Administrative Structures

Jointly sponsored training programs in New York State have evolved a variety of structures for making decisions about the day-to-day administration of programs and the delivery of services. Broad policy agreements are normally incorporated into the collective bargaining agreements that fund these programs. At this level both unions and management participate equally. There are marked differences, however, between the state and the city in the administration of program services.

Not surprisingly, programs that were initiated by the unions are administered largely by union-appointed personnel and day-to-day decisions about content, methods, and delivery systems are made by union policy makers with the concurrence of management, which has a rarely exercised veto power. State programs that were initiated by management have established structures for administration in which unions have a strong voice with respect to the selection of content, administrative personnel, and contractors; nonetheless, the major initiative for change tends to come from management. In part, this may be influenced by the continuity and expertise of the

OER training staff; also important is the OER role in policing the fiscal controls of New York State.

Educational and training services for both state and city programs draw on in-house capabilities but also reach out to educational institutions and independent contractors. The city unions tend to rely on their own resources for job-related training and basic education programs while tapping the resources of local universities for college credit and degree programs. State programs make greater use of consultants and independent contractors, and the administration of the PEF program is delegated to Rockefeller College, which in turn contracts for services with other institutions of higher education. The extent to which these administrative structures are based on the mission of the programs and how much has happened by accident or through the sometimes chaotic process of collective bargaining and organizational politics is critical but difficult to determine. Programs such as these not only deliver training but also shape the relationship of labor and management, influence the public and proprietary educational system, and often influence the political fortunes of union leaders and government officials. Given the monetary, organizational, and personal impact of these programs, the following questions appear worthy of further study: Under what conditions is third-party administration necessary or desirable? What administrative structures and reporting requirements give the parties the oversight they need to discharge their legal and organizational responsibilities yet are not unnecessarily disruptive? What can be learned from private sector training and development efforts about jointness in administration and the use of outside contractors?

Conclusions and Future Directions

New York State and New York City have almost twenty years of experience in the co-sponsorship, design, and administration of educational and training programs. The value of these programs is evidenced by the continuing support they command from their sponsors, the growth in enrollment, and the expansion of funding even during periods of fiscal stringency. Both government and union leaders speak glowingly about what Tom Hartnett, New York State Commissioner of Labor and former director of OER, described as the "better product" that results from joint involvement in the selection of content, methods of teaching, and systems of delivery, as well as the union commitment to promotion and recruitment of participants. Two of the programs (District Council 37 and PEF) have been evaluated by independent analysts and rated as unusually effective.[6] Further research is required to determine the link between these union-management training programs and their stated goals—increased productivity and employee satisfaction, improved morale, and upward mobility.

Whether the New York experience can be transferred to other public sector jurisdictions remains to be seen. The high degree of unionization and union acceptance by management at both state and city levels in New York may make replication in other parts of the country difficult. Also unusual is the unions' willingness to make long-term investments in member education a collective bargaining priority. Nonetheless, the positive results in New York should encourage other public sector unions to develop their own experiments.

There is wide agreement among experts that the United States faces critical challenges, including coping with its changing role in the world economy, accommodating to labor force shortages, and replacing an aging infrastructure. Labor and management are asking that training and development address more of these concerns. Unions increasingly equate education with empowerment and dignity for their members. Employers see education as essential to maintaining the quality of their work force. Both parties need more information on how to administer their training and development resources. The New York experience demonstrates that working together, public sector unions and employers can enhance the quality of life in the work environment.

---

6. The district council program was evaluated in 1984 by staff of the New York State School of Industrial and Labor Relations at Cornell University and the results presented in an unpublished report. The council's college-degree program, offered in cooperation with the College of New Rochelle, was analyzed by faculty of the Wharton School of the University of Pennsylvania. These results were presented in a report funded by the Carnegie Corporation of New York in 1975. Both studies were very positive in their assessments of the impact of district council programs on the self-image and potential for upward job mobility of their members. The PEF program has been the subject of ongoing research by faculty of SUNY at Albany. Preliminary results are reported in Foerman, Quinn, and Thompson 1987. The principal conclusion was that the flexible format fits the varied needs of participants.

7 · JOINT TRAINING OF DISLOCATED WORKERS: WHAT DOES IT TAKE?

Michael G. McMillan

For many years federal legislation relegated unions to a secondary role in providing services for displaced workers, while supporting the role played by corporations and public agencies. As this chapter discusses, with the rise of jointism and other changes in the arena of collective bargaining, unions have become increasingly and positively involved. Written by an executive director of a union-based human resources institute, this chapter should be of particular interest to practitioners and human resource planners who seek to enlarge options for all workers, whether active or displaced.

Since the enactment of the Job Training Partnership Act (JTPA) in October 1982, practitioners, government officials, and academic experts have come to agree that the most effective programs for dislocated workers are those that include a significant degree of cooperation between labor and management. Although this view may appear self-evident today, it was not always widely accepted. Early studies and pilot projects in the field of training for dislocated workers focused on private sector involvement, ordinarily defined as leadership or input from business. A 1982 report by the Congres-

This article benefited greatly from the ideas and experience of Daniel Marschall, Iles Minoff, Laura Perlman, Jane McDonald Pines, and Markley Roberts.

sional Budget Office, for example, cites several advantages of involving employers in the adjustment process (pp. 51–54) but barely mentions the role of labor unions.

In late 1982, the U.S. Department of Labor established six demonstration projects for dislocated workers, to be operated by private industry councils (PICs) and Comprehensive Employment and Training Act (CETA) prime sponsors. The key players in these programs were employers, PICs, local governments, community colleges, the Employment Service, and for-profit consultants. Only one program included a union—the United Auto Workers in California's Alameda County—as a partner (Abt Associates 1983).

Conventional wisdom in the employment and training field has come a long way since then. Research and practical experience have demonstrated that programs operated by unions and/or employers are the most effective. When the U.S. General Accounting Office (GAO) tabulated survey results from 563 dislocated worker projects operating between October 1982 and March 1985, it found that those operated by employers or unions attained a higher average placement rate than those conducted by public agencies, PICs, service delivery areas (SDAs), or educational institutions. The average wage level for the employer-union projects was $7.62 per hour, compared to $6.61 for all projects (1987a:66). A related GAO study of eighty exemplary projects for dislocated workers concluded that "projects operated by employers and/or unions had above average results about three times more often than projects operated by other organizations, such as service delivery areas" (1987b:1).

A renewed emphasis on labor-management cooperation in the planning, implementation, and administration of programs for dislocated workers has emerged from these and other findings. In 1985, Secretary of Labor William Brock charged a tripartite task force (including six labor representatives) with the task of making public policy recommendations on the dislocated worker problem. Their final report (December 1986) describes "responsible behavior guidelines" for companies in the process of closing plants, including working with labor unions on alternatives, providing advance notice, and establishing worker-management committees to oversee outplacement activities. "Because adjustment is best accomplished by those directly involved," the report concludes, "whenever possible a employer-worker committee should be established at each plant closing or larger permanent layoff to coordinate the delivery of readjustment services to displaced workers" (U.S. Department of Labor 1986:31–32).

Labor-management cooperation has existed for many decades on many levels: in entire industries, across communities, and in individual companies. In addition, many states are actively promoting the formation of area labor-management committees (Siegel and Weinberg 1982). Extolling the virtues of labor-management cooperation, however, often obscures a harsher reality: labor-management committees are not feasible in all plant closing situations. The illusion of management cooperation sometimes covers up less noble goals. Whatever the particular situation, such cooperation is not a substitute for the collective bargaining process. As AFL-CIO secretary-treasurer Thomas R. Donahue told an audience at a 1982 conference on the quality of work life: "To the labor movement, the collective bargaining process is the cornerstone to honest labor-management cooperation. Any action that weakens a union, distorts the balance in its relationship to management, or its ability to represent its membership will damage that union's ability and desire to participate in committees of any kind with a particular management."

This principle helps guide organized labor's participation in training programs for dislocated workers. Authentic labor-management cooperation in actual or potential plant closing situations requires trust on both sides. It necessitates a willingness by companies and industry associations to provide the information needed for unions to assess business conditions and management decisions. In addition, state government officials and service delivery area administrators must view organized labor as a valued partner in the adjustment process. At the federal level as well, legislation must create structures in the job training field that strengthen the integrity and independence of labor-management committees.

Labor organizations are now widely involved in program operations. Since its formation by the AFL-CIO in 1968, the Human Resources Development Institute (HRDI) has intervened in hundreds of plant closings, working closely with local unionists to design training relevant to their members. HRDI has served more than 340,000 individual workers through job search assistance workshops, counseling, job development programs, instruction in basic skills, training seminars, conferences, and other activities. In 1986, AFL-CIO unions, central bodies, and HRDI sponsored programs funded at more than $86 million. More than thirty state federations have labor-JTPA coordination staffs and/or operate programs. Many valuable lessons have been gleaned from this experience.

For labor-management cooperation to be effective in particular plant closings, the unions involved should have access to technical assistance and back-up resources from a larger union-sponsored program. Such assistance may be available from several sources. Permanent statewide, labor-operated job training programs such as exist in Colorado, Michigan, and other states (see chapter 8 on state efforts in Michigan to sponsor joint labor-management training programs) are among the best sources of assistance. State AFL-CIO federations may foster such programs by creating internal employment and training committees. Expertise may also come from international unions through their preexisting labor-management efforts at the national, industrywide level; such is the case in the automobile, communications, and steel industries, among others. Finally, under limited circumstances, technical assistance is available from HRDI.

This chapter presents several case studies that illustrate how labor-management cooperation can flourish in an environment of mutual trust and full involvement by organized labor in the employment and training system. Such cooperation includes a willingness by state government to grant funds directly to labor organizations.

Programs for dislocated workers are of particular importance because of the Economic Dislocation and Worker Adjustment Assistance (EDWAA) Act, effective July 1, 1989. The act mandates that state units for dislocated workers promote the formation of labor-management committees in response to plant closings. EDWAA funds may be used to cover start-up costs for the committees as well as operational expenses.

Labor's Statewide Effort in Colorado

The activities of the Colorado AFL-CIO provide a good example of how a comprehensive labor-operated job training program can facilitate the formation of labor-management committees during plant closings or layoffs. The conditions of the Colorado economy has provided fertile ground for new approaches, and for years the state federation there has been practicing what EDWAA preaches. Widespread cutbacks in mining jobs, along with mass layoffs by packing houses, airlines, refineries, and other manufacturing facilities, have displaced some seventy-five thousand workers throughout Colorado over the past decade.

As far back as the early 1980s, the Colorado AFL-CIO used CETA funds to conduct job search workshops for laid-off employees. Whenever possible, the state federation works closely with individual employers and other organizations to develop cooperative mechanisms. In addition, an employment and training coordinator was hired in 1980. The coordinator has intervened in more than fifty plant closings.

In 1984, the coordinator learned from UAW Local 766, which represents employees at Martin Marietta, that the company was seeking skilled machinists and installation mechanics to work on defense projects at its aerospace facility near Denver. HRDI and the state federation helped place a number of dislocated workers in these positions. Some were discharged later, however, because they were unable to fulfill the precise construction and assembly standards.

The UAW local proposed a retraining program to equip the dislocated workers with the needed skills. Working with HRDI staff and representatives of the labor-sponsored Rocky Mountain Work project, the coordinator explored the concept with Martin Marietta's training specialist and secured agreement from the company to participate. The group undertaking the effort then obtained a grant from Title III, the section of JTPA that funds dislocated worker training, through the governor's Job Training Office.

The program design hinged on providing customized training at community and technical colleges in the Denver area. The Colorado AFL-CIO coordinated the project and focused on outreach and recruitment. To customize the training to Martin Marietta's specifications, college instructors spent three weeks at the facility learning about work processes, and once classes began they visited the company regularly to update their information. In addition, the company sent its quality control specialist to classroom sessions to monitor the training.

This small-scale training effort was a great success. As of 1984, the company had hired sixteen of eighteen program graduates. The joint labor-management approach ensured access to qualified applicants and helped guarantee that training would be directly targeted to meeting Martin Marietta's requirements.

The Martin Marietta experience set the stage for future labor-management cooperation. When AT&T announced plans in 1985 to abolish more than four hundred jobs at its information systems division in Denver, Local 8412 of the Communications Workers of America worked with the company and the state federation to survey the needs and interests of members. An early intervention strategy was developed, and career continuation classes were held for three months during worktime before the layoff. Funding sources included the governor's Job Training Office, the Arapahoe County SDA, and the Colorado AFL-CIO. While labor involvement maintained the credibility of the effort among dislocated workers, AT&T's knowledge of the labor market and close contact with other employers buttressed the placement component.

Organized labor's employment and training efforts were institutionalized in 1987 when the Colorado AFL-CIO obtained funding for a statewide program. With resources from JTPA Title III and the Wagner-Peyser Act, twelve labor staff from three AFL-CIO offices were integrated into the state's rapid-response activities. As a result, the state federation operates workshops on early intervention for those affected by closings of union and nonunion plants, followed by other services, such as counseling and job search workshops. Participants interested in classroom occupational training are referred to SDAs.

The state federation's labor-management approach culminated in services to workers at Gates Rubber Company, which produces rubber belts for the auto, mining, and agriculture industries. In April 1987, Gates announced the layoff of 850 workers from its outdated Denver plant, scheduled to close in 1989.

Given substantial advance notice, the Colorado AFL-CIO took the lead in establishing a labor-management committee composed of three union officers, three company officials, and a neutral chairperson. Management and Local 154 of the United Rubber Workers (URW) agreed at the outset to keep grievances and other strictly collective bargaining issues out of the joint meetings. Workers scheduled to be laid off participated in four-hour unemployment survival workshops held on company time at the plant site. They then had access to one-on-one counseling, skills assessment, placement assistance, and referral to educational institutions for classroom training.

The labor-management committee at Gates played an active role in program oversight. Participants could choose from various education and retraining options, but funds were disbursed by the AFL-CIO only with committee approval. "Virtually anything is open to them, as long as it's approved by the committee. There are no restrictions," Bob Greene, employment and training coordinator for the Colorado AFL-CIO, told the *Employment and Training Reporter* in 1988 (p. 282). Services were coordinated with an array of institutions, including community colleges, the job service, SDAs, and local school systems.

The joint effort at Gates Rubber would not have been feasible, say union representatives, if the Colorado AFL-CIO had not established a statewide program. It provided essential experience in the formation of joint committees and the legitimacy needed to obtain full cooperation from SDAs. The joint structure helped cement commitment from both sides.

Authentic labor-management oversight of job training programs in Colorado has been successful because of the proactive stance taken by the state federation, the number of willing employers, and the value the state government puts on labor's participation in the system. "If you don't have labor-management committees," concludes Bob Greene, "employers would take full control of these programs and decide who gets the training. You have to have local unions involved to make sure their membership is protected. It's awful easy for other institutions to believe every word that employers say. You need a counterbalance."

Labor-Management Committee for Safeway Workers

In some cases the best intentions and cooperative attitudes of union and management are undermined by existing structures in the employment and training community. Unless state government agencies and key actors in the JTPA system support the integrity of the cooperative process, services to workers laid off after plant closings will face needless obstacles.

In Dallas, Texas, union workers at Safeway became victims of one of many corporate takeover campaigns. Safeway was once America's largest grocery store chain, with some two thousand stores and more than 165,000 workers, many organized by the United Food and Commercial Workers (UFCW) union. In the wake of a hostile take-over bid in 1986, Safeway management retained control through a leveraged buyout and assumed $5.6 million in corporate debt. To maintain the cash flow needed to pay off the debt, Safeway adopted a strategy of selling off its stores in selected markets. Within one year of the buyout, the number of Safeway stores had dropped from 2,330 to 1,874 (Weinstein 1987). The UFCW estimates that some thirty-seven thousand of its unionized Safeway workers faced the prospect of lower-paying jobs or no jobs at all (Greenberg 1988).

With only several weeks notice, Safeway shut down 141 stores in April 1987, eliminating more than 8,800 jobs in the north central region of Texas. About 4,800 of the laid-off workers were repre-sented by UFCW Locals 368R and 540. With the assistance of the U.S. Department of Labor's Bureau of Labor-Management Relations and Cooperative Programs, representatives of the UFCW interna-tional union led the formation of a joint labor-management commit-tee to oversee services for displaced workers. Along with Safeway representatives and state government officials, the new committee included officials from locals of the UFCW; the Teamsters; the Bakery, Confectionery and Tobacco Workers Union; the Retail, Wholesale and Department Store Union; and the International As-sociation of Machinists.

The joint committee immediately drew upon its combined re-sources to plan a comprehensive program. Safeway provided de-tailed information on job titles, wages, and employee demographics, and with assistance from the UFCW international union, the com-mittee developed a detailed three-page survey to obtain information from workers on their counseling needs, desire for job search assis-tance, and interest in specific occupational training. The survey in-dicated that 81 percent of the displaced workers were interested in retraining, especially in technical and electronics occupations. The union used this and other information to design a customized pro-gram, to which the company donated a training center, office space, furniture, and personnel time. The unions, which eventually negotiated more than $10 million in severance pay for their members, focused on communicating with their members and gearing up to train them to provide direct services to their peers.

Other aspects of the adjustment process did not proceed as smoothly. The UFCW initially sought a JTPA Title III grant directly from the state, but the union dropped the idea when it became clear that the state was interested in giving Title III grants only to SDAs or state agencies. (At the time, the state allocated 60 percent of its Title III allotment to SDAs by formula; the remaining 40 percent was used for rapid-response activities, and grants were funneled through SDAs or the Texas Employment Commission.) When interviewed, union staff cited several barriers to program start-up that the joint committee encountered. Unionists recall one instance in particular in which an SDA staff person pulled aside a Safeway representative and apparently tried to discourage him from cooperating with the union.

The process of obtaining a Title III state grant dragged on for months after the Dallas Safeway closed in April 1987. When the state convened a public meeting of its rapid-response team, composed of staff from five state departments, a UFCW representative attended the session to present program funding needs. She was ejected from the meeting, in violation of state regulations. Only after a grievance was filed and a new meeting held did the state offer to commit $750,000 to get the program started—but not without one final condition: a training center would have to be up and running in three weeks. Union and company staff met the deadline; the doors opened on October 1, 1987.

Despite the succession of barriers, the joint labor-management program for Safeway workers operated successfully through early 1989. The $750,000 in state funds was later combined with a $1 million Title III grant from the U.S. secretary of labor, with all funds flowing through the local SDA to the UFCW as a subcontractor. Participants obtained a wide variety of services, including skills assessment, counseling, workshops on job search skills, on-the-job training, classroom instruction, and job development, placement, and support services, such as child care. Program staff, drawn from the ranks of dislocated Safeway workers, received intensive training from HRDI and UFCW international representatives in all aspects of service delivery.

According to union representatives, the state government's experience with the Safeway effort led to an improvement in their attitudes toward organized labor as a partner in responding to plant closings. Unions in Texas are now included in response activities more frequently, say union staff, and labor representation on PICs has increased.

The negative aspects of the Safeway experience highlight the barriers to labor-management cooperation intrinsic to the JTPA and EDWAA. Under the highly decentralized structure created by EDWAA, the majority of funds for dislocated worker programs are directed to "substate areas." In the overwhelming majority of cases, according to surveys conducted by the National Governor's Association, the substate areas are the same SDA administrative entities that operate JTPA programs for disadvantaged clients. Each SDA is governed by a private industry council, 51 percent of whose members by law are from business and industry. Earlier experience with job training programs has taught HRDI that the domination of PICS by business interests discourages the full participation of unions, central labor bodies, and AFL-CIO state federations. Moreover, state policies and government attitudes toward labor participation change from one governor's term to the next. Instability and inconsistency have thus been built into the system, all to the detriment of productive collaboration by the two sides affected most directly by dislocation.

Industrywide Approaches at the National Level

The scope of this chapter does not permit a full examination of jointly sponsored training programs at the national level, which have been undertaken in several major industries. The economic conditions that led to the inclusion of Title III in the JTPA—widespread worker displacement, rapid technological change, heightened international competition, and related conditions—also spurred the private sector to develop new training structures. A number of unions and companies have developed labor-management mechanisms to promote "continuous learning" for employees. "These joint programs benefit management, union, and the worker," explains one summary of this trend.

Management benefits by raising the level of worker competence and by increasing the motivation, commitment, and performance of the work force as a whole. . . . Unions gain a deeper role in advancing the careers and performance of their members, causing them to be viewed as a major factor in employment security and in the sustained improvement of wages, benefits, and working conditions. Employees gain self-improvement, self-esteem, greater employment security, and increased participation (Rosow and Zager 1988:75).

When implemented at the nationwide level in collective bargaining agreements, these efforts frequently yield dividends at the local plant site. Such programs also provide the technical assistance and backup resources necessary to engender meaningful labor-management cooperation after specific closings and mass layoffs. Experiences have been especially noteworthy in the automobile, communications, and steel industries.

The 1982 collective bargaining agreement between the UAW and Ford Motor Company established the unique Employee Development and Training Program to serve the training and career development needs of both active and displaced Ford employees. Financed through a "nickel fund"—a five-cent payment per hour worked by UAW employees—the EDTP offers a battery of specialized services: prepaid tuition, career counseling, basic skills training, technical education, preretirement planning, and customized training. Intended to be a "real working partnership" between labor and management, the effort is coordinated by a six-person joint governing board. Professional staff provide technical assistance, augmenting local EDTP committees, in determining local training needs. More recently, the UAW bargained similar programs with General Motors and Chrysler (Kassalow 1987; see also chapter 4 on the UAW-Ford program and chapter 5 on the UAW-GM Paid Educational Leave program).

The utility of the form of jointism pioneered by the UAW and Ford was powerfully demonstrated at the company's San Jose, California, assembly plant, the site of a massive plant closing in 1983. The company provided six months advance notice. Both sides were committed to a cooperative approach and formed a local EDTP committee, with the UAW as a full partner in planning and implementation. Within one week of the announcement of the closing, in November 1982, an employment and retraining center was operational. Located on the plant site, the center was accessible to employees during working hours, and orientation meetings, seminars, and vocational exploration courses were also held at the plant site. The local EDTP carried out an extremely systematic process of consulting workers on their needs and interests, planning a sequence of services, coordinating contacts with educational institutions and state government, and monitoring operations. Flexibility and responsiveness to workers' needs stand out as hallmarks of the effort, fueled by the labor-management approach, suggesting, in the words of analyst Gary B. Hansen (1984:16), that "control and direction of a plant-closing program by responsible, capable company and union personnel who are prepared to invest the time and resources necessary to do the job right makes for better and more successful programs."

The positive impressions Hansen gained soon after the closing were substantiated when he conducted a follow-up survey two years later. Only 17 percent of the employees were still unemployed. Among the workers who were employed, those who had engaged in substantive education and vocational training were making 85 percent of their Ford wages. Workers' perceptions were overwhelmingly favorable toward the program: 96 percent believed it had been effective in its training and retraining activities (Hansen 1987b).

"Collective achievement through individual empowerment" captures the approach of the Alliance for Employee Growth and Development, a cooperative venture of AT&T, the Communications Workers of America, and the International Brotherhood of Electrical Workers. Evolving out of the collective bargaining process in 1986, on the heels of the divestiture of AT&T, the Alliance reflects a shared understanding that a highly skilled work force is the true foundation of job security—not to mention a critical component of AT&T's capacity to compete successfully with new telecommunications firms. In recognition of the problems associated with large bureaucracies, AT&T's union and management negotiators created structures in which local components were important (Treinen and Ross 1989; see also chapter 3). The Alliance is a separate, nonprofit corporation that is governed by a committee composed of an equal number of representatives from labor and management. Alliance local committees are the "cornerstones" to planning and implementing customized local programs.

Like programs in the auto industry, the Alliance is geared to the needs of both working and displaced employees. Participants have access to an extensive array of services: training in new communications technologies, basic skills upgrading, career planning, prepaid tuition, and family relocation. As of September 1988, the Alliance had fostered a nationwide network of 219 local committees in forty-one states. More than sixteen thousand AT&T workers were involved in program activities. In a statement that clearly revealed its long-term orientation, the Alliance reported that it "is emerging as a career development strategy for AT&T's future staffing needs, not just as a tool for downsizing" (Alliance, *Annual Report* 1988).

The steel industry has extensive experience in union-management cooperation, dating back to 1960 when a human relations committee was formed "to plan and oversee studies and recommend solutions" (Siegel and Weinberg 1982). Massive industry layoffs in recent years have provided fresh impetus. From 1980 through 1988, members of the United Steelworkers of America made enormous sacrifices—contributing more than $4.5 billion in inflation-adjusted lost wages and benefits—toward company efforts to eliminate excess capacity. During this period the number of production jobs in steel mills was cut in half, from 332,000 to 166,000 (USWA Policy Statement 1988b).

In 1983, USWA president Lynn Williams created an International Headquarters Task Force for Dislocated Workers Program Development to coordinate union involvement in dislocated worker projects. At district and local levels, often working with HRDI, the union has been closely involved in the operation of more than sixty-five worker assistance centers across the country which as of August 1988 had enrolled nearly thirty thousand unemployed steelworkers. While union and company contributions have totaled more than $6.9 million, these resources have leveraged nearly $50 million in JTPA grants.

The firsthand experience of the USWA in planning and implementing such programs has provided a solid base on which to pursue new labor-management initiatives. The 1983 Basic Steel Agreement contained a provision (appendix O) pledging company cooperation in seeking job opportunities for displaced workers. In 1986 agreements with individual steel firms, the USWA bargained for annual cash contributions from companies to operate centers for dislocated workers, as well as company-union advisory councils to oversee operations. As of mid-1988, advisory councils governed eleven separate assistance centers. Their work is reinforced by the Top Advisory Council, which meets regularly to study industrywide initiatives (USWA 1988a).

The USWA approach illustrates how a union, having accumulated grass-roots expertise in serving the training-related needs of un-employed members, now has decisive input into the use of funds contributed by companies—all accomplished through collective bar-gaining and creative labor-management cooperation. The USWA is moving to create a steel tripartite commission of government, in-dustry, and union representatives to develop national policies, as well as to establish an apprenticeship and training system to meet the need for "skilled and technically proficient employees to operate and maintain modern steel facilities" (USWA Policy Statement 1988b).

Labor-Management Cooperation: What Is Most Effective?

HRDI's experience in labor-management cooperation and in de-signing comprehensive programs for dislocated workers has led to a number of conclusions about what works best. Dislocated workers have unique needs, different from those of disadvantaged clients, and require specially tailored services. Labor organizations, having formed long-standing "human contracts" with the workers they rep-resent, are often in the best position to spearhead the planning, de-sign, and operation of programs for their former members and others who are permanently displaced.

Although there is no single optimal approach to serving dislo-cated workers, successful programs tend to share several character-istics. Hiring formerly displaced workers provides a local program with staff who are thoroughly knowledgeable about the specialized needs and occupational skills of their cohorts. Local unions and AFL-CIO central bodies have a credibility with workers that make them highly effective at recruitment and outreach. Following a comprehensive skills assessment, participants should have access to a mix of services, including basic skills training, prior to involvement in occupational skills instruction. Workers who appear likely to benefit from skills training should be given the option of enrolling in on-the-job training or classroom training. Needs-based payments and other income support allowable under Title III and EDWAA should be utilized to ensure that displaced workers who are among the long-term unemployed receive the training necessary to secure well-paying jobs.

Programs operated by labor organizations frequently secure their members higher wages at placement than programs conducted by other organizations. This is partly because labor representatives have access to industrial job opportunities that afford workers comparable wages. Programs staffed by unionists have a strong commitment to seeking out and securing jobs in the unionized manufacturing sector. Because dislocated workers often are compelled to accept lower-paying employment on a transitional basis, especially in depressed labor markets, programs should keep in contact with participants after initial placement in the hopes of placing them in higher-paying jobs over the long term.

Promoting joint labor-management committees in response to plant closings must be viewed as one part of a comprehensive, humanistic approach that values the lives of workers ahead of raw statistics and performance standards. Only the federal government has the resources to ensure help to all those who need training and job opportunities. It is unfortunate that the highly decentralized and business-dominated structure of the JTPA tends to inhibit the effectiveness of the nation's employment and training activities. Nonetheless, organized labor is fully committed to playing an active role in making JTPA meet the needs of workers as well as possible.

Although the EDWAA Act increases the representation of organized labor on a statewide advisory body, it perpetuates the JTPA's decentralized and business-dominated approach. A majority of EDWAA funds allotted to states go directly to substate areas whose administrative entities (the substate grantees) ordinarily are the same industry-dominated private industry councils that were created by JTPA. Despite language encouraging labor-management committees, the basic structure of EDWAA tends to undercut such collaboration between key private sector players.

To achieve authentic labor-management cooperation requires that national-level, industrywide joint organizations be established in key industries. The seeds of such organizations have already been planted. EDWAA has the potential to provide the start-up resources to cultivate them. To meet training needs in a cohesive and coordinated fashion, without pitting company against company or state against state, cooperative mechanisms with a national viewpoint are essential.

Labor-management cooperation and jointism must be viewed not as ends in themselves but as part of a strategy that centers on continuous, long-term investment in our nation's human resources. If U.S. firms are to regain a competitive edge, job-specific training must be flexible and adaptable to the ever-changing nature of new technology and work processes. This perspective necessitates increased reliance on the workplace as the central arena for training. Private industry and the federal government must go beyond platitudes and political rhetoric and make significant resources available for worker training, retraining, and skills upgrading. In the final analysis, the skills of the American work force will be the measure of our achievements.

8 · JOINT STATE-LEVEL RESPONSES TO WORKER DISLOCATION

Richard Baker

This chapter discusses state-level initiatives that foster a union-management approach to assisting dislocated workers. After reviewing legislative efforts, Baker discusses how a Canadian approach to dislocation has been applied at several Michigan sites. The core of the Canadian program is the delivery of resources and aid through government-sponsored experts to a joint labor-management committee at the plant level. The essay should be of particular interest to practitioners and policy makers in human resource development and to state officials in training and economic development agencies.

America's belief system justifiably celebrates the ability of the individual to make a difference, to combat the odds and succeed where others have failed. While this belief is perhaps true in general, it is often untrue in particular situations. Plant closings are one such situation. In closing after closing, workers blame themselves, and are often blamed by others, for events over which they have no control and about which they had neither information nor the power to make changes.

This chapter highlights a series of state-level initiatives aimed at fostering joint union-management approaches to worker dislocation. These efforts are excellent examples of how the rhetoric of participation and institutional initiative can be linked through concrete actions.

Background

If management controls 80 percent of what a worker does, as the modern management guru Edward Deming states, then it is unfair to assign blame to the worker when there is a closing. In fact, the wide range of events that cause plant closings generally have nothing to do with individual workers or with the quality of the product they produce. Mergers and acquisitions often result in excess or duplicate capacity. Manufacturing technology becomes obsolete. Mature product lines are slow to be replaced. Industries decline. And, finally, automation leads to changes that minimize the role of the individual worker.

The Bureau of Labor Statistics estimates that from 1981 to 1986 about 5.1 million workers (defined as persons who worked for three or more years for their last employer) were displaced as a result of plant closings and mass layoffs. The statistics for 1987 show that although the figure may have dropped to about 750,000 for that year, the trend was quite steady. Including workers who were employed for less than three years doubles the average per year to over 2 million (Secretary of Labor's Task Force 1986:7).

In 1970, the goods-producing industries were 33 percent of nonagricultural payrolls. By 1985, they were 26 percent and services were 74 percent. Imports have also increased dramatically, from 4 percent of the U.S. market in 1948 to 13 percent in 1985, and they continue to increase (see, for example, Secretary of Labor's Task Force 1986). Similarly, yen-to-dollar ratios, virtually unchanged from 1950 to 1969, have swung dramatically since then. And interest rates and energy prices, both stable for generations, have become major catalysts for significant changes in our national as well as our world economies.

The effects of these changes have been striking throughout the society, but they have been particularly traumatic and debilitating for American workers. Millions who only a few years ago were firmly in the middle class are seeking employment, with few alternatives or resources to help them.

When the first wave of closings began in the late 1970s, first in steel, then machine tools, and then the auto industry and its suppliers, there was little or no awareness of the magnitude of the change that was occurring. There had been layoffs before, even for extended periods, but there had always been recalls, too. Not this time.

Except when the closing resulted in layoffs so massive as to mobilize an entire community, as in Gary, Indiana, or Akron, Ohio, workers were usually alone in searching out services and assistance agencies. Most agencies were set up to deal with the chronically unemployed or other persons who were difficult to place. They were not set up to deal with successful middle-class people who happened not to have a job.

Legislative Responses

The government's response, in general, has been to develop a tentative yet gradually more comprehensive program targeted at dislocated workers. The Trade Adjustment Act (TAA) of 1974 provided income maintenance benefits, training, and relocation and job search assistance to persons dislocated because of import competition. Reaching a peak in 1980 ($1.63 billion) and in 1981 ($1.45 billion), funds from the act declined to $109 million in 1982 and to $54 million in 1983–85 (General Accounting Office 1986:20).

The Job Training Partnership Act (JTPA), Title III, was enacted in 1982 specifically to help dislocated workers find jobs. Beginning with the 1982–83 fiscal year, appropriations ranged from $94 million for 1983–84 to $223 million in 1984–85 and 1985–86, then decreased in subsequent years to $169 million and to $100 million in 1987–88. The General Accounting Office (GAO) estimates that even in 1984 (the highest JTPA Title III funding year) JTPA Title III and TAA combined reached only 7 percent of the estimated 2.23 million workers who were dislocated that year (GAO 1987c:13).

One of the reasons for this low rate may be the process by which funding was distributed. Under TAA, a lengthy process of certification by the federal government was required to establish that a closing or mass layoff was indeed caused by foreign competition. By the time approval was obtained, months, and sometimes years, had passed during which the workers waited for assistance. In addition, the assistance addressed only workers who were directly affected, seldom the employees of related suppliers and subcontractors who were subsequently dislocated.

Similarly, under Title III of JTPA, states were given 75 percent of the annual federal funding to distribute as they felt appropriate. Some states used a formula for distributing funds to each local service delivery area (SDA) or private industry council (PIC). More commonly, funding was distributed on an individual project basis as closings occurred. Although the response time was cut, the program still missed those workers who were not at the work site. The result was that a sort of "creaming" often took place whereby more assertive or aggressive workers obtained services.

Another method of distribution is to fund organizations that serve a group of specific workers. The AFL-CIO Labor Education and Development (LEAD) program is an example of this approach. The program receives an annual grant that is used to provide services to dislocated workers, including help in writing resumés, job search skills training, and assistance in job development and placement. But, once again, the aggressive and the assertive tend to be the winners in this process.

Only about 15 percent of the employers involved in plant closings offered displaced workers a comprehensive assistance package of income maintenance, continued health insurance, counseling, and job search assistance. Only 5 percent provide a comprehensive assistance package and give thirty or more days advance notice of the closing or mass layoff. In a 1986 survey, the GAO found that about 60 percent of employers provided some assistance to their dislocated employees, usually severance benefits (54 percent) or continuation of health insurance benefits (43 percent). About 31 percent provided job search assistance. Most of the outplacement assistance and benefits went to white-collar workers, however. For example, 53 percent of the white-collar workers got severance pay but only 34 percent of the blue-collar workers; 42 percent of the white-collar workers had their health benefits extended but only 32 percent of the blue-collar workers (GAO 1987c:77–86).

To summarize, although some assistance has been available, not many workers have utilized it. As a result, although many workers quickly found new positions, more than 40 percent were unemployed for more than six months, and perhaps as many as 20 percent had not gone back to work after several years. Older workers, women, minorities, and those with nontransferable skills or who lacked basic math and reading skills were most seriously affected (GAO 1987c:12).

The Canadian Model

The Canadian Immigration and Naturalization Service has for twenty-five years housed what is now known as the Industrial Adjustment Service (IAS). Its purpose is to help businesses and workers "adjust" to the effects of change in the workplace. IAS helps companies during plant closings and mass layoffs but also during periods of growth and expansion, when it provides help in upgrading equipment, manufacturing methods, and product lines and in improving the efficiency and training of employees.

The IAS employs approximately eighty industrial adjustment consultants throughout Canada. Representing hundreds of years of combined expertise as business executives and labor leaders, they are the initiators and catalysts for the government's response to plant closings.

Upon learning of an impending plant closing or layoff, the IAS contacts the company and the union to arrange for a joint meeting to discuss the situation and to determine the extent to which assistance may be required. In over 85 percent of the closings, the company and the union (or a delegation of workers in unorganized sites) agree to establish an adjustment program at the plant. This consists of a Joint Adjustment Committee (JAC) of four to eight persons, equally representing labor and management and appointed by their respective peer groups. With the assistance of the IAS consultant, the committee selects a third party from outside the company and union to be a neutral chair.

The purpose of the JAC, its objectives, the procedures to be followed, and the process whereby the JAC's costs are shared equally by the company and the government are contained in an Assessment Incentive Agreement (AIA) signed by all three parties—the government, the company, and the union. This is in contrast to most U.S. initiatives whereby workers receive assistance from either the government, the union, or the company but seldom from a program involving all three.

In general, the purpose of the JAC is to assist workers and their company in adjusting successfully to a plant closing or massive layoff by helping the workers get new jobs as quickly as possible. The JAC focuses its efforts on identifying the jobs needed by the workers and on ensuring that they have the resources necessary to find those jobs and get hired.

The differences between the system prevalent in the United States and the one in Canada are evident. In general, two-thirds of Canada's dislocated employees are working again within six months, at a cost of about $200 Canadian per placement. In contrast, on average, between 1981 and 1985 only 45 percent of the displaced workers in the United States were reemployed within six months after a layoff or plant closing (Task Force on Economic Adjustment 1986:10). The average cost per placement for persons participating in the various federally funded, state-operated dislocated worker programs in 1986–87 was just over $2,000 American (National Alliance of Business 1988:16). The contrast between what might be defined as the client-driven system in Canada and the agency-driven system in the United States is striking.

These dramatic differences encouraged the U.S. Department of Labor and the National Governors' Association to sponsor an eighteen-month demonstration to see if the Canadian process could be replicated in the United States. Six states—Michigan, New York, New Jersey, Ohio, Utah, and Iowa—were selected to test the approach.

Several aspects of the Canadian IAS approach appear to have contributed to the program's success. First, the program is joint and equal: both labor and management are represented equally, they select their own members for the JAC, and they work together on the shared goal of assisting their co-workers. Second, labor and management operate under a joint agreement (the Assessment Incentive Agreement) that sets forth the relationship, defines how the committee will work and its jointly agreed-upon objectives, and provides for the source and use of funds by the committee. Third, participation is voluntary and can end with thirty days' notice by either party.

These criteria parallel what are commonly cited as the base requirements of quality of work life and employee involvement programs, in which the establishment of trust and a consensus decision-making process are seen as essential to success. In operational terms, this means that each decision is jointly arrived at and supported by all the participants.

The Michigan Model

The Michigan Governor's Office for Job Training (GOJT) was one of six U.S. agencies selected to implement demonstration projects. GOJT staff had experience and training in quality of work life and employee involvement programs. They had also provided consulting assistance to quality circle projects in both public and business settings and had assisted in establishing two areawide labor-management committees. The following cases highlight both the joint nature of the process and the specific steps taken by the parties.

Ore-Ida

Located in a rural farming region, Ore-Ida's Michigan plant was modern, highly productive, and profitable when it closed on May 15, 1987, dislocating 517 workers. A producer of potato products, fresh-frozen for distribution to retail outlets, the employer had developed a complex facility since its establishment in 1962. It grew potatoes on land it owned and contracted with area farmers for their crops as well. During production, the plant processed 1 million pounds of potatoes a day, and by the end of a season it had consumed more than 40 percent of Michigan's annual potato crop. The firm had invested an estimated $10 million in new facilities and equipment over the preceding five years to remain competitive and reduce costs.

Unfortunately, projections of consumer demand did not match long-term investment decisions, and by 1988 four plants were operating at about 65 percent capacity. The firm's other plants, in Oregon, Idaho, and Wisconsin, were more versatile. Thus, if the Michigan plant were closed, those plants remaining would operate at 85 percent capacity—an ideal level of production. If one of the others were closed and the one in Michigan left open, operational capacity levels would be 100 percent, a relatively inefficient level for a food processing factory. The decision was to close the plant in Michigan.

The reasons behind this decision contrast with popular mythology about why plants close: wages were competitive with other sites (the average wage was $8.35/hour); labor-management relations were good; absenteeism was low; productivity was high; the use of quality circles was expanding; the plant was modern; reinvestment was occurring; and the firm was profitable.

The attitude and responsibility shown by this company were unique. Once the decision was made in the fall of 1986 to close the plant in May 1987, the company made a sensitive and caring effort to help all involved adjust to the impact of the closing.

Initial steps taken. The Michigan Governor's Office for Job Training initially contacted the plant manager in December and proposed that Ore-Ida follow the Canadian model. The managers at the plant had never gone through a closing before and were interested in a solution that gave them some control over the situation. Management had been deluged with consultants and outplacement firms eager to assist them, but it did not feel any had proposed a method that fit the unique characteristics and needs of their workers. After considerable discussion, the firm's management team agreed to meet with GOJT representatives in Idaho. The outcome of the meeting was that the company agreed to provide the JAC with $30,000 to meet half its costs and to provide support services, materials, and space as needed. A meeting was then arranged with the president of the union, who quickly agreed to participate on an equal basis.

In February 1987, the union and company had signed an Assessment Incentive Agreement, copied almost verbatim from the Canadian model. The essential elements were that the union and company would each appoint its own members to the committee; the committee would select a neutral third-party chair; and the company and GOJT would share equally the costs of the committee (members' wages and the neutral chair's expenses as well as expenses of the committee for newsletters, printing, and other supplies). The purpose of the JAC was to help workers adjust to the closing, with the details to be developed by the committee. The Assessment Incentive Agreement also provided that any party could leave with thirty days' notice without penalty. The company and the union then each appointed three members and two alternates to the committee.

GOJT made a conscious decision to trust the process and empower and enable JAC members to develop their own program while providing them with the technical assistance needed to achieve their goals. GOJT recognized, for example, that all JAC members needed group process skills if they were to have an equal opportunity to affect the outcome of the program both positionally and informationally.

Committee members received training in win-win processes, consensus decision making, group problem solving, brainstorming, and prioritizing. Information and activities to improve levels of participation and communication were provided as well.

Since the JAC was essentially a task force with a defined product to be produced (an adjustment program), GOJT dictated the process by which the project would proceed. The process emphasized utilization of a problem-solving approach, decision making by consensus, and other techniques commonly used in such groups. The goal was to ensure that the experiences and expertise of all the members were drawn into the discussion, that the relative power positions of management and workers were neutralized in the decision-making process, that participants' skill levels were similar, and that there was a sense of teamwork and shared commitment to the content of the program.

The first activity of the JAC was to select a third party as neutral chair. Drawing upon each member's experience, members defined the characteristics they thought were best and worst in chairs. After prioritizing and reaching a consensus on these qualities, the JAC developed a series of interview questions and a process by which the JAC would interview candidates. Ten local men and women were identified. Of these, five were interested and four were interviewed. A hospital planning consultant was selected by consensus after a day-long interviewing session.

This initial use of group processes was reinforced with the more formal training described above, which was provided by the industrial adjustment consultant from GOJT. He continued to provide technical assistance to the JAC and guided its deliberations throughout the project (see figs. 8.1 and 8.2).

The JAC then adopted a mission statement to express its purpose: "To provide a network of services to assist the firm's employees in their job search, and provide necessary resources and assistance as needed." A survey was developed to determine employees' concerns, needs, and future plans. The members brainstormed scores of concerns and problems, which together with tabulated survey results

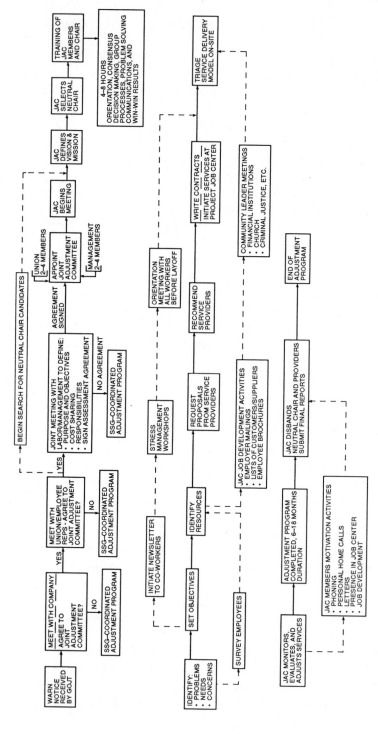

Figure 8.1 JAC's Organization and Program Delivery Process

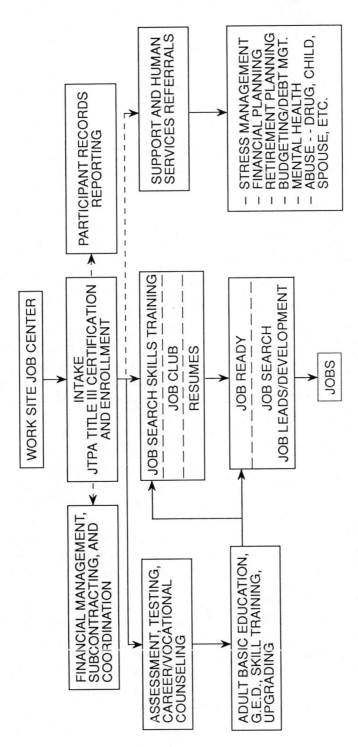

Figure 8.2 Service Delivery Triage Process

were used to reach an understanding of the magnitude of the situation they confronted. Representatives of area agencies and educational institutions were then invited to meet with the JAC to describe their services and how they might assist the JAC in achieving its mission. This process enabled the JAC both to educate service providers as to the magnitude of the problems the committee confronted and to familiarize committee members with the types and quality of resources available to assist them.

Prior to this step, the JAC had sent requests for proposals to all area service providers, inviting them to propose program areas they could provide to Ore-Ida's dislocated workers. The program areas were administration of the job center, to be established on-site at the company's facility; intake, testing, and counseling; job search skills training; and job development and placement services.

A decision to use competitive bidding met with mixed reactions from some of the public agencies. As long-time taxpayers in the community, JAC members relished the idea of competition, and they proved to be tough negotiators. Because they knew the problems and had become educated about the range of resources available, they fashioned a program that was focused, economical, and, most important, effective.

A local intermediate school district was selected to administer the program and provide intake, testing, and counseling, and the local branch office of the Michigan Employment Service was selected to provide job development and placement services. An independent consultant was subsequently selected to offer job search skills training through the intermediate school district. The local community mental health office provided free classes in stress management as well as crisis intervention services. These services were provided through the JAC's one-stop job center, located in the company's vacated office and training areas.

The JAC monitored its program in weekly meetings with program operators and by helping out on-site. The unique strength of the JAC was constantly reaffirmed as the program unfolded over the next seven months. As special problems were identified among various populations of employees, the JAC would bring together people from the service agencies with people from other community resources to create special services to address these concerns. The following examples are typical:

Orientation Day, held on a Saturday morning, introduced employees and their spouses to the service providers and job center. A nationally known motivational speaker, who happened to live in the town, provided the enthusiasm needed to move the event in the right direction.

A slick brochure touting employees' skills and attributes was developed and delivered to thousands of employers. Many employees used it to introduce themselves at interviews.

A weekly newsletter was published and distributed in the plant and mailed to the workers' homes after the layoff.

A job fair was held at the plant at which over fifteen employers were present.

A Golden Opportunities for Golden Years program was held for those fifty-five years and older to introduce them to special services for senior citizens and to provide them with assistance in their job search.

JAC members and volunteers staffed phone banks and made in-home visits to motivate employees to use the services.

Meetings were held with representatives of local financial institutions and members of the criminal justice system to sensitize them to the needs of the dislocated workers. These meetings addressed special credit needs, child support concerns, and stress-related behaviors.

Results. The results in January 1988, after eight and a half months, were impressive. Of 511 employees, 351 had enrolled in the program, including 30 of the 39 who had retired. Twenty-seven were still in classroom training, and 331 were employed. Nineteen had moved out of the area, and 19 had refused all assistance. Eleven could not be contacted to determine their status. Six were in disability rehabilitation or welfare programs. The remaining 59 were still unemployed when the project ended in January 1988. Only 12 percent of the original work force who wished to be employed remained on layoff. About half of these were second-income providers who did not need to work.

On average, workers earned $5.87 per hour at their new jobs, versus $8.35 at Ore-Ida, a 30 percent reduction. Those who were willing to drive to Grand Rapids, twenty to thirty-five miles to the southwest, were receiving hourly wages in the $7 to $10 range, while those who stayed in their hometown were receiving between $4.25

and $6.00. For most workers, decisions were made based on commuting time and family situations.

The cost of the program, including OJT contracts, classroom training, and the $30,000 provided by the company, was $400,000. The cost for each participant who was enrolled was $1,140; the cost for each enrollee who obtained a job was $1,794. If all workers who obtained jobs are included (many used the job center's services but were not enrolled), the cost per placement drops to $1,246 each.

There had been considerable concern at Ore-Ida that labor and management might have difficulty working together. In this instance, however, because the closing was permanent, participants were able to set aside their traditional positions and work together to achieve a common goal and outcome from which all would benefit.

Hydreco

For over forty years, Hydreco had manufactured hyraulic pumps for a variety of construction, earth-moving, and agricultural machinery. At one time over 500 employees had worked at this plant, but when GOJT learned in December 1987 that a closing was scheduled for May 1988, Hydreco had only 110 employees. Faced with competition from imports and changing product requirements, it had been sold by its parent company to another conglomerate that now planned to close the facility and move the remaining contracts and products to a facility in Georgia.

Initial steps. As at Ore-Ida, there was a great deal of lead time—almost six months—in which to plan and implement a joint adjustment strategy. Initially, GOJT did not have sufficient monies to fund the JAC, so Hydreco agreed to fund 100 percent of the JAC's costs, at least until public funds could be secured. The union proved to be equally enthusiastic and responsive, and an Assessment Incentive Agreement was signed in January 1988. A discretionary grant of $130,000 was received subsequently from the U.S. labor secretary's reserve fund for the project.

The work force at Hydreco was quite different from the one at Ore-Ida, which was two-thirds female. At Hydreco, all but a few office staff were men; about one-third were salaried. The youngest hourly worker was forty-two, and average seniority approached thirty years. Most were skilled craftsmen or had other technical skills. Most had never worked anyplace else except for the armed forces (45 percent were veterans).

A four-member JAC of two labor and two management people along with one alternate apiece was selected. The committee selected as chair a professor of industrial engineering who had worked with all of them fifteen years before as an engineering sales manager. The process of providing small-group training in problem-solving processes, consensus decision making, and related skills was utilized in the same manner as at Ore-Ida.

Keeping within the model for a client-designed, client-driven adjustment program, the JAC requested proposals to provide services to the employees. The local Job Training Partnership Act service deliverer was selected to serve as the lead agency and to keep financial and participant records. The local branch office of the Michigan Employment Service Commission was hired to provide job search skills training and job placement services. A private business school provided testing, assessment, and career counseling, and another private company provided stress management training and counseling. The local town provided space for a job center in return for a donation from the company of a case of paper towels and a case of toilet paper.

The Hydreco project proved to be more contrary—and more typical—than the one at Ore-Ida. The plant did not cease production in May 1988. In fact, it was still producing special orders in February 1989. Workers got laid off one by one, so that the sense of solidarity and urgency was lost as the closing date kept changing. The company also received certification for the receipt of Trade Readjustment Act benefits, which made most employees eligible for an additional twenty-six weeks of unemployment pay. While these benefits were welcomed and deserved, many workers now felt even less urgency about undertaking a job search. They had also bargained for substantial severance pay (often more than $10,000) and a year of health benefits, further reducing the sense of urgency.

Results. In spite of the formidable disincentives, including the workers' age and lack of job search experience, the initial results were quite positive. By November 1988, forty-three workers had been laid off. Of these, thirty-five had participated in the program. Seventeen had new jobs at an average wage of $9.55, versus $10.34

at Hydreco after thirty-plus years. Additionally, several were enrolled in classroom training to acquire new or upgraded skills.

In response to the results of its employee survey, the JAC had conducted a series of seminars on starting a small business, a retirement and Social Security seminar, an orientation program, numerous get-togethers at the job center, and a pot luck dinner. Mailings, focused on employers that needed the specific occupational skills of Hydreco employees, were utilized to generate interviews, as was a targeted mailing of the project's "Resumé Book." Through phone calls and personal visits, JAC members encouraged co-workers to participate in JAC activities. Finally, a monthly newsletter, mailed to all former employees, helped ensure that the Hydreco social network remained functional and helpful.

The closing had a dramatic impact on the ability of the union and management to work together toward goals that both perceived to be the same. As one labor member stated, "If we had been able to work this way out in the plant over the past years [thirty-two years for him] like we do up here in committee, this plant probably would have never closed."

The University of Michigan School of Social Work Employment Transition Program, under the leadership of Jeanne Gordus, initiated a long-term longitudinal study of the dislocated workers at Hydreco. The initial study found that the employees' perceptions of the company and the union as well as of the JAC were very positive; the program had enhanced their opinions of each.

The Hydreco project was completed in June 1989.

G. R. Manufacturing, Inc.

G. R. Manufacturing, founded at the turn of the century as Leonard Ice Box Company, was a pioneer in the development of refrigerators and grew into a major national company, which then merged with Kelvinator in the 1920s. After World War II, it was sold and resold to several companies before it was finally sold to White Consolidated Industries, an international conglomerate. In late 1987, it decided to close the Michigan plant and move production to Tennessee. The plant, which had over five thousand employees shortly after World War II, was down to eleven hundred by June 1987. At that time, the company laid off about six hundred workers and announced that it would close in the summer of 1988. Then, in early December, it announced that it would close in less than thirty days—on New Year's Eve.

Initial steps. The company and union invited GOJT to assist in the formation of a JAC in early December. Working with a local community task force that was already assisting the workers, initial efforts at forming the committee and selecting a neutral chair quickly got bogged down in power struggles between the company and the union. These were left unresolved, and the dispute influenced the selection of the neutral chair. Both sides sought to obtain control over the process to the exclusion of the other.

The JAC declined offers of training or technical assistance in the development of its adjustment program, and after four months there was still no program and the project was drifting to an undefined end. A job fair was held at which attendance was high but which resulted in few jobs being secured. The project lacked a focus or a presence that encouraged workers to believe they would be successful in their job search as a result of their participation in the project.

A discretionary grant of $441,000 was obtained from the secretary of the Department of Labor in March 1988. This coincided with the resignation of the original neutral chair, who was replaced shortly after by the retired personnel director of the company. Committee members had all worked with him during his thirty-two years with the firm, and he had their deep respect. Several people who had opposed his appointment originally had since left the JAC, enabling the selection to be made.

The JAC embarked on a goal-setting process to redefine its problems in the context of the current situation, in which the work force had now been out of work for three to nine months. Because the need to put a program in place was seen as urgent, GOJT did not provide training at this point. Fortunately, the trust and esteem in which the members held the neutral chair permitted him to move the program quickly forward. By now the plant was closed. Members of the committee who had tried to exert control and who had prevented the JAC from developing a range of programs responsive to the needs of the employees were now gone. Those who were left were truly volunteers—people with a commitment to saving their co-workers from further disaster. The result was a much more harmonious and open working relationship among members of the JAC, and, as a consequence, a full-service worker assistance program was implemented.

Service providers were given space and facilities in the UAW's union hall across from the plant, and the UAW/G. R. Manufacturing Worker Assistance Center began operations there in June 1988.

The members of the JAC were hired by the project on a full-time basis to implement the program. They certified applicants' eligibility for the program and referred them to appropriate services at the worker assistance center. Subsequently, in addition to processing paperwork to meet JTPA requirements, they also assisted employees in gaining access to social service providers and made extensive phone and personal contacts to motivate them to participate. Because of an agreement with the Leonard Ice Box trust fund, a holdover from the days when profits from the company store were used for charitable activities for company employees, the JAC was able to provide various support services. These included money for gas and for haircuts and food baskets on holidays. Coffee clubs, pot luck dinners, and a newsletter were used to maintain communications.

Results. The program exceeded its goal of three hundred participants; more than 340 were enrolled. The goal of finding jobs for 180 proved difficult, however, in that one-third of the work force had less than a high school education and 22 percent— eighty—read at less than a sixth-grade level. Only three of these eighty employees got jobs through the program, even though there were extensive on-site services. Two employment specialists from the Michigan Employment Service Commission were stationed on-site, on-the-job training was used extensively to obtain placements (over eighty), and a highly skilled job search skills trainer was employed at the site for six months. Unfortunately, less than a dozen employees were able to take advantage of these formal classroom training opportunities. The fact that most employees had exhausted their unemployment insurance benefits by the time the project got started probably prevented most of them from considering classroom training as an option.

When the project drew to a close in March 1989, several successes were apparent: of the 1,161 workers who had been laid off starting in June 1987, 450 had found work without the help of the JAC. Working mainly with those who were left, beginning in June 1988, the JAC had helped 189 find full-time jobs and another 43 find part-time jobs. Over 150 had retired, another 72 were not looking, 26 were on sick leave, and 53 had moved out of the area. At the end of the project, 5 were still in classroom training. Only a handful— less than 30—were still actively looking for jobs. They were referred to local agencies for extended assistance. The JAC was unable to locate 140 of the workers who had been laid off.

Lessons from the Michigan Projects

The following section discusses the lessons learned as a result of the programs conducted at the three plants described above as well as four other plant closing projects that have used joint adjustment committees. While some of these lessons may be applicable to a variety of worker dislocation programs, they are critical to joint union-management initiatives.

Selecting Members and a Chair

The objectives of the JAC are embodied in the Assessment Incentive Agreement and made real by the requirement for consensus decision making and the requirements that there be a neutral chair, equal representation by both union and management on the JAC, and financial support to carry out decisions. These conditions appear to enable committee members to work together even at work sites that have a long history that would seem to mitigate against cooperative ventures.

Committee members should be volunteers who do not have a history of animosity toward labor or management. They should be team players whom people enjoy working with, informal leaders whose opinions are valued by others. Management members should be assured that they are respected by their superiors, that they will be able to make decisions on the committee, that they will have some independent authority, and that within limits their independence will be respected. Similarly, union members must have the freedom to make their ideas known and to act independently, even though they have to answer to the union, too.

If any member has a hidden agenda or is out for self-aggrandizement, the ability of the JAC to operate on a consensus basis will be seriously impaired. It may even be negated completely.

Choosing the chair of a JAC must be undertaken carefully. The desire to assist and be part of a cooperative effort is important, as is the ability to respect and appreciate the purpose and viewpoints of both labor and management. A demonstrated ability to lead voluntary participants is a unique attribute, as is the ability to draw out the best from every member of the committee.

Several other guidelines should be followed as well:

• The independence of the chair must be unquestioned.

• Persons from local agencies will be seen to favor labor or the company and are therefore unacceptable, as are persons under contract either to the union or the company.

• The whole JAC must be involved in the process of interviewing and selecting a chair.

• Selection of the chair must be by consensus. Otherwise, members may plot how to get even later on. The process must be win-win.

• The chair must be paid. Otherwise, the JAC may not be a priority. The chair can donate the salary to charity if he or she does not want it.

• The chair should be from the neighborhood. The chair will often have to establish or forge alliances with agencies and other services. Knowing the players and their agendas is important.

• The chair must conduct himself or herself in a businesslike manner and prepare reports on time and completely. Similarly, agendas and minutes are requisite to effective committee work.

Training the Committee and Chair

Labor and management members come to the JAC with very different perspectives (givers versus takers of orders), sources of power (elective versus appointment), and skills in group processes (democratic versus position and staff work). Effective committee membership involves the use of learnable skills, structures that ensure open participation, and guidelines that all agree will be followed:

• Processes must be put in place that enable people to voice their opinions and ideas freely, without fear of being ridiculed or ignored.

• Training in brainstorming, prioritizing, group problem-solving, and consensus decision making ensures that all members have the skills necessary to participate. Experiential training, intended to

give JAC members a chance to apply newly learned skills, builds familiarity as well as a team spirit supportive of their use by all.
• Knowledge of the ways in which participation is enhanced or stultified enables members to participate equally and effectively.
• Training all the members enhances the neutral chair's capacity to work effectively and efficiently with all of them.
• Training builds commitment to the process itself and to the importance of individual involvement in the program.

Importance of Time

The ability to plan a coherent and effective program takes time. If the JAC has only a few days to react, it cannot develop expertise or build confidence among co-workers that they should use the program. Much of the success of jointly sponsored programs appears to center on their ability to respond to individual needs of a work force: are workers young or old, skilled or unskilled, parents or empty nesters, in need of retraining or adequately skilled? Furthermore, research shows that the longer people are out of work, the greater the likelihood that they will never go back to work again. Various pathologies such as abusive behavior toward oneself and others also tend to increase and self-esteem decreases. Putting programs in place prior to a closing or layoff helps people feel they can cope with the change and get on with their lives.

Involving International Representatives or Business Agents

The international representative or business agent has access to a broader perspective on the union's policies toward joint labor-management efforts than does local union leadership. The former may have experiences germane to the particular site that can help the program succeed. Involving these people is more than a courtesy; it represents an effort to provide political support for the local union's efforts in participating in the JAC. Lack of support may close several areas of assistance.

Training the Neutral Chair

Projects to date have been fortunate in that they generally had qualified, adaptable chairs. Chairs benefit from leadership training, however, particularly in the concepts and skills involved in being a participative leader of a team such as the JAC with its unique membership and decision-making processes. Even the most well-meaning

JAC needs guidance from an experienced industrial adjustment consultant; he or she is the keeper of the process.

Impact of the Demonstration Project

The lessons learned from the demonstration project found a receptive audience in the U.S. Congress of 1988. Few if any of the positive aspects of the experience failed to find a place in the two new laws passed during that session. The Economic Dislocation and Worker Adjustment Assistance Act amended Title III of the Job Training Partnership Act as it pertained to workers dislocated by plant closings and mass layoffs. This very aggressive piece of legislation conveys with urgency that the situation of dislocated workers is serious and that state governments and local recipients of funds should make every effort to respond quickly, cooperatively, and effectively to their plight. Paramount is its recognition of the importance of rapid-response teams if services are to have a positive impact.

A companion piece of legislation, the so-called "Plant Closing Law" or Worker Adjustment and Retraining Notification Act (WARN), requires companies with more than one hundred employees nationwide to provide sixty days' notice of their intent to close or lay off a substantial number of employees. This notice must go to the employees or their unions, the local government, and state dislocated worker units. States in turn are mandated to respond within forty-eight hours on-site to prepare an assessment and plan of action with local officials, the company, and employee representatives. Similarly, Title III funds are now available to provide services to workers before they are laid off instead of making them wait until they have their pink slips.

The use of labor-management committees is explicitly encouraged as a first option that the rapid response team should explore with the company and workers when they meet on-site. Lessons learned about the need for a written agreement and the importance of having the JAC choose its members and a neutral chair, participate equally, and share committee-related financial responsibility with the company are all set forth in the law and its accompanying regulations. The legislation suggests that the industrial adjustment consultant may provide a list of neutral chairs for the JAC to consider. In all cases, however, the JAC decides who the chair will be. Furthermore, whether a JAC is established or the local JTPA provider (called a substate grantee) is given responsibility for providing services, a seamless web of services should be readily available.

Work sites vary, as do the causes of layoffs and closings and, most important, the characteristics of each work force. The new legislation recognizes this as well. No one particular response is favored over another, although the joint labor-management approach is strongly encouraged. The rapid response team is charged with making an assessment and recommending a response. There are no practical limits to the variety of options it may suggest, provided they give workers access to the tools and resources that will enable them to adjust to the closing.

Future Prospects

As of early 1989, more than fifteen states had experimented with forms of the joint labor-management approach, including some unorganized facilities. And, in addition to the experiments described above, four more Michigan sites have used the approach with positive results. It appears that the Canadian IAS model can be replicated in the United States with favorable outcomes.

The model seems to have implications for situations other than just plant closings and layoffs. For example, Canada has for many years applied the model so as to help companies and their employees adjust to the effects of changes in technology, markets, and products and to find new ways to compete more effectively. To paraphrase one JAC member, "If we worked this way all the time, maybe we would have to close fewer plants and we could build more jobs for all of us."

Conclusion

When labor and management join together with government to provide services, the benefits are clearly greater than when one party has to deliver services alone. The success achieved by those who have used the Canadian IAS model confirms both the validity of the approach and its applicability to the United States. As a result of the enactment of WARN and EDWAA, the model has now been endorsed at the highest policy-making levels. The stage is now set for its use in a variety of situations in which labor and management need to work as partners to achieve a common goal.

9 · JOINT PROGRAMS FOR LIFELONG LEARNING

Jeanne Prial Gordus, Cheng Kuo, and Karen Yamakawa

This chapter examines whether providing counseling and advising increases rates of participation in adult education. Specifically, the authors address whether the life/education advisors (LEAs) in the UAW-Ford Education, Development and Training Program influence individuals to participate in the adult education program at rates higher than would be observed in similar locations where emotional and informational assistance are not provided. The study on which this chapter is based represents one of the few efforts to quantify the results of joint training. The chapter should be valuable to researchers and policy developers, particularly insofar as it illustrates how the adult learning model can be successfully applied to studies of joint training programs.

Is it possible to increase participation by industrial workers in adult education by providing counseling and advising? And, if so, what is the mechanism through which this increase in participation occurs? The relevance of these questions to public policy are sufficient to justify our research. The special conditions under which our exper-

The authors acknowledge the support of the UAW-Ford National Education, Development and Training Center. Besides financial support for program and monitoring efforts, the cooperation of UAW-Ford staff, LEAs, and UAW-represented Ford employees was indispensable to this effort. Members of the survey, interviewing, and analysis team, far too many to name here, helped develop these data. We thank these collaborators but retain claim to all errors.

iment took place also make this research relevant to a study of union-management workplace interventions.

This chapter presents results from research on one of a series of program initiatives known as the Education, Development and Training Program (EDTP), developed and implemented jointly by the United Automobile Workers and the Ford Motor Company. The EDTP is just one of an array of joint UAW-Ford program initiatives, ranging from employee assistance programs to help workers deal with life situations to health and safety and employee involvement programs.

Over the past decade much attention has been directed toward the joint aspect of the programs since this characteristic is so important. Less attention has been focused on their dramatically changed and enlarged scope. Many, if not most, programs in the 1970s were directed toward problems and deficiencies in physical health, mental health, or skills. By the mid-1980s, the emphasis had changed from remediation to enhancement and development. The underlying response to programs changed accordingly. No longer was program participation a sign that an employee had something wrong but rather that he or she was becoming better. The ideological shift and the inclusion of the entire work force in the new support structure has not escaped the notice of UAW-represented Ford workers. Their view of the programs and its joint sponsorship is extremely positive.

Although the joint nature of the UAW-Ford Education, Development and Training Program is not in itself a major focus of this chapter, it is important to note that this complex of programs could not have been implemented without a carefully designed joint structure. Under this structure, each party contributes important resources that might be withheld in the absence of a commitment to jointness. Life/education advisors must be selected jointly, and the failure of one party or the other to be involved makes implementation impossible. A program that is supported by either the company or the union but not by both will lack crucial support. For example, the space allocation role of the company and the union provision that it will grant LEAs access to workers are both indispensable. Finally, since the co-chairs of local joint committees must sign the monthly reports of LEAs, both the union and company are kept informed of the LEAs' work.

The LEAs are a visible symbol of jointness since they are employed by neither the company nor the union but respond to joint direction from both on a daily basis. Important messages are sent to employees about the value of education and self-development since union leadership and upper management are evident at graduation and recognition ceremonies, during education fairs, and at other important events, such as the opening of learning centers. Measured approval by the LEAs of the union and the company is very high and statistically identical: they view jointly developed education programs as evidence that joint programs can work and that they are good for individuals and for groups.

This chapter has six major sections. A brief description of the UAW-Ford Education, Development and Training Program is followed by a description of the development and implementation of the Life/Education Planning Program (L/EPP). The third section outlines the hypothetical framework that guided the study design; the fourth presents the results of a survey of UAW-represented Ford employees on their prior attitudes, educational attainment, current participation, psychosocial well-being, and levels of satisfaction; and the fifth presents a linear structural relationship (LISREL) covariance analysis of these data in relation to the model. The final section presents some conclusions and an agenda for the proposed next phase of research.

The EDTP

During collective bargaining negotiations in 1982, Ford and the UAW agreed that jointly developed and provided training and retraining programs should be made available to UAW-represented Ford workers. Funded with five cents for every hour worked by every hourly worker, the program soon came to be known as the nickel fund. At first, the focus was almost exclusively on the needs of laid-off workers, but as those needs were addressed and the industry rebounded, new initiatives were developed to address the interests and needs of current Ford employees.

There are three central organizational features of the program. First, in all respects, all the programs are joint efforts. Second, in each major facility, program direction is under the authority of a joint local Education, Development, and Training Committee. And third, all programs are participant-driven.

At the time of our survey, six major program areas had been developed under national guidelines:

Education and Training Assistance Program (ETAP). A tuition assistance program that provides workers with up to $2,000 per year.

Skills Enhancement Program (SEP). A broad program including adult basic education, high school competence, English as a second language (ESL), and other enrichment services.

Successful Retirement Planning Program (SRPP). A preretirement planning program.

College and University Options Program (CUOP). A program to facilitate college entry and success.

Targeted Education, Training or Counseling Program (TETCP). A program for trying out innovative pilot projects.

Life/Education Planning Program (L/EPP). A counseling and education/life planning program.

In conceptualizing how the program areas are related to each other, a central role is given to L/EPP as a point of access to other programs.

In the early period of working with laid-off workers, the UAW-Ford experience provided important lessons about the advising and counseling function. First, it became clear that other program elements had to be available before advising could best be utilized. Second, the success of the individual and group career counseling and job search skills program, which featured highly supportive counselors who assisted laid-off workers to develop a positive assessment of their prior experiences and their future potential, suggested that a similar participant-driven approach would be successful for active workers as well. Thus L/EPP was designed, developed, and implemented after ETAP, CUOP, SEP, and SRPP had been launched.

The Life/Education Planning Program

In the spring of 1985, the University of Michigan recruited professionals to become life/education advisors to serve about 70 percent of the hourly workers who were employed in about forty of the larger Ford locations. Most of the workers in the remaining facilities were scheduled to be served by the L/EPP in the summer of 1986.

After prescreening, the university presented the dossiers of the top applicants for each LEA position to a local EDTP committee so that it could recommend candidates for that location.

In July 1985, thirty-four highly qualified professionals from a number of disciplines and backgrounds were hired, trained, and assigned to the locations. The central focus of their job was personal advising and counseling, which was to be strengthened by their second role as providers of specially designed workshops. They were also expected to make referrals, provide program and service information, and administer the program. Fundamentally, the LEA's assignment was to help UAW-represented Ford workers assess their resources, consider or reconsider personal goals, and outline ways in which those and other goals could be met using many resources, including the UAW-Ford programs.

The choice of outside professionals to work within the context of a joint labor-management program was deliberate. I. L. Janis (1983) and others have emphasized the importance of trust and referrent power in the helping relationship. Because the LEAs were strangers in the plants, initial steps to promote trust were undertaken by joint local committees, to whom the LEAs report on a daily basis. Further steps were taken after their training to impress upon the LEAs that their primary objective was to help individuals develop and achieve life and education plans. LEAs have high levels of education, many are still furthering their educations, and they have special counseling skills, all of which are important in promoting their roles as experts. Their roles are undertaken, however, under the guidance of local joint committees to ensure that programs are developed to match the needs of each location.

Profile of the LEAs

The first group of life/education advisors who entered the facilities was interesting and diverse. At the time of the survey on which this analysis is based, the group was almost evenly divided between men and women, and about 20 percent were minority group members. The typical LEA was 39.5 years of age, held a college degree, and had more than seven years of experience in advising and adult education. About 85 percent held a degree from a four-year college. More than half had master's degrees, and a few had Ph.Ds. The age range at the time of the survey was from twenty-seven years to sixty-seven years. Many were enrolled in programs to advance their education and skills. A review of the LEAs' professional experiences and professional development activities reveals a commitment to education, training, and advising.[1]

LEAs' Workday

To provide some detail of what LEAs do, we asked LEAs to send us their diaries for a typical workday. What follows is a composite of several of those diaries.

7:30 A.M. Checked my mail and checked messages. Read the mail and waited until 8 A.M. to return two calls from schools that were responding to questions asked by workers.

8:15 A.M. Had an advising session with a worker who wants to return to college. Helped him with the application.

8:35 A.M. Called the admissions office to obtain the name of the admissions officer. At the same time, made an appointment to visit that office next week to discuss challenge exams for workers at this location. Gave worker the name and phone number.

8:45 A.M. Worked on an article for the UAW local newsletter. Three workers came to the office with questions about attending in-plant courses or participating in other EDTP initiatives.

9:30 A.M. Called the community college to make last-minute check on the details for the start-up date of one of our in-plant classes. Drafted a letter to all the workers at the plant who plan to enroll in that class and made photocopies.

10:45 A.M. Addressed and personalized the letters to seventy workers who are planning to enroll in the class. Mailed the letters.

---

1. These sections are drawn from *Center Report 6: Life/Education Planning Program—A Status Report on the UAW-Ford Program* (Dearborn, Mich.: UAW-Ford National Education, Development and Training Center, November 1987). Used courtesy of the UAW-Ford National Education, Development and Training Center.

Noon   Suddenly it became very busy. Several assembly line workers came to my office. Two workers need help tracking down their Education and Training Assistance Plan forms (the forms used to request that the National Education, Development and Training Center [NEDTC] pay for a course). I'll call the UAW-Ford NEDTC this afternoon. Three other workers came in and wanted to know about courses. I helped them with the enrollment forms.

12:45 P.M.   Noted in my monthly contact report that I had seen nine workers so far today.

1:00 P.M.   Called UAW-Ford NEDTC about the ETAP questions. Went into the plant and located the two workers who needed the information and gave it to them. Got stopped five times by workers. Noted three questions that workers had which require follow-up. Made appointments with other workers for advising sessions later this week.

1:30 P.M.   Returned to the office and got materials for the EDTP committee meeting today.

1:45 P.M.   Put up posters in the plant for upcoming College and University Option Program workshop and handed out my monthly newsletter. Tracked down two workers who had just started college to see how things were going and to offer encouragement.

2:30 P.M.   Had an advising session with a worker.

3:00 P.M.   Another advising session with a worker; this time a referral is in order. Called and got information for the worker.

3:30 P.M.   EDTP Committee meeting. Acted as facilitator and resource person. We agreed on the on-site courses to be offered next semester and began planning for an education fair.

Two themes emerge. One is that there is constant direct contact between LEAs and employees. The other is that there is consistent dependence on informal joint efforts, namely on the national center and on the local joint EDTP Committee for guidance and assistance in implementing programs.

Theoretical and Conceptual Frameworks in Adult Education

Adult education—who participates and why—has recently become an important area in public policy. The growing complexity of the workplace, emerging in part because of new computer-aided processes, has made continuing education crucial to the smooth and productive provision of goods and services in an increasingly competitive environment. New technologies are not limited to "hard technologies"; problem solving has become an important skill as well.

The recession of the late 1970s and early 1980s revealed that many displaced American workers had either deficient or rusty skills in a number of areas and that about 20 percent had serious deficiencies. Analysis of national data revealed that high educational levels were positively associated with rapid and positive posttermination adjustment (Podgursky and Swaim 1987). Yet, as other analysis shows (GAO 1986), only 6 to 7 percent of those eligible take advantage of adjustment programs, and only a small fraction engage in either skills or basic education training programs. These issues have created additional interest in research on adult education.

The adult education literature has traditionally addressed community-based programs. Only recently has it begun to examine the dynamics of corporate or joint educational endeavors. Likewise, until relatively recently, virtually no systematic attention has been given to the complex theoretical issues involved in motivating adults with limited time and energy to participate in education.

New interest in empirical and theoretical issues in adult education research is emerging, however. Several important literature reviews and critical analyses (Charner and Fraser 1986; Scanlan 1986; Nordhuag 1987) draw attention to the barriers and incentives to participate in adult education. Several studies, including the work of K. P. Cross (1979, 1981), draw together findings that strengthen the process of hypothesis formation.

Economic hypotheses have long been important in discussions of participation in adult education. A significant amount of economics research (Schultz 1961; Becker 1964; Welch 1975; Fuchs 1983) emphasizes the return to investment in education. While high educational attainment is regarded as an investment that yields returns in the form of higher earnings, rational decision making and optimal utility also play important roles in participation behavior. It fits within this framework that the vast majority of postschooling education takes place as on-the-job training, work experience, job search, and migration or employer-sponsored training involving present cost with the expectation of increased future earnings. In addition, the age range of twenty-five to forty-four years, during which the majority of this activity takes place, is also consistent since after the age of forty-four, workers have fewer years during which an economic return to investment can be expected. This return to investment framework undergirds a great deal of case study research (Taylor 1967; Weigand 1966; Puetz 1980; Castle and Story 1968; Kay 1982). Much of the recent adult education research has veered away from the economic formulations, however, toward psychological or psychosocial models, which view benefits, values, and expectations more broadly.

Three relatively recent psychosocial formulations, called composited or multivariate by one reviewer (Scanlan 1986), are quite similar. The recruitment paradigm (Rubenson 1977) focuses on the interactions of personal variables; needs associated with tasks during the life cycle; environmental constraints, both objectively and subjectively experienced; the values of potential participants and their reference groups; and institutional barriers or facilitators. Actual situations in this formulation are screened through individuals' responses. Behaviors are therefore associated with three sets of intermediate variables: active preparedness, perceptions of the environment, and perceived personal needs. Crucial to the operation of the model are other interactions such as the perceived value of education, the probability of participation, and the perceived values and benefits expected to arise from participation.

In a slightly different formulation (Cross 1981), attitude toward self and attitudes toward education are central, and perceived value and expectation of benefits are involved. In this incremental model, participation is considered as one action in a continuum in which information plays a significant role in linking internal psychological variables and external environmental conditions. Life transitions are included within this model, as are variables influencing both objective circumstances pertaining to the needs for education and perceptions of need and opportunity.

More recently, another framework, the Psychosocial Interaction Model (Darkenwald and Merriam 1982), considers participation in adult education as occurring along a continuum of responses scaled from high to low through which personal characteristics and prior experience can be thought to be processed. These constructs include socioeconomic status, the degree to which learning is required by the individual's environment, the perceived value and utility of education, readiness to participate, stimuli to participation, barriers to participation, and, finally, probability of participation.

While no one formulation was considered irrelevant to our experiment, none appeared to be completely appropriate for testing. Because of the special characteristics of the UAW-Ford EDTP, some barriers to education such as travel time were eliminated since classes were often on-site. Costs, except in time, were also eliminated. To some degree, standard economic incentives were eliminated as well in that these educational opportunities are directed toward personal development and not toward career change or mobility. Further, these programs coexist with but do not replace company-sponsored training, which is directed toward job performance. To a significant degree, therefore, barriers and incentives were removed, providing an opportunity to explore the mechanisms through which individuals, in the absence of many complicating factors, vary their behavior so as to engage in new productive behaviors.

The L/EPP also features a comprehensive reporting and monitoring system in which the comments of LEAs are carefully coded and analyzed. As the research plan progressed, this rich data source suggested that, although participation in adult education was the topic to be addressed, the processes revealed by LEA reports seemed much closer to a psychosocial phenomenon known to assist individuals to make productive changes in behavior. Such changes range from smoking cessation, weight loss, and exercise regimens to coping behaviors associated with productive adaptations to life changes. Thus, in effect, although the experimental design was initially developed broadly so as to test an economic theory of adult education and several hypothetical frameworks developed specifically to describe participation in adult education, as the program and research progressed a more basic theoretical approach emerged. This construct was nearly identical to a well-researched and tested hypothetical framework—the notion of social support—which had already been used in workplace research. No new hypothetical framework emerged. Instead, several rather complex, specific, and applied hypothetical frameworks were investigated and rejected in favor of a relatively new basic theory in social psychology.

The proposed social support model was designed to investigate whether a social support agent, the LEA, could influence individuals to participate in adult education at rates higher than would be observed in similar locations where appraisal and informational and emotional assistance were not provided. To influence individuals to make a new and different decision, the perceived value of education would need to be increased, while perceived barriers to education would need to be decreased. Also considered was whether lower educational attainment might negatively influence individuals so that their feelings of personal effectiveness in the arena of education would need to be increased to meet the new educational challenge. Other variables included age, seniority, years of educational attainment, and number of dependents, all of which were assumed to have effects on participation. Prior participation in education and training was also considered to be important.

Research Design and Survey Findings

The LEAs were assigned to the Ford facilities in two groups almost a year apart, enabling us to use a quasi-experimental research design (Cook and Campbell 1979). Both the program and the research design involved a framework in which social support had a major positive impact on participation. Instrumental assistance in the form of programs and tuition was available to both experimental and control groups for a year, while the other three forms of social support—information, appraisal, and emotional assistance—were available from the LEAs to the experimental group only. (Potential sources of support are shown in table 9.1.)

The pretest/posttest research strategy called for random sampling from four control facilities carefully matched along a number of dimensions, particularly worker demographics, with four experimental facilities. A telephone survey was completed shortly after the first year of the program and before the L/EPP was implemented in the control facilities. The survey focused on demographics, educational history, family structure, employment and unemployment history, prior participation in adult education, participation in training

Table 9.1 Potential Sources of Social Support

Sources of Support	Content of Supportive Acts
Spouse/partner Other relatives Friends Neighbors Supervisor Co-workers Service/care givers Self-help groups Health/welfare professionals	Emotional support (esteem, affect, trust, concern, listening) Appraisal support (affirmation, feedback, social comparison) Informational support (advice, suggestion, directives, information) Instrumental support (aid in kind, money, labor, time, modifying environment)

Source: House 1981:1–23.
Each social support can be general versus problem-focused or objective versus subjective.

during layoff, participation in company- or union-sponsored programs, measures of personal efficacy, personal valuation of education, barriers and benefits associated with education, and attitudes toward the L/EPP and toward the union, the company, and joint labor-management programs. A substantial number of the workers had unlisted telephone numbers, which partly explains the response rate (about 60 percent). Comparisons were made between respondents and the total sample and between the respondents and the universe. No significant differences could be detected in age, seniority, or other potentially influential variables, revealing little response bias.

Questions were asked about participation in all types of programs. Certain educational opportunities available to workers—retirement planning and the L/EPP itself—were excluded from the outcome variable, a composite measure of program participation.[2] Participation in what is called adult education in this research design therefore includes college courses for credit, noncredit college courses, other community noncredit courses, and programs in general education, such as skills enhancement.

---

2. The outcome variable, current participation (Eta 5), is a composite measure of worker participation in four educational programs—ETAP, TETCP, SEP, and CUOP.

Table 9.2   Experience in Adult Education by Program Status and
Program Participation

		Adult education	
	Total	Participants	Nonparticipants
Program status			
Column %			
Total	100.0%	100.0%	100.0%
	(921)[a]	(74)	(847)
Program facilities	49.9%	66.2%	48.5%
(experimental group)	(460)	(49)	(411)
Nonprogram facilities	50.1%	33.8%	51.5%
(control group)	(461)	(25)	(436)
Row %			
Total		8.0%	92.0%
Program facilities		10.7%	89.3%
Nonprogram facilities		5.4%	94.6%
Program participation[b]			
Column %			
Total	100.0%	100.0%	100.0%
	(203)	(33)	(170)
Participants	28.1%	63.6%	21.2%
	(57)	(21)	(36)
Nonparticipants	71.9%	36.4%	78.8%
	(146)	(12)	(134)
Row %			
Total		16.3%	83.7%
Participants		36.8%	63.2%
Nonparticipants		8.2%	91.8%

Two-way cross-table analysis was used to test the relationship between respondents' participation in adult education and their program status (experimental group versus control group) and between respondents' participation in adult education and advising/counseling program. The hypothesis of independence was rejected at .001 level.
[a]Number of respondents.
[b]Participation in counseling/advising program.

Table 9.2 reveals that more than 28 percent of the respondents in the program or experimental group had participated in the L/EPP advising and counseling program. This participation, as well as enrollment in a retirement planning program, was specifically excluded when participation in adult education was considered. The data also show that participation in adult education in program facilities was roughly double such participation in nonprogram or control facilities, 10.7 percent versus 5.4 percent. Significantly, those participating in the counseling and advising program participated in adult education at a very high rate (36.8 percent).

Hypothesis Development, Theoretical Model, and Analysis

Two hypotheses were developed for testing after the data from 932 completed survey instruments were processed and preliminary tabulations run: (1) the LEA would increase worker participation in adult education; and (2) the LEA would increase worker participation in adult education indirectly through intervening variables, for example, by increasing the efficacy of workers or decreasing perceived barriers to education, and through the interaction probability of adult education participation.

The University of Michigan's Panel Study of Income Dynamics has for many years used a set of questions to measure personal efficacy, which can be defined as a combination of how effective a person is at achieving goals and how effective that person perceives himself or herself to be at goal achievement. These variables have been shown to correlate with economic and occupational status and mobility. We have relied on the work of M. S. Hill and her associates for the measures of efficacy that have been used in the University of Michigan's Panel Study of Income Dynamics (Hill et al. 1985). Respondents were asked whether they "usually felt pretty sure their life would work out the way they wanted," "when they make plans ahead, do they usually carry them out," and whether they "nearly always finish things once they start them."

To ascertain whether the structural relationships between the program or intervening variables and the dependent variable were genuine, it was necessary to control for certain social and demographic characteristics. These variables were controlled because they differed significantly across groups (see table 9.3).

A theoretical model of social support was proposed and tested using LISREL covariance analysis. LISREL is a very versatile approach for analyzing causal models involving multiple indicator variables, reciprocal causation, measurement errors, and correlated errors (Fornell 1982). One of LISREL's strenths is that it may be used to evaluate the plausibility of causal models using nonexperimental data (Anderson 1978; Maruyama and McGarvey 1980). LISREL consists of two major parts: the structural model and the measurement model. The structural model refers to relations among exogenous and endogenous variables, which are usually latent theoretical constructs. The measurement model specifies the relations between latent constructs and observed variables. LISREL

Table 9.3   Selected Background Variables of Respondents (experimental group)

Variables	Male	Female	T-statistic
Age	46.1	43.8	2.8[a]
Seniority (years)	18.9	13.9	8.7[a]
Education (years)	11.3	11.7	-2.0[b]
Number of dependents	2.5	2.1	2.4[b]

[a]Significant at .01 level in t-test.
[b]Significant at .05 level in t-test.

is superior to other multivariate analytical methods because it can achieve the following two objectives at the same time: first, by analyzing the correlation among observed indicators of a latent construct, the measurement error of each indicator can be estimated; and second, the correlation between indicators of different latent constructs can provide estimates for the structural relationship between the latents.

The structural part of the model is presented in figure 9.1. The dependent variable (Eta 5) is the worker's participation in current education programs, which was reflected by a composite measure. The impact of the LEA (Eta 1), measured by two items indicating the frequency of consulting with the LEA, is the primary causal agent affecting participation. In addition, three psychosocial variables—efficacy (Eta 2), perceived value of education (Eta 3), and perceived barriers to education (Eta 4)—are the intervening variables.[3] The observed indicators of the latent constructs along with the Cronbach alpha of each scale are presented in appendix A to this chapter. Based on the social support framework, LEAs may have direct as well as indirect effects on enhancing workers' participation in education programs.

To control some important antecedent factors, four social structural variables are also included in the LISREL model—age (Ksi 1), seniority (Ksi 2), years of school completed (Ksi 3), and number of dependents (Ksi 4)—which are all reflected by single indicators. Finally, a concern for possible continuation effect was also examined

---

3. "Education value" and "education barriers" were measured on a five-point scale constructed by the Survey Research Team (Gordus et al. 1987).

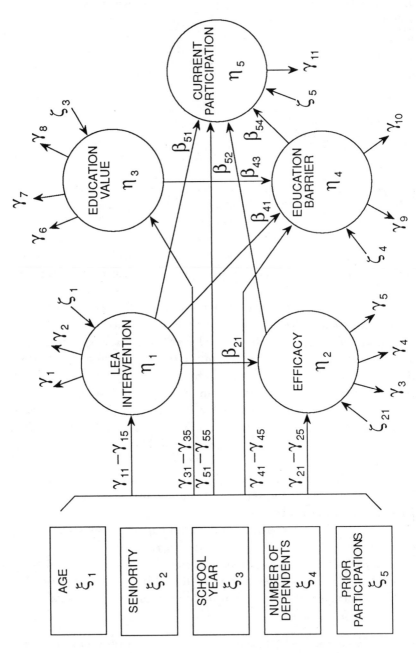

Figure 9.1 Theoretical (LISREL) Model of Workers' Participation in Adult Education

by including an exogenous variable—prior participation in similar programs (Ksi 5)—in the model.[4]

The proposed model was tested on both the male and female samples. In our previous research, the LISREL covariance analysis was used to attain some understanding of the process by which the psychosocial, personal background, and program-related factors interactively influenced workers' decision to participate in programs (Gordus, Kuo, and Yamakawa 1987). Findings from that research showed that the social support agent, the LEA, was the most important causal agent in encouraging program participation. It is possible, however, that males and females may have different concerns in mind when they consult with the LEA. As a result, the social support mechanism may affect the participation decision of males and females differently. This analysis aims to describe these differences.

Based on the overall goodness-of-fit indices, six nested LISREL models were tested and compared to assure that the factorial structures of the measures were invariant across groups. If the measurements were not compatible across groups, then we would not have been able to tell whether the observed differences in path coefficients were due to gender or measurements. Table 9.4 presents the overall goodness-of-fit indices of the six nested models. The LISREL technique depends on several assumptions (Joreskog and Sorbom 1984; Liang and Bollen 1985; Baltes and Nesselroade 1970). The parameter estimates of the selected model (model 3) are presented in appendix B.

Several measures were used to assess the goodness of fit of the models because a consensus had not emerged on which measure was the best one. The first one was a Chi square measure, which assessed the probability that the observed covariance matrices could have been generated by the hypothesis model. The smaller the Chi square, the better the overall fit. The Chi square statistic is sensitive to violations of the multinormality assumption, however, and is proportionate to sample size. We therefore needed to examine the Chi square ratio, namely the Chi square divided by its degrees of freedom. In practice, a Chi square ratio of three or less is considered indicative of an acceptable fit (Carmines and McIver 1981). The

---

4. Prior participation is another composite measure of workers' participation in company-/union-sponsored programs.

Table 9.4 Comparison of Six Nested Models

Model	Measures constrained to be invariant across groups	Measures freely estimated	Chi square (df)	Chi square/df ratio	GFI	
Model 1	All (Eta 1–Eta 4)	None	225.53 (df = 142)	1.59	.947	.938
Model 2	None	All	208.01 (df = 136)	1.53	.953	.940
Model 3[a]	Eta 2–Eta 4	Eta 1 (LEA impact)	213.33 (df = 141)	1.51	.951	.940
Model 4	Eta 1, Eta 3, Eta 4	Eta 2 (efficacy)	224.84 (df = 140)	1.606	.948	.938
Model 5	Eta 1, Eta 2, Eta 4	Eta 3 (value of education)	225.18 (df = 140)	1.608	.947	.938
Model 6	Eta 1–Eta 3	Eta 4 (barrier to education)	222.71 (df = 141)	1.580	.949	.938

[a]The model selected for reporting.

third measure, the goodness-of-fit index (GFI), was devised by K. G. Joreskog and D. Sorbom (1984). GFI is relatively robust against departure from normality and is a measure of the relative amounts of variances and covariances jointly accounted for by the entire model. A separate GFI was printed for both male and female subsamples.

Comparing the first two models, the differences in Chi square values between model 1 and model 2 indicate that some measurement structures were indeed different (Chi square = 17.49, df = 6, p value < .01) across groups. Among the six nested models, model 3 was the one chosen to be reported because it had a relatively better overall fit when compared with the other models in which one measurement structure was freed. Comparing model 3, in which the lambda Ys of Eta 1 (LEA intervention) were freed, with model 1, in which none of the lambda Ys were freed, we observed that the Chi square is significantly improved at a .001 level (Chi square = 12.2, df = 1, P value < .001). It indicates that the measurement structure of LEA intervention (Eta 1) was significantly different across groups but that all the other measures were relatively stable across groups.[5]

Table 9.5 presents a list of the predicted direction of the structural relationship between the dependent variable and each explanatory variable. Both models have a good fit with the empirical data, as indicated by the Chi square ratio (1.51) and the GFIs (.951, .940) listed on table 9.4. About 18 percent of the variance in male workers' program participation has been accounted for by the model, whereas approximately 25 percent of the variance in participation among females was explained. This is a high level of explanatory power, but it also suggests the need for further research.

Consistent with our hypothesis, the social support agent, the LEA, showed a significant direct effect on workers' participation in educa-

---

5. The distribution of the two indicators of the impact of the social support agent (Eta 1) was skewed (i.e., skewness ranges from 3 to 7). The authors have tried using the log transformation to improve the skewness. The result was not very satisfactory. Besides, the log transformation reduced the size of the variances and covariances and caused a problem of rounding errors. The authors decided to stay with the original scaled values. The difference in the measures of this construct between the male and female samples could have resulted from the unequal degree of skewness in the distribution (the distribution of these two variables for the male sample are much more skewed compared with the female sample) and the unequal degree of variations in the two variables. As a result, it is not appropriate to loosen the invariant constraint on this particular measurement. The overall fit improved a great deal when the constraint was lifted.

Table 9.5 Selected Variables and Their Directional Impact on Workers'
Participation in Education Programs

Social structural variables	Intervening variables	Predicted sign	
		Male	Female
	(n1) LEA intervention	+[a]	+[a]
	(n2) Personal efficacy	+	+
	(n3) Value of education	+	+
	(n4) Barriers to education	−[a]	−
Age		−	−
Seniority		−	−
Education		+	+
Number of dependents		+[a]	+
Prior participation		+	+[a]

[a]Significant at .05 level.

tion programs in both male and female samples (betas = .345, .317).[6] The magnitude of the path coefficient is the highest one compared with that of the other explanatory factors. It was not surprising that the impact of the social support agents turned out to be the most pronounced in that one of their major objectives was to motivate workers to pursue their educations. In essence, we found that the LEAs significantly increased the likelihood that workers would participate.

The hypothesis that the social support agent had an indirect impact by way of the psychosocial mediators was only partially supported. No relationship between LEA activity and personal efficacy was found for either group. LEAs were able to reduce the perceived education-related barriers in both male (beta = −.189) and female (beta = −.167) workers. In turn, the perception that there are fewer barriers to education may enhance program participation among males (beta = −.138) but not females. To summarize, the social support agents had a direct influence on the females' participation in education but had both a direct and indirect influence on the males by reducing perceived barriers to education. Indirect enhancement

6. Researchers usually report the unstandardized parameter estimates when a multivariate comparison is conducted. We chose to present the "within group standardized solution," however, because it usually has a value ranging from 0 to 1. It is thus easier to compare the relative strength of the causal paths within the group.

of their participation was not achieved by increasing their sense of efficacy, however.

The relationships between the social structural antecedents and program participation were somewhat different for males and females. For males, age was found to result in higher appreciation of the value of education (gamma = .161) but had little effect on their sense of efficacy. For females, age had a significant effect on their sense of efficacy (gamma = .264) but had nothing to do with their attitude toward education.

Our hypothesis that high risk leads to program participation was rejected. Seniority was found to have no impact at all. Such perceived risks as low seniority may motivate workers to improve or upgrade their skills by enrolling in education,[7] but such a trend was found to lead to more frequent consulting with the social support agents among males (gamma = .166) but not among females.

Educational attainment was found to be an influential antecedent factor. In both male and female samples, high educational attainment (or more years in school) was found to increase the frequency of consulting with social support agents (gamma = .196, .135) and to be positively related to participation in previous training programs (phi = .180, .167). In addition, educational attainment was found to increase female workers' sense of personal efficacy (gamma = .235); it had no such effect on males.

With regard to the hypothesis on the impact of potential family economic need on program participation, the study found that those males with more dependents had a decreased appreciation of education (gamma = −.143) but were motivated to participate in the program (gamma = .126). Both male and female workers who had more dependents tended to consult with the social support agents less frequently (gamma = −.117, −.153).

Our hypothesis concerning the continuation effect—that workers who once participated in training programs would be more likely to enroll—is supported among the females but not the males. The re-

---

7. A cursory analysis was undertaken as a preliminary step toward modeling. Our inquiry was guided by the "risk" hypothesis. Individuals with lower seniority (less than fifteen years) were separated from those with higher seniority. Another stratification, with respect to the risk status of the facility, was added. Across all eight facilities, those at highest risk (low seniority-high risk) participated at rates nearly triple the rate for those at lowest risk (high seniority-low risk) (Gordus, Kuo, and Yamakawa 1987).

sults indicated that female workers who had participated in programs were more likely to consult with an LEA (gamma = .298), to appreciate the value of education (gamma = .189), and to participate in current education programs (gamma = .221). The results indicated not only a clear continuation effect but also that prior participation in education programs contributed to increasing the active search for social support from LEAs and to developing a more positive attitude toward education in general and toward participation in education. For males, participation in previous programs failed to demonstrate any effect on either current program participation or the psychosocial mediators.

The two education-related constructs were found to be negatively associated with one another among both males (beta = −.244) and females (beta = −.433). It is likely that a worker would be motivated to overcome the barriers and difficulties associated with attending school if she or he valued education highly.

The results from the LISREL covariance analysis yielded substantial evidence to support most of the proposed hypotheses. In particular, the research supports the contention that the social support agent serves as a positive social force who can directly encourage workers to participate in current education programs and reduce perceived barriers and difficulties related to participating. The result could be a greater propensity to participate among males. The social support agent is able to encourage participation directly and to increase the propensity to participate indirectly by reducing the perception that there are education-related barriers to participation.

In contrast, female workers seem to be more self-determined and to gain a higher level of personal efficacy as they grow older. Those who had participated in educational programs tended to seek out information and advice from the social support agents and to remain in the programs. The social support agent provided mostly informational aid. The LEAs were able to reduce the females' perception that there were education-related barriers, but this shift did not translate, as it did among the males, into a greater willingness to participate.

Social structural antecedents had different and mixed effects on the workers' decision to participate and on the intervening psychosocial variables. Among the males, a greater economic need tended to lead to participation, but this was not so among the females. That is, male workers who had a greater economic need (i.e., more dependents) were found to be more likely to participate in current education programs. This could be because males traditionally play the role of breadwinner for the family and hence are more sensitive and responsive to "economic imperative" situations. Although participants were specifically told that enrollment in the educational programs would not necessarily get them a better-paying job, the improvement in job-related skills and expansion of knowledge may have made the workers feel more secure psychologically. It is widely known, and especially well known to these workers, that a better education means better chances in the labor market.

This research has answered the major questions posed at the beginning of the chapter. Even in the absense of career-related incentives, it is possible to motivate working adults to participate in lifelong education. This can be done by removing traditional objective barriers such as costs and, through the provision of prepaid tuition assistance, inconvenience. Additional barriers associated with time and travel to school can be lowered by offering on-site classes. But even when such objective barriers are removed or reduced, powerful psychological barriers may remain. This research has also highlighted that a social support structure that provides instrumental assistance in addition to other forms of aid such as information, appraisal, and emotional support, through the services of a social support agent, can have a powerful positive impact on adults' willingness to participate in education. The mechanism through which social support operates is different for males and females. This is an interesting and provocative result that requires further investigation.

As noted above, there is some concern about the measurement of the endogenous latent constructs. The value of some of the lambda Ys indicated that the measurement had a poor interitem reliability. In addition to changes and refinements in measures, the next phase of this research could tackle the intricate problem of how educational attainment increasingly changes the attitudes, values, and perceptions of working adults and in turn how these changes are reflected in patterns of behavior.

Proposed New Directions in Programs and Research

While social psychology has long had close ties to industrial relations, an experimental program designed as a social support mechanism and focused on life enhancement for an entire work force is not a traditional approach in practice or research. Such approaches are generally associated with employee assistance and health and are somewhat limited in scope and clientele.

While both union and company clearly benefit from having a more educated work force, the freedom of choice in educational offerings that a participant-driven, professionally supported program demands is truly unusual. Even more striking in some ways is that such a program removes many barriers to education. The program and the associated research work are freed by this program design from the necessity of dealing with such mundane yet implacable barriers as inconvenient class locations, problems with tuition reimbursement, and shifts and overtime that play havoc with class attendance. Instead, the program and research can focus on addressing central subjective barriers to and personal values about education. It is difficult, however, to conceive of such a broad-based, comprehensive program succeeding in settings where it is not jointly implemented.

Until this point, this chapter has left one important question not only unanswered but unasked: why do people seek out LEAs? There appear to be several answers. Their friends at work suggest it. Their supervisors acknowledge their value; many even arrange for LEAs to make presentations in department meetings. Others such as the employee assistance coordinator may "talk up" the L/EPP program. One facility has a college club; those going to school get together and talk about what they are doing and do some self-help. Education fairs, often annual spectaculars, bring out the whole family. Many people first go to an LEA to get information for a youngster getting ready for college—and stay around to enroll themselves. Often the parent wishes to be a role model for his or her children. In Table 9.6 we show the validated forms of social support provided by the LEA, taken from the survey, and other reported forms of social support.

Earlier, we discussed the context for the LEA's intervention. It is possible now to speculate about the context recreated through this and other interventions. Not only has the L/EPP moved from the

Table 9.6 Observed Forms of Social Support

	Source of Support								
Content of supportive acts	Spouse or partner	Other relatives(s)	Friend(s)	Neighbor(s)	Work supervisor	Co-worker(s)	LEA(s)	"Self-help" group(s)	Health/welfare professional(s)
Emotional support (esteem, affect, trust, concern, listening)	Y		Y		Y	Y	X	Y	Y
Appraisal support (affirmation, feedback, social comparison)	Y		Y		Y	Y	X	Y	Y
Informational support (advice, suggestion, directives, information)	Y		Y		Y		X	Y	Y
Instrumental support (aid in kind, money, labor time, modifying environment)	Y						X		Y

X = validated in survey.
Y = reported in monitoring data for some participation.

idea of deficiency to the idea of development, but the program clearly has the potential of engaging employees as supporters of themselves and their co-workers and families and as mobilizers of support and resources. A substantial body of evidence supports this assertion, although even more is required.

In late 1988, some facilities had employed LEAs for forty months, and the remaining facilities had for twenty-eight months. To a limited degree, the outside professional LEA has become an institution. As workers become more proficient at mobilizing and providing support for themelves and each other, will the need for this institution diminish? Or will it increase as workers and the workplace change?

This chapter has focused on the short-term impact of a counseling and advising program on participation in other educational programs, the correlates of participation, and a few outcomes of participation. What will the individual and organizational outcomes of such programs be, and what will the interaction be between personal development and learning and organizational development?

To develop a program that permits an unprecedented range of personal choices for education and development, specifically excluding work-required training, is an enormous organizational change. The degree of trust in workers' good judgment is high, while the level of change is deliberately quite low. What effect does the continued existence of high-trust/low-control programs have on the entire working environment? And what will the impact be on specific plants and local unions of working together jointly at something that is highly approved, conceded to be beneficial to all, and designed to underline respect for the potential of all workers? Will other new efforts emerge? Will jobs grow to match workers' new intellectual and personal skills? And, finally and most important, how will jointly administered programs for personal development be integrated with a changing union-management relationship?

Appendix A to Chapter 9:
Observed Indicators of the Latent Constructs

η_1 (Eta 1) LEA intervention

    y_1 Frequency of consulting with life/education advisor

    y_2 LEA impact (number of program activities participated in)   Cronbach α = .797

η_2 (Eta 2) Personal efficacy

    y_3 Feel pretty sure life would work out the way wanted

    y_4 Usually carry out things the way planned

    y_5 Nearly always finish things once start them   Cronbach α = .398

η_3 (Eta 3) Perception of value of education

    y_6 People should continue education throughout their lives.

    y_7 People should go to school because it improves life all around.

    y_8 Going to school helps with family and home.   Cronbach α = .580

η_4 (Eta 4) Perception of barriers to education

    y_9 Going to school while working is just too hard to do.

    y_{10} Going to school takes too much time from family and home.   Cronbach α = .677

Appendix B to Chapter 9:
LISREL Covariance Analysis

Male Sample Results

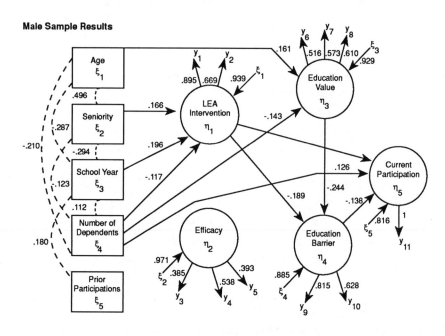

Female Sample Results

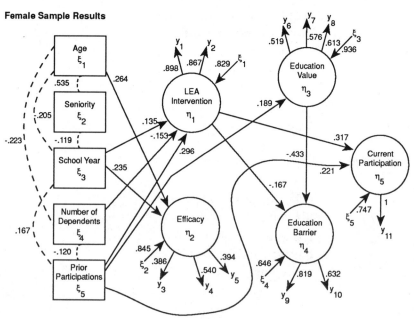

10 · SERVICE DELIVERY IN JOINT TRAINING PROGRAMS

Louis A. Ferman and Michele Hoyman

The authors of this chapter contend that, insofar as joint training programs are participant-driven and derived from contractual arrangements, their approach to service delivery is different from that in other training programs, such as company-supported or large-scale publicly supported efforts. Practitioners and researchers should find this chapter of interest as a planning document and as background as they develop research hypotheses.

Models and designs of service delivery have been well studied in traditional human service organizations, including hospitals, schools, and employment and training agencies. The focus of this research is usually on how the services are planned, organized, and delivered to program participants, as well as how participants are recruited and processed through the program. In contrast, the thrust of this chapter is how jointism as a philosophical concept, value, and practice serves to modify traditional models of service delivery and give rise to new ones.

The very assumptions of jointism in training—local voluntarism, local autonomy, local empowerment, decentralized decision making, and local service networks—together with the control accorded joint local committees lead to the development of certain structures and relationships not apparent in the service delivery designs of such traditional human service organizations as employment and training agencies. Central to these new models and designs are six basic factors:

1. The two organizations involved—the union and the corporation—have different cultures and interests yet are linked in an institutional arrangement so as to provide employment and training services to a distinct population of workers. Decision making at all levels of the program is codetermined so that input into decisions is required from both sides. Thus decisions are more likely to be the result of consensus-building than mandated from the top of the organization or by a system of rules.

2. Joint training programs bring together personnel from diverse backgrounds with different expertise and perspectives—union and management staff, employment and training specialists, consultants and educators. The service delivery system that develops is a result of the interactions of these actors.

3. Joint training programs are not exclusively training or human resource development programs but are grounded in labor relations concerns with employment security and are contractually mandated. Emphasis may be on ensuring employment security for individual workers by providing skills upgrading, vocational training, and/or basic skills development. Thus the focus may be on protecting the individual by guaranteeing him or her a job in the same company, training the person for a new job, or equipping the person with the skills for an outplacement. The labor relations context is therefore an important consideration in the development and implementation of a service delivery system.

4. The critical link in service delivery is the local joint committee, in which local initiatives and options are planned and implemented. Such committees have equal numbers of members from the union and the company. The intention is that the local committee should be empowered to plan, develop, and implement the local program with minimum input from national headquarters. For the most part, committee members are not professional employment and training specialists and do not have backgrounds in human resource development. It is therefore necessary to provide committee members with training in issues and operations of human resource development.

5. The empowerment of the program participant is of paramount importance in joint programs. He or she must be actively involved in making choices and specifying needs and thus interactive with the program rather than simply a recipient of services.

6. Services should be tailored to the needs of the individual participant rather than to the needs of the local labor market; the latter is the focus in traditional employment and service agencies. In contrast, joint training programs are participant-driven and focus on the needs and interests of the individual.

Major Dimensions of Joint Training Programs

Joint training programs can be examined from three different perspectives. The first is an *employment security perspective.* The thought here is that joint training programs can be instrumental in helping workers develop a stable and productive lifetime career that will insulate them from the turbulence of the economy and labor market. Historically, programs focused on career development have been targeted at professional and technical workers and have generally overlooked industrial and lower-level white-collar workers. Training for the latter was confined to preparation for a specific job, not for a lifetime of work. In contrast, joint training programs make career development programs available to unionized industrial workers.

The second perspective is a *human resource perspective.* The assumption here is that offering a package of services jointly administered as a result of a union-management agreement can enhance the labor market adjustments unionized workers must make both within and outside the firm. Beyond this there is a concern with the enhancement of the quality of life for these workers both within and outside the workplace and with the development of life education options and plans. The central tenet of this perspective is that monies generated by the work of active employees should be used to support the training and development of *both* active and displaced workers.

The third perspective is *a conflict-reduction perspective.* The assumption here is that joint training programs create situations and conditions in which union and management personnel interact in a cooperative, problem-solving mode and thus reduce the conflictful nature of industrial relations. These programs may be considered to have positive consequences beyond fulfilling the employment needs of program participants, including the extent to which employment security is enhanced; the extent to which the labor market and personal outcomes of program participants are improved; and the extent to which the programs contribute to jointness and cooperation.

Some other features of joint training programs are also relevant:

1. Although programs are usually aimed at both active and displaced workers, in most cases the negotiated contracts stipulate that the company must make a financial contribution to the program based on the hours worked by union-represented active workers or the number of unionized workers who are employed in a given time period.

2. Programs go beyond skills development for specific jobs and encompass personal and career-related skills in an effort to improve the quality of life for workers and their families. Monies can be put to diverse use; use is not limited by the skills requirements of workers' current jobs. The objective is to prepare workers for a long-term career by improving both their vocational and social skills.

3. Participation is *voluntary* and, it is assumed, will be governed by conditions and needs at local sites.

4. Control of the program is at the grass-roots level. Joint union-management committees at the local plant determine worker needs, select and organize training resources, and set training priorities.

5. Training activities do not replace existing union or company obligations. Funds are not to be used to support apprenticeship training, a company obligation, or labor education programs, an obligation of the union.

6. In each case we have studied, program administration was assigned to parallel labor relations departments in the union and in the company and not to organizational development or training and education departments. This suggests that, although the programs stressed training, the emphasis was on *jointness* and program development under the special institutional arrangements established in the contract.

7. Considerable emphasis is placed on employing local community service networks to provide the training. Thus most training is delivered by local vendors under contract to the program.

8. Programs are structured so as to avail themselves of both union and management staff who work side by side on a fixed-term basis.

Other resources of both the union and the company are drawn in to fulfill planning, recruitment, counseling, and other operational tasks.

9. Workers, whether active or displaced, are eligible for a *total* package of services rather than for a *single* service.

10. Monies are made available based on seniority. Active workers have fixed monies available for training in any given year, whereas displaced workers generally have fixed-sum allocations to be used on a short-term basis.

Structural Features of Service Delivery

Joint training programs represent innovative and pioneering attempts to serve the unionized worker in a workplace that has become increasingly turbulent and unpredictable. The structure of these programs is predicated on a desire to increase the employment security of the worker as well as the competitiveness of the firm. The aim is to serve workers in transition, whether they are changing jobs within the company or leaving the company for other employment.

One useful way to highlight the structural features of joint training programs is to compare and contrast them with those of other training programs. Two such programs are plant-based company training programs and publicly supported training programs. In every large company, there is a concern and some provision made at the plant level for training new workers, for upgrading the skills of other workers, and for sharpening the skills of still other workers. There is also a concern with keeping the firm competitive by introducing new technology and providing training in how to operate it. Such training is provided for in the overall plant budget.

Publicly supported employment and training programs are financed by taxes and offer a wide variety of services to unemployed workers, displaced workers, minority group members, the disabled, and older workers. Beginning with the U.S. Employment Service, funded in 1935 under the Social Security Act, and continuing through the current Job Training and Partnership Act, these programs use a combination of federal and state tax monies to deliver employment and training services to recipients as mandated by legislative guidelines.

Table 10.1   Comparison between Company Training Program and Joint
Training Program

Company training program	Joint training program
Underlying assumptions	
Provide opportunity for mobility in internal labor market	Provide an opportunity for career development and lifetime employment training and education
Develop or upgrade workers' skills to fill current/future job vacancies or technology demands within the plant or company	Develop an opportunity for life-long training and personal development of the worker
Enlarge workers' skills within a given line of job progression	Enlarge workers' skills outside a normal line of job progression
Training costs are a line item in total plant operating budget	Costs are negotiated as a company contribution based on worker effort (e.g., number of hours worked)
Training available both to unionized and nonunionized workers in the company	Training is restricted to union-represented workers
Operations	
For unionized workers, inclusion in training program is a function of seniority, bidding rights, and recommendation of supervisors	All unionized workers (as specified in the contract) are eligible for services and training
Training is mostly conducted in-house by company training department	Training is mostly vendored out to local operations
What to train for is a managerial decision	What to train for is based on joint committee determination of workers' expressed needs and aspirations
Effectiveness of training is based on subsequent job performance	Effectiveness of training is based on career development progression and satisfaction of the individual worker

Both programs have distinct features that can be contrasted with those of joint training programs.

Company Training versus Joint Training

Table 10.1 contrasts company or plant-based training and joint training programs. The former are concerned with the internal labor market and with making the company more competitive by increasing the human capital stock of its workers. The goals are to provide for mobility in the internal market by developing or upgrading workers' skills so as to fill existing or future needs of the plant or company. Workers are usually trained in a given sequence of skills. The budget for training is usually a line item in the operational budget of the plant, and training in various forms is extended both to unionized and nonunionized workers.

In contrast, joint training programs are participant-driven. The emphasis is career development and lifetime employment, education, and training. The program is structured based on the expressed needs of the worker, not the job needs of the plant. In addition to technical training, the focus is on personal development, which is seen as an important component of lifetime career development. Costs for the program are negotiated as a company contribution based on worker effort (e.g., the number of hours worked). Finally, joint training is restricted to union-represented workers.

There are also differences in how the two programs operate. Inclusion in a company training program for unionized workers is a function of seniority, bidding rights, and the recommendation of supervisors. Most of the training is conducted in-house by a company training department, although some may be vendored out. In the final analysis, what is trained for is a managerial decision and the effectiveness of the training is measured by subsequent job performance. These operating features contrast sharply with those of a joint training program, in which all union-represented workers can elect to receive services and what to train for is determined by a joint committee based on the expressed needs and aspirations of the workers. Training is usually vendored out, and the effectiveness of the training is based on fulfillment of goals set in a personalized employability plan for career development.

Traditional Employment and Training Programs versus Joint Training Programs

Tables 10.2 contrasts traditional employment and training programs and joint training programs.[1] We will focus on four features: the

---

1. Traditional employment and training agencies are usually organized around community services for the unemployed or job seekers and are not for active workers. Two prototype programs are the Comprehensive Employment and Training Act (CETA) of 1973 and the Joint Training Partnership Act (JTPA) of 1980.

Table 10.2   Selected Characteristics of Traditional Employment/Training Programs and Joint Training Programs

Traditional	Joint
Underlying assumptions	
Emphasis is on job finding and job security	Emphasis is on career development and employment security
Local office implements uniform, canned program developed centrally	Local committee is empowered to initiate, plan, and organize program tailored to needs of local work force
Program participant is limited in job choices and routed to available job openings	Program participant is to be empowered by giving him/her choices and options for employment development
Emphasis is on skills development of program participant	Emphasis is placed both on skill and personal development of program participant
Participant processing	
Batch processing of program participants	Processing of participants is individualized and personalized
No plan for employability development	Specific employability plans are developed with specified resources and targeted outcomes
Fragmented and uncoordinated management of services	Centralized case management of services with emphasis on "one-step" servicing
Fixed, uniform services based on organizational technology and expertise	Vendored variable services depending on participant's needs
Eligibility is legislatively mandated, and services are based on categorical designation	Eligibility is contractually defined, and services are based on participant's needs
Recruitment of program participants is largely passive and restricted to formal channels of communication (letter writing, newspaper ads)	Recruitment of program participants is active, using both formal and informal channels of communication
Assessment of program participant is based on standard assessment testing	Assessment of program participant is based on paper trail of work history (union and company records plus standardized testing)
Routing decisions for services are based on serial recommendations of organizational professionals	Routing decisions for services are based on specific employability plan
Creaming of program participants for services (i.e., only top prospects are processed)	Each program participant has equal access to services
Service giving restricted to organization professionals	Extensive use may be made of participant peers to deliver services
Administration	
Planning and development of local program is mandated from central guidelines	Local committee is empowered to control planning and development of program

Administration (cont.)

Well-defined table of organization with multilevels of authority (pyramidal)	Flattened authority structure with considerable discretionary authority
Well-defined and rigid division of labor based on fixed expertise	Collegial organization with much job switching
Decisions are based on rules	Decisions are based on consensus-building

Operations

Services are mostly in-house with few vendored services	Most services are vendored out to community resource agencies
Few provisions for relocation assistance to other job markets	Relocation assistance to alternative jobs within company
Labor market information services provided	Labor market informative services provided
Industry and company job vacancy surveys to identify training services	Worker surveys to determine personal aspirations and needs for the development of training services
Program evaluation focuses on staff effort measures	Program evaluation focuses on participant outcome measures

underlying goals, processing of participants, administration, and operations.

Underlying Goals

The underlying assumptions of traditional employment and training agencies are to identify job openings in the local labor market and fill these jobs with job seekers. The emphasis is on *matching* job seekers with job openings. If a job seeker lacks requisite skills, an attempt is made to provide him or her with the skills for a particular job through a training program. The focus is on moving a job seeker into a particular job, and the training is dictated by the skills required to do this job. Consequently, the job seeker's choices are determined by the jobs that are vacant. The employment and training agency develops uniform programs in an effort to fill these jobs. Such programs are developed by "experts" in the higher echelons of the organization and are sent on to local offices to be implemented. Local office staff are concerned with interpreting and executing the programs in a uniform manner that does not violate organizational guidelines.

In contrast, joint training programs focus on employment security (or lifelong careers). The emphasis is on providing workers with a combination of personal and technical skills not for a single job but for a lifetime. The starting point is what each worker needs and expects to know for a lifetime of work. His or her aspirations, desires, and needs, rather than the immediate needs of the job market, shape the program. The objective is to empower the participant and let him or her shape his or her work life. For this reason, joint programs emphasize *both* personal and skills development and empower local committees to plan and organize the program based on participants' needs. In joint programs, the program is participant-driven, beginning wtih the grass-roots actions of local committees and their constituencies.

Processing of Participants

Traditional employment and training agencies rarely personalize or individualize program participants. The typical agency has a maze of service stations through which the client is routed. At each station, a diagnosis is made or a service provided or a routing decision made. Encounters between provider and participants are restricted to the service being given or the decision being made. Consequently, providers learn little about participants beyond the information generated in these fleeting encounters. A wide geographical distribution of stations can add to the alienation.

Traditional employment and training agencies emphasize batch processing (i.e., participants are processed in groups rather than as individuals). The reasons are simple: there is a tendency to reduce individual needs to group needs (e.g., all unskilled workers need training); and there is an organizational economy of scale in treating participants in groups, particularly when large numbers of people are involved. Processing may be further complicated by the lack of individual employability plans to guide selection of services and the fragmented and uncoordinated management of services that often occurs in a multistation service situation.

Other processing problems occur in traditional employment and training programs. First, the programs have a fixed, uniform set of service options that often represent only one aspect of the organizational culture. Traditional service options are considered to be best and are reinforced by both the technology and expertise within the organization. Few new service options are introduced by vendors. The result is that participants are shaped to service options rather than able to shape them.

Second, in public employment and training programs, eligibility and the service options that are available to a particular category of participants are legislatively mandated. Thus, even if certain services are perceived to be needed, legislative mandates may preclude obtaining them.

Third, broad-based assessments are almost nonexistent; assessment is based on standardized testing. The result is a limited view of the skills and capabilities of participants.

Fourth and finally, "professional expertise" is the basis of most decisions in the programs. This can result in limiting the options for action. For example, "creaming" (considering only the most capable prospects) for program participation may occur because college-educated professionals are likely to place their bets for success on more educated participants and ignore others.

In contrast, in joint training programs, processing of participants is individualized and personalized. Each participant has an individualized employability plan based on self-interest inventories, personal counseling on career development, and personalized assessment information. Of central importance, in most cases the local committee and its associates have both a workplace and a nonworkplace relationship with participants, often representing years of acquaintance.

Joint training programs are also characterized by a centralized case management of services with an emphasis on "one-stop" servicing. The focus is on participants' employability plans. The local committee acts as a core resource that coordinates services, bearing in mind participants' needs and goals as set forth in the plan. For the most part, services are vendored out through a competitive process to local contractors. The result is generally service of high quality.

Recruitment of program participants is done both formally and informally. In-plant TV consoles, union and management newspapers, community television, and union meetings are used as formal means of contacting workers and marketing the program. Equally important are the informal channels. These may include reachingworkers through informal leaders who hold no official position but are nevertheless influential in their work groups and through informal social occasions such as picnics or sporting events. Because it uses the workplace as a focus for communication, recruitment for joint training programs is far more extensive than the effort used for public employment and training programs.

Joint training programs are also in a better position to assess participants' abilities. Besides standardized assessment, local committees can learn about a participant from union and company records, providing a broad, in-depth picture. This picture can be supplemented by the personal observations of peers who have a knowledge of the participant's skills and performance in the workplace.

Creaming—a characteristic of many large-scale employment and training programs—is unlikely to occur in joint training programs in that the decision to participate is in the hands of the worker rather than organization administrators. Equal access to services is guaranteed by the collective bargaining contract.

Finally, joint training programs can make use of a participant's work peers to deliver services (counseling, training, recruitment, and social support). In many cases, having services delivered by trusted and familiar figures who have a special relationship to the participant can be a decided advantage.

Administration

Employment and training programs are characterized by a traditional administrative structure. There is a well-defined organizational structure with multiple levels of hierarchical authority. There is also a well-defined and rigid division of labor based on expertise. The planning and development of the local programs is mandated based on central guidelines, and local decisions are more often based on rules than on local initiative. The staffs of these programs are hired for their credentials and expertise. Decisions are apt to be based on theoretical models rather than on grass-roots know-how.

In joint training programs, the local committee is empowered to control planning and development of the program based on the input of program participants. In employment and training programs, planning is top down; in joint training programs, it is bottom up. Since authority relations are joint at all levels, decisions are developed by building consensus rather than from fixed rules. This situation breeds collegial relationships in which there is considerable job switching and blurring of authority lines.

Three characteristics foster these more flexible relations and movement away from traditional administration. The first is that the beneficiaries of the joint program *own* the program. They are not passive recipients of services but an active force in the shaping and development of the program. This is the essence of participant empowerment. Such a situation precludes the development of distance between program administrator and program participant. The second characteristic is that neither the union nor management has ultimate authority in operating the program. The result is the development of more collegial relationships. Third, joint training programs often operate in a turbulent environment in which responding to a crisis (e.g., a plant shutdown) is the order of the day. Immediate decisions and actions are necessary, including job switching, to reallocate organizational effort. To make such decisions often requires discretionary authority as well as a blurring of job boundaries.

Operations

Employment and training programs stress services that are available in-house rather than vendored. The services to be delivered are usually identified after reviewing industry and company job vacancy surveys. Training is provided primarily to meet the needs of the local economy and secondarily to meet the needs of program participants. Most employment and training programs seek to identify jobs in the local community, and labor market information is focused on the local economy. Few programs are designed to deliver intensive assistance in relocating. Finally, evaluation is apt to document the effort of the program (e.g., the number of training sessions, number of participants served, and staff time spent on an activity) rather than whether program participants attained their goals.

In these respects, joint training programs are significantly different. Most services are vendored out to local community agencies in a competitive process that stresses the quality of the service and the qualifications of the vendor. There is a contract with the local service provider, enabling the local committee to monitor service delivery and to exert pressure when necessary to improve or cancel the service.

Joint training programs tend to emphasize employment possibilities both in the internal labor market of the company and in the external labor market of the community. The program is privy to information on jobs within the company that would not be available to public employment and training programs.

Finally, in evaluating joint programs the emphasis is on whether program participants attained their goals as outlined in their personalized employability plans. Since participants' aspirations and needs determine the operations of the program, the focus in an evaluation is on the extent to which program services have contributed to fulfilling these needs.

Participants' Experiences

In the final analysis, the experiences of participants in joint training programs provide the best understanding of these programs. The following three experiences illustrate two common themes. The first is that "change is opportunity." In each case the participant was confronted by an event (or events) that destabilized his or her employment situation. But as threatening as the prospect of change was, it provided new opportunities for career and job development. The second theme is that the joint committee and its associates can provide much social support. In each case the local joint committee was an administrative agent for program development and coordination, but it also provided much-needed psychological support.[2]

Barbara B.

Barbara B. came from a working-class family in a small midwestern community. She began working at the local telephone company as a backup operator while still a junior in high school. She was married shortly after high school, and by the age of twenty she was at home with two children. Because of financial pressure, she decided to apply for and subsequently accepted a position as a temporary operator at the local telephone company. Although she characterized herself as "having a job" and not pursuing a career, her involvement with the company put her in touch with the job opportunity network and thus with information about possible permanent employment, tuition programs, and opportunities for promotion.

---

2. The examples were compiled based on the experiences of several participants undergoing similar job transitions.

By the time she was twenty-five, Barbara B. was separated from her husband and had set up household with her two children. By now she had a full-time job at the phone company. About this time, the company and the union negotiated a joint training program. A local joint committee was set up and Barbara was appointed co-chair with a union counterpart. One of the committee's first actions was to survey the work force about their skills, work preferences, and aspirations for the future. Influenced by the results of her questionnaire, Barbara set up several career counseling sessions with a local vendor. This activity, combined with discussions with peers, altered her view of her relationship to the world of work and she began to view her job as a stepping-stone in a career.

Her career counseling sessions also indicated that she had "a head for figures." This realization encouraged her to use a tuition refund feature of the joint program to complete two classes in business math at a local community colllege. For the first time, she felt she had a skill other than knowing the switchboard. She also underwent a change in self-image as friends and family came to regard her not only as a worker but as a college student. Barbara credited her expanded thinking about her career to the members of the joint committee and her work peers, who "egged her on."

At the urging of several work peers, Barbara signed up to take the test for a job in the comptroller's office, although she had resisted for some time. She was the only woman to take the test and was convinced she had not understood it, but subsequently she was notified that she passed, was interviewed for the job, and was hired. Again she experienced a great lift in self-image and sense of accomplishment. And again she credited her work peers and members of the local joint committee with urging her on.

In her new job Barbara volunteered for several special assignments, motivated by the desire to be challenged and by her belief that each new assignment would be a building block in her career. One of these assignments required that she develop and write a training manual on phone use for the hearing impaired. Although her last writing assignment had been a term paper in high school, she found the task challenging and stimulating. Meanwhile, she attended more classes under the tuition refund program.

There were few opportunities for promotion at Barbara's workplace, so she began to identify job opportunities elsewhere. Again the local committee was her main source of information. She availed herself of classes on job search and relocation, sponsored by the committee, and found this information useful in her decision to move.

She then bid for and obtained a job as an assistant manager approximately fifty miles from her community. Using the relocation services provided by the committee, Barbara arranged to defray the costs of the move. The committee also provided psychological support during this transition.

Barbara was at the new site for two years when the facility was closed. As in the case of her earlier relocation, her new job search activities were difficult but not traumatic, and when the local committee developed a program designed to relocate, retrain, and reemploy displaced workers, Barbara followed up leads for herself and also helped her peers. Again she credited her committee and peers with giving her social and resource support.

As a result of her job search, Barbara was relocated to an office in a distant state as a branch manager. She learned about the job through the activities of the joint committee, which assisted her in relocating.

Barbara credited the program with bringing about three distinct changes: the development of her view of work as a career rather than just a job; her willingness and ability to accept and explore new job opportunities; and her heightened self-awareness and confidence in her ability to master problems in her work life.

John F.

John was thirty-nine years of age and had worked on a grinder machine for twenty years in a plant in the Midwest. He was married at twenty and was the father of four daughters. He left school in the ninth grade and admitted that he had limited abilities in reading and math. He expressed little hope of doing more than semiskilled work. He felt intimidated by classroom work and considered his lack of reading, writing, and math skills his biggest barrier to job advancement. He reported that for most of his life he had hidden his illiteracy from family, friends, and co-workers.

In July 1986, the management at his plant announced it would close. John saw few chances of transferring to another plant, so he discussed his illiteracy and poor reemployment prospects with several co-workers. One was a member of the local joint committee. He urged John to attend an orientation meeting on generic skills programs. John was reluctant but attended "after being badgered and hog-tied" by his friend. He was also desperate and somewhat curious about the program.

The orientation made two points that John found interesting. The first was that a literacy test would be administered and help given as needed. The second was that as a program participant, he would be eligible for a computer-based literacy system (PLATO) within the plant. PLATO was self-paced (John could go as fast or as slow as he wanted), was supplemented by an instructor, and provided instant feedback. John saw this approach as more satisfying than the traditional classroom situation.

John registered in the generic skills program and in a mechanical application program given in the plant after hours. Thus John's literacy training was conducted as it applied to work, not in a vacuum. The basic skills program was sequential, so that John moved to a new learning module only after mastering the previous one. John saw his basic skills training as enabling him to climb a ladder of opportunity to technical training, and this perception was reinforced by an individualized employability plan that was developed for him.

Chris R.

Chris R. had lived in a small midwestern community for most of his life, as had two generations before him. He had twice held jobs for a short time elsewhere, but in both cases he had become homesick and returned to his hometown. He described himself as a "stay-at-home" who had no desire to go elsewhere. His wife, who was brought up in the community, had similar attachments and so did their two boys, aged ten and twelve.

It came as a real shock when management announced that the plant where Chris worked would be closed within the year. Chris had worked there for nineteen of his thirty-nine years. The people at the plant were "a second family."

The local plant had a joint committee that provided a number of services: orientation sessions about separation benefits, counseling, career development meetings, brochures detailing available training programs, assessment of skills, labor market information, and relocation assistance. These services became available about seven months before the scheduled shutdown.

Chris was most interested in information about job openings in the community, preferably with the company. He was least interested in relocating. But after an intensive job search, he had to face two hard facts: there was no alternative employment in the community, and the company was opening a new plant where there would be openings but it was some eight hundred miles away. Because of his skill classification, his seniority, and contractual provisions, Chris was near the head of the list for employment. Although he and his family initially rejected the idea of moving, as the date of the shutdown grew nearer, they began to regard it as a viable possibility.

Through contact with the local committee, Chris was referred to the relocation assistance unit at his plant, which provided counseling so that he and his family could discuss the move and deal with the associated emotional trauma. Orientation sessions were held in which the history, culture, demographics, and social amenities of the new community were discussed in great detail, and long-time residents as well as a relocation assistance counselor were available to answer questions and provide contacts with real estate firms and moving companies. Low-interest loans were available to finance the move, and exploratory trips to the new community were financed through a special fund.

Chris and his family finally made the move, using relocation assistance services in both his hometown and the new community. A relocation assistance counselor was available at the new plant site to counsel him and the other newcomers and to help them adjust to the new community. The local committee at the new plant site organized an "adopt a newcomer family" program in which plant workers would oversee a newcomer family during the transition period and provide advice on schools, transportation, real estate, and social services. In addition, an 800 hotline was open twenty-four hours a day to answer questions.

After about a year, Chris had adjusted favorably to the new community. He had even developed an employability plan. It was then that the second shock occurred. The company reopened the closed plant in Chris's hometown to manufacture a new piece of equipment. Chris and his wife yearned to return but felt "locked into the move." Discussions with the relocation assistance counselor made it clear that this was not the case. Chris and his wife are now considering using the relocation assistance services to help them return to their hometown.

Making work transitions obviously requires more than skills training. It also requires social and psychological support. In the cases described above, both were forthcoming from the local committee (and its associates) and from work peers. One decided advantage a local joint committee may have is that it functions *both* as a coordinator of services and as a source of social support. It may be necessary to reduce the emotional trauma of a work transition before beginning technical training. Equally important, the relationship between a worker and his or her work peers can be important in career development. In addition to offering social support, peers can also function as recruiters for the program, marketers of the program, and sources of job leads and employment strategies. Finally, insofar as the workplace is a social organization that can offer both psychological and functional aid during work transitions, such transitions will be more effectively managed if the workplace rather than a community-based organization is the focus of intervention.

Case Studies

Any selection of case studies of joint training programs is bound to be arbitrary and thus raise the charge that they are biased. There is considerable variability, and no case is truly typical. The cases discussed below were selected to illustrate specific operational issues.

Case 1: A Community-Based Reemployment Assistance Center
In the mid-1980s, a large firm and union in the Midwest undertook to enlarge its joint training program by establishing several reemployment centers where displaced workers could avail themselves of a variety of services (counseling, assessment, referral to training, relocation assistance, job placement, and job development). Designed to serve displaced workers from a number of plants, the centers were accessible by bus as well as car. An applicant for the program would be given preliminary screening and services in a satellite facility and then referred to a center for more intensive services.

Each center was staffed by employment and training professionals from a nearby nationally known human resource development agency, members of the national joint training program, members of the local union, and personnel from a nearby community college. Day-to-day management of the center was handled by a community college administrator who reported to top officials in the national training program. The latter had overall responsibility for the center and coordinated the various actors that served the operation.

Counseling and career development staff came from the private human resource agency, job coaches with responsibility for ongoing contact with participants from the local union, and the coordinator for all services (internal and external) from the national training program, as did the relocation assistance counselor/coordinator and information processing personnel. Two additional staff, who were employed directly by the center, were responsible for job development and job placement. The overall strategy was to make available the fullest range of services possible.

This service delivery arrangement had five obvious advantages: (1) participants had easy access to services; (2) many service organizations were represented; (3) services and benefits from the joint program were coordinated with those offered by other sources (the community college, JTPA, public employment programs, and company fringe benefit programs); (4) participants had access to resources of both the union and the company; and (5) participants received a mix of the "grass-roots" expertise of union and management staff and the "elite" expertise of employment and training professionals.

There were also disadvantages to this arrangement. First, because a wide range of expertise was represented, there were turf struggles over strategy. Union personnel had a pragmatic view (services should be immediately job-relevant), which clashed with the more long-term view of the employment and training personnel. The second problem was authority. Most personnel had ties to "parent organizations," making it difficult for the center's director to have complete authority over them. On numerous occasions the director had to bargain with personnel to obtain compliance. Third, few personnel were willing to make a complete commitment to the center's goals since they recognized that the center would close if its main goal—placement of all the displaced workers—was met. Even with these disadvantages, however, the program represented an innovative approach to servicing displaced workers.

Case 2: A Program for Displaced Workers

After fifty years of operation, a small facility (eighty employees) was targeted for closing. The company did not have a joint training program or a local committee, but both the company and the union informally organized a joint committee to work with displaced workers. The committee developed a four-step strategy: (1) a survey would be conducted aimed at identifying workers' skills, needs, desire for training, and job plans; (2) negotiation would begin with a state agency so as to make career development counseling available free of charge at the work site; (3) information would be obtained about job openings in the company in the immediate area; and (4) a counseling program would be established to provide relocation assistance. Frequent and personalized contact with each of the displaced workers was an important element in the program. At least one hour-long interview with each worker was the goal. These interviews were focused on both explaining service options and providing social support.

An important dimension of this program was the exploration and identification of job openings beyond formal channels. The cochairs of the committee initiated informal contacts within the company (particularly in branch offices) to identify possible job openings. This network of contacts was expanded by enlisting the help of other committee members as well as their associates. As a result, 80 percent of the displaced workers had new jobs, most with the company, by the time of the shutdown.

Two features of this program stand out. First, the committee was successful in finding workers new jobs because its members developed a network of job contacts that went beyond formal channels. Committee members had an in-depth knowledge of the job seekers and a personal relationship with potential employers, greatly facilitating the job search process. Second, the committee identified local service resources and made good use of them. A knowledge of training available at the local community college was helpful in processing program participants and expanding service options. Committee members viewed their work as a personal crusade to save their peers and went beyond conventional channels to help them.

Case 3: A Peer-Based Literacy Program

In a plant within a large company, there had been a recurring problem because the literacy level of some participants in the joint training program was so low that they were excluded from technical training programs. Although literacy programs were available both inside and outside the plant, workers resisted attending them. Under the guidance of a nearby university, an experimental program was initiated to use peer workers to recruit, counsel, and train illiterate workers in verbal and mathematical skills. Foremen and stewards identified a number of workers as "natural leaders" (individuals who had a strong social standing in the plant). In addition, workers identified or nominated other workers who had influence in the informal life of the plant.

Once identified, the natural leaders from several departments underwent a series of training sessions on sensitivity awareness, interpersonal communication, and programs to reduce illiteracy (both computer-based and one-on-one). They were then given the task of identifying workers with low literacy skills and recruiting them into the program. They also provided both information and social support. Periodically, they would also review the program, help solve problems, and suggest resources and strategies for improvement. The plant was not directly involved in the literacy program; both planning and operation were peer-based.

Case 4: An Education Fair for Active Workers

A local committee had been in place for almost a year in a large midwestern plant, but participation in the joint training program had been low. In an effort to improve the situation, the local committee ran a series of education fairs in the plant garage once every two months on Friday afternoons during working hours. Refreshments were served, and workers who wanted to attend were excused from work. The fair consisted of a number of booths, each staffed by a local vendor who offered educational or training services. Each booth had brochures, and one had a slide show to explain course offerings, registration procedures, and class hours. Particular emphasis was placed on the possibility of offering in-plant classes if registration was sufficient. An innovative feature of the fairs was that those workers who were interested in taking courses could register on the spot. A simple job interest inventory was also available.

High-level officials from both management and the union were visible, as were stewards and foremen, members of the local committee, and job counselors associated with the committee. Participation by these people had three positive results: (1) it legitimized the importance of the fairs and indeed of the joint training program; (2) it provided an opportunity for many important people in the plant to learn about the community service options in the community; and (3) it provided an opportunity for an informal flow of information between potential program participants, vendors, and important actors in the plant.

Follow-up information was made available in a variety of ways: through personal contacts between counselors and participants, through feature stories in plant and union newspapers, through spot announcements on the in-house TV system, and through interviews on the local TV station.

Case 5: A Mobile Classroom
In this case, a plant in the South was closing. The local committee had developed a program of career counseling and training for displaced workers, initiated a year before the shutdown. The program depended on local community resources, however, and because the three communities involved were in remote areas that had few services, the committee was concerned that services would not be delivered. The committee therefore organized a "floating classroom" that consisted of a trailer truck with a large van that could be opened into a thirty-person mini-auditorium. The van carried a library of training manuals, audiotapes and VCRs with videocassettes, and various machine simulations. Staffed by instructors from a nearby university, the van circulated regularly from one facility to another, thereby enabling participants in remote facilities to avail themselves of the program.

Several conclusions can be drawn from these brief descriptions. Joint training programs are far more flexible than traditional employment and training programs in adapting operations to the social realities of program participants. Reaching out to isolated participants (mobile classrooms), providing one-stop assistance (reemployment and assistance centers), and bringing vendors to the participants (education fairs) are all innovative delivery techniques. Instead of being restricted by bureaucratic red tape, some administrators are swiftly and decisively initiating programs that lead to results.

These cases also suggest that the workplace can be an important locus of intervention in that unique resources of both the union and company can be mobilized. Beyond this, the cases indicate that joint training programs can be the focus of considerable experimentation in human resource management. These cases can be viewed as the first in what could become a set of rigorous studies of work transitions.

Summary

On at least three dimensions, joint training programs differ significantly from large-scale, publicly funded employment and training programs. First, joint training programs are participant-driven, suggesting that service delivery is responsive to the needs and aspirations of program participants. Further, participants have some control over the direction and content of the program as well as over the quality and offerings. Second, the intense involvement of the union and company in such programs suggests that resource networks in both organizations can be mobilized to provide unprecedented informal support for participants. These networks can be used in recruitment, marketing of the program, and assessment and can provide social support to a degree not possible in publicly supported programs. Third, joint training programs make it possible for industrial workers and low-level white-collar workers to plan a strategy for the development of a lifetime career rather than merely prepare for a specific job.

The psychology of joint training programs also differs significantly from that of publicly supported programs. First, because programs are participant-driven, participants have a sense of ownership of the program. Participants often develop an attitude of personal empowerment that translates into a sense of involvement with the workplace. The oft-cited stereotype of the alienated worker may actually give way to an involved worker who cares and strives to have input at work. Second, heightened empowerment at work may lead to heightened empowerment outside work (e.g., in the family, neighborhood, and community). Technical and social skills developed in joint training may be applied to nonwork settings. Increased literacy, for example, may lead someone to become a more active community citizen. Thus the thrust of joint training is to reorient the worker's perspective from a short-term concern with preparing for a specific job to a long-term focus on meeting lifelong career needs.

This chapter has emphasized the innovative nature of joint training programs and their ability to mobilize both union and management resources on behalf of the active and displaced workers of a specific company. Unfortunately, such programs can at most play a limited role in solving the human resource problems of our society. They are restricted to unionized work forces, or at most about 16 percent of the working population. Furthermore, not all unionized companies have been able to avail themselves of such programs. Small and medium-sized companies frequently do not have the necessary resources (monetary or personnel). Even if we generously assume that about one-third of all unionized work forces will be able to have such programs, this means that only about 5 percent of the labor force will be able to participate and the workers involved will be concentrated in larger, wealthier companies. Thus unionized and nonunionized workers will continue to be trained either in company-sponsored, union-sponsored, or publicly sponsored programs.

The Comprehensive Employment and Training Act of the 1970s and the Joint Training Partnership Act of the 1980s were enacted to deal with the problems of disadvantaged workers, not of active workers. The former had little or no work histories or chaotic work histories. The tasks for these public programs were far more formidable than for joint training programs, and thus the potential for success was lower. In contrast, displaced workers in joint training programs have stable work histories and proven work skills. In comparing joint training programs and public programs, the labor market characteristics and the potential of program participants must be kept in mind.

Joint training programs can be viewed as a vast experimental laboratory in which different technologies and techniques (e.g., recruitment, client processing, and counseling) can be tried out. Seen in this light, joint training programs may have a significance beyond their immediate constituencies in developing rigorous research that could benefit the entire field of human resource development.

11 · THE GOVERNANCE OF JOINT TRAINING INITIATIVES

Ernest J. Savoie and Joel Cutcher-Gershenfeld

This chapter was written by an academic who has an intimate knowledge of joint training programs and by a practitioner who has developed such a program. The thesis is that the governance of joint training programs can be understood only in the context of the parties' labor relations. Specifically, the chapter focuses on four closely linked elements of joint training programs: (1) accepting and refining the mixed motive relationship; (2) crafting forms of governance for specific areas of mutual interest; (3) jointness as an emergent strategy; and (4) providing dynamic leadership. The chapter should be especially useful to researchers and policy developers.

For many labor and management leaders, establishing and serving on a board or committee that administers joint union-management undertakings, including worker training programs, represents a substantial departure from their experiences with collective bargaining. This is because the formal rulemaking and enforcement that characterize most union-management relations do not ensure the successful operation of joint endeavors, particularly those directed at providing an ever-evolving service such as education and training.

When labor and management leaders share responsibility for large-scale initiatives, such as joint worker education, they must design entirely new forms of governance; respond to a multiplicity of worker interests and needs, which tend to change during workers' lifetimes; and often adjust the training to demands of a dynamic environment that includes shifting business strategies, emerging technologies, redesigned work systems, fragmenting world markets, and deep demographic changes (Piore and Sable 1984). In these complex milieus, strict pattern bargaining or the imitation of provisions in other agreements, the hallmark of most collective bargaining, is not usually serviceable as a template. When a company and a union are undertaking a major joint project, tailoring, innovation, and watchful adaptation, including revitalization—a heuristic approach—are requisites for success. For the most part, an evolutionary path is necessary, progressing from fairly simple applications to those that are more comprehensive and integrated. In essence, the parties must engage in a process of crafting new social institutions. This process has deep implications for the way the parties interrelate and for the governance of their joint initiativies.

While specific choices about formal structures and the way authority is delegated are important elements of governance, this chapter does not provide taxonomies or comparisons of such features. Interested readers can refer to discussions of specific programs in this volume if they wish to explore this issue and to Ruttenberg (1990) for a comprehensive study of joint governance structures. Using the specific case of health and safety committees, Ruttenberg reviews committee composition, size, member roles, selection, tenure, minutes, schedules, pay, funding, functions, disputes, agendas, priorities, results, and opportunities. More general information on joint committees can be found in Cohen-Rosenthal and Burton (1987). Service delivery issues associated with joint training issues are discussed in chapter 10 of this volume.

The thrusts of this chapter are the general principles that underlie the operation of joint endeavors and the governance of education programs in unionized workplaces. We use the term *governance* to capture the complexity of labor-management relations in an era when large-scale joint training and many other large-scale joint programs exist side by side with traditional negotiations and contract administration. In this era, labor and management must address all the classical issues of governance. These include distinctions among executive, legislative, and judicial decision making; coordination of central, local, and regional administration/relationships; designating accountability, planning, decision making, and implementation; assuring funding and providing staffing; promoting communication and enlisting participation/membership and constituency support; exercising leadership and handling the succession of leaders; operating with checks and balances; maintaining stability while allowing for growth and responding to crises; managing human and fiscal resources; and achieving legitimacy, performance, and renewal. Our goal is to identify some of the principles that underlie the broad range of labor-management activities associated with governance as we have defined it.

Specifically, we will focus on four closely linked elements of large-scale joint worker training programs that we see as critical for success: (1) accepting and refining the mixed motive relationship, particularly as it manifests during pivotal events; (2) crafting forms of governance for specific areas of mutual interest; (3) perceiving jointness as an emergent strategy; and (4) providing dynamic leadership. The interplay of these elements, rather than any single one, is especially critical. Indeed, each of the elements is interdependent. Together they establish governance as one of the central challenges facing labor and management leaders interested in joint training initiatives.

The analysis in this chapter is based on the experiences described in this volume as well as detailed and wide-ranging discussion with practitioners and participants involved in joint training. Savoie has been directly involved as a governing member of several major joint undertakings, including the joint governing body of the UAW-Ford National Education, Development and Training Center. Cutcher-Gershenfeld has been involved in a major evaluation research study sponsored by the Ford Foundation on leading national joint training initiatives and in a collaborative research project on training involving Michigan State University and the state of Michigan, as well as a variety of other research projects (employing a mix of quantitative and qualitative methodologies) concerned with new developments in labor-management relations.

Accepting the Mixed Motive Relationship

Joint worker training is shaped by both the common and the conflicting interests of labor and management. It represents a special application of a core principle of collective bargaining: the view that all parties have a mixture of common and competing interests (Walton and McKersie 1965). Thus, while there are aspects of joint training for which there is common agreement, conflicts involving training will also arise. Sometimes joint training activities will lead to far-ranging joint gains, while at other times there will be fundamental conflicts centered on training issues. As a result, attempts to establish worker training (or any other major joint initiative) as a separate activity, totally independent of collective bargaining, hold little likelihood of lasting success.

Building on the mixed motive theme, experience indicates that the governance of joint training initiatives is a double-edged process. That is, governance involves both the successful identification and pursuit of common concerns and the effective identification and resolution of points of conflict.

The importance of jointly pursuing common concerns is illustrated, for example, in the selection of outside vendors for the delivery of training programs and in the monitoring of costs and the quality of service. The use of outside vendors, ranging from community colleges, to professional associations, to independent vendors, to secondary schools, to universities, is common. Crossed signals and worse consequences are likely if each party tries to select and monitor vendor performance independently. Thus the success of the joint training initiative may depend on the company and the union accepting their common concern with cost and quality, as well as developing a coordinated approach to selecting vendors and monitoring performance.

The importance of resolving conflict effectively is illustrated, for example, when labor and management disagree over the desired mix of occupation-specific training and generic skills building and education. Unions frequently press for transferable training (for example, the operation and maintenance of new technologies) so as to increase employees' abilities to adapt to future changes and their opportunities in the labor market. In contrast, employers often seek to tailor training to the unique characteristics of their work site and equipment so as to reduce training time, increase success, and limit the investment associated with employee turnover. If the parties do not address such points of tension, one or the other is likely to exhibit a decreasing level of commitment. That, obviously, could be fatal to a joint initiative.

Taking Advantage of Pivotal Events

Because mixed motive relationships have this double-edged quality, the evolution of many joint initiatives is characterized by a sequence of pivotal events (Cutcher-Gershenfeld 1988). The successful pursuit of joint training initiatives reinforces joint activities in areas other than training, while failure to pursue an opportunity may constrain the options of the parties. Similarly, successful resolution of a conflict can produce deeper mutual understanding, while inadequate resolution can undercut joint activities. From a research perspective, it is through pivotal events that the mixed motive aspects of the relationship are most visible. From a practitioner perspective, pivotal events represent a series of choices on which to some extent the future of the joint initiative hangs. Pivotal events are inevitable. The challenge is to recognize the pivotal nature of situations as they arise so that broader consequences can be taken into account.

It is possible to create pivotal events, either to further a joint initiative or to obstruct it. For example, the Ford/UAW joint training programs have sponsored day-long training events open to the entire population of a facility. Such events had the potential to be pivotal to the extent that they reinforced and extended joint training initiatives.

Identifying and Pursuing Joint Concerns

Part of the mixed motive approach to labor-management relationships involves identifying and pursuing joint concerns, a process many labor and management leaders find uncomfortable. On a practical level, relatively few labor or management leaders have much experience in working together in a problem-solving mode. They are more used to forms of collective bargaining in which information is closely guarded, a spokesperson controls the flow of communications, controlling the agenda is of paramount importance, and the outcome is a product of power and leverage.

Thus a key practical issue in the governance of a joint training program is the parties' level of interaction as they brainstorm, make group decisions, and perform other aspects of problem solving. Effective interactive skills will enhance problem solving, while inadequate skills will undercut it. It is therefore important that the parties ensure that there is continual problem-solving training for key participants.

Related to this issue is another key practical matter: whether there is turnover among either labor or management leaders. Turnover is particularly an issue if the replacements do not have the same level of experience or skill in interacting as their predecessors. Thus union appointments or elections and management rotation or promotion can be pivotal events for joint training programs.

The process of identifying and pursuing joint concerns also poses certain challenges. Here the challenges involve, on the one hand, working together closely to develop and administer the training program and, on the other hand, maintaining sufficient independence to ensure that valid special interests are served. This political dynamic arises from the fact that both labor leaders and managers are responsible for constituencies that do not attend the joint meetings, that cannot be part of the detailed decision-making process, and that may not even fully accept the wisdom of the joint endeavor. It is thus important to educate and inform the constituency constantly and to attend to events that may have an impact on some or all of that constituency. It is important to respect not only the reality but the perception that independent interests are fully represented.

The best joint training programs provide promotional, advertising, and information-sharing activities to ensure widespread internal communication about the programs. Thus the volumes of brochures, video tapes, and other materials distributed by employers and unions engaged in joint training reflect more than just the need to reach nontraditional audiences with technical information. They also reflect a political need to keep constituents informed of the scope and direction of joint activities.

Identifying and Resolving Disputes

The means by which program differences and disputes are resolved is also important to the mixed motive approach to labor-management relations. Generally, labor and management find that ongoing administrative responsibility for a training program (involving a wide range of parties and interests) requires a different form of dispute resolution than is typical of either the periodic, bilateral process of collective bargaining or the episodic, formal rule-enforcement process of contract administration. Instead of resolution via economic power or the application of precise rules, the dispute resolution process takes on more of a clinical, case-by-case quality in which the pressures are more subtle, the common interest is more appreciated, and the logic of argument is more salient. Typically, the parties establish dispute resolution mechanisms specifically for the joint initiative, usually involving various levels of review by local, regional, and national joint committees, and do not use existing contract grievance procedures. The development of effective dispute resolution mechanisms is a pivotal activity. Their presence can foster deeper understanding of each side's priorities, or their absence (because of a lack of understanding) can undercut the joint initiative.

A second concern can arise if, because of their successful experiences, the parties so emphasize the common interest in worker training that legitimate criticism or disagreement is interpreted as a lack of support. While the hard threats of collective bargaining may not be appropriate for joint training meetings (at least not very often), the parties' capacity to disagree and confront one another is still essential if the interests of each side are to be served. Conflict is not enmity and is not always destructive. There is constructive conflict, which facilitates the sharing of different ideas, experiences, viewpoints, and facts. Indeed, in retrospect, it often becomes clear that the result of conflict was a superior product and longer-lasting accommodation.

A dilemma arose at the Xerox Corporation, for example, during the implementation of a corporatewide training program in what the company has termed Leadership through Quality (LTQ), which, broadly defined, is centered on identifying the needs and capabilities of internal and external suppliers and customers. When it came time for training to take place in the manufacturing operations, which are organized by the Amalgamated Clothing and Textile Workers Union (ACTWU), the union demanded that the training be designed and administered on a joint basis. At first the corporation was reluctant to open the issue for discussion since a corporatewide design had already been developed and approved by many internal management stakeholders, materials had already been developed and were in use, and a team of LTQ trainers was already in place. The union prevailed, however, and the resulting modification in the design was better fitted to the unionized manufacturing operation. In addition, a whole cadre of union-appointed quality of work life trainers proved to be highly skilled in conducting the LTQ training. If management had conducted the training on a unilateral basis with standardized materials as it preferred, the implementation of LTQ probably would have been less effective.

Linking the Pursuit of Common Concerns and the Resolution of Conflict

The two elements of governance highlighted here—the pursuit of common concerns and the resolution of conflicts—are, of course, interrelated. Training programs are by their nature demand- and opportunity-driven. The demands and opportunities come from multiple sources and can be both complementary and competing. For example, in the course of training tied to the introduction of new technologies, a need for remedial training in math and reading often surfaces. While the new training needs may delay the introduction of the technologies, a deeper set of hidden organizational restraints is brought to light. Further, while the new set of needs is being addressed, the format shifts, requiring different instructors and different educational approaches.

Increased experience with problem solving around common concerns can lead to a greater willingness and capacity to address points of conflict or stalemate. At the same time, increased experience in resolving conflict can lead to higher levels of confidence in bringing broad, common concerns to the surface whose outcomes cannot be fully anticipated. In this sense, the pursuit of common concerns and the resolution of conflicts are interrelated and indispensable elements of governance in employment relations.

Crafting Governance

The most visible aspect of governance is the formal structure for decision making. In larger firms, this formal structure is often a series of joint committees at local, regional, and corporate levels. Linked to the committees are professional staff, outside vendors and educational institutions, and various channels for input by interested internal constituencies (such as workers, line management, and industrial relations/human resources staff). It is important that these structural arrangements not be viewed as immutable. In fact, they reflect a series of choices by the program's founders as well as subsequent adjustments. The process of making these choices is the process of crafting governance. Before discussing this process, we will review a number of contextual aspects of governance that set the stage for the crafting process.

The first such aspect of governance involves the topic areas for training and the populations to be trained. These two elements are intertwined—the topic areas will vary depending on whether the workers are displaced or active, in skilled trades or production, in the office versus the factory, nonexempt versus supervisory, and so on. Some issues, such as computer literacy, may cut across all groups. The impact of topic areas and population on governance is twofold. First, different topic areas impose different time constraints on decision making. For example, training for dislocated workers is segmented into training before and after dislocation. Second, the subject matter chosen as the common area of mutual interest (e.g., literacy training) will influence the degree of staffing by outsiders, the need for previously unavailable expertise, the use of professional vendors, and partnering with other institutions and providers.

The second aspect of governance involves the governance systems of the partner institutions. These will be especially important in determining whether there are national, local, or regional committees; how these committees interact and to whom they report; the level and quality of the staffing; the funding; and oversight and accountability procedures.

When parties have agreed to establish more than one joint initiative, which is frequently the case, a third aspect of governance involves the relationships among these joint initiatives. What, for example, is the relationship between the joint training initiatives and employee involvement programs, safety and health programs, apprenticeship programs, joint strategic planning efforts, and so on? In some cases, the efforts are linked together nationally and/or locally under a general joint body. In other cases, the initiatives are independent but are united by common membership and reporting at the top. There are advantages and disadvantages to each arrangement. Multiple, concurrent joint committees may have the advantage of keeping each program from becoming vulnerable to conflicts that emerge in the others. For example, in some automotive facilities, there is a measure of internal division among workers regarding issues of employee involvement and team-based forms of work organization, raising the question of whether joint training activities can (or should) be kept distinct from such debates. A common structure for all such programs will increase the likelihood of links being made. The lack of a common structure, however, means that more politically controversial programs are more vulnerable and also introduces complex issues of coordination.

The fourth component of joint governance centers on the range of discretionary authority accorded the committees. At one extreme, the committees are little more than contract-enforcement bodies, operating under strict guidelines. Many of the earlier joint benefit committees and apprenticeship committees were of this type. At the other extreme are committees with very broad charters; extensive staffing, authority, and influence over counterpart local bodies; and extensive special funding under the direct control of key union-management decision makers. These committees arose in the 1980s and are found most notably in the automotive and communications industries.

The fifth component of governance involves change over time. For example, the parties in many labor-management relationships have increased their funding and staff for joint training activities in successive negotiations. They have extended the domain of their educational activities, stressing personal development and generic skills as well as technical and workplace operations. Today, joint training programs encompass a wide range of special topic areas, such as basic reading and mathematical skills, public speaking, general computer literacy, preretirement planning, personal financial education, and technical literacy. Services may include guidance and counseling and educational assessment on-site or through prepaid tuition plans. For dislocated workers, the services include job search, worker retraining, placement, loans, and moving assistance. Expansion of the scope of joint training inevitably raises questions regarding the adequacy of some early governance structures for service delivery.

Questions about shifts in the governance structure usually arise in the context of a planned or unplanned pivotal event. As the number of professional staff with training expertise (employed by the company and union) increases, for example, the status of these third parties in a union-management structure becomes increasingly salient. The result is joint discussion not only about the programs but about the structure within which the programs reside.

As the parties fashion each new program, they expand their own participative skills and enrich their environments. Working with internal professionals and outside experts, they develop employee interest surveys, conferences, workshops, conventions, and numerous forms of evaluation. They learn to encourage feedback, recognition, and celebration. In some cases, the parties learn to use high-tech aids, including satellite conferencing, interactive video, and computer-based training. Many of these new skills can be used in other areas of responsibility. Thus a sixth dimension of governance involves the application of joint experiences to the respective union and management organizations.

A seventh component relevant to the crafting of governance involves increased recognition of adult learning principles and techniques, as well as adoption of the goal of lifelong learning. Early on, many parties discovered that the traditional policies and practices at many academic institutions tended to inhibit adult learning. These practices included the location of classrooms, the pedagogy, and the methods and criteria for selecting and training instructors. To be successful, program designers had to create new delivery systems. Joint education initiatives, as partners with the educational community and other educational providers, offer a fertile ground for experimentation, pilot programs, and demonstrations. There is an eye on the future, on preparing for change, and on building the skills, competence, and commitment needed for the 1990s—a decade of even more intense global competition, and shorter product cycle times.

Governance in the 1990s will involve continuous give and take on a broad variety of topics within complex national and local environments. There will be a multiplicity of administrative structures. At a given work site, one or more steering committees may be responsible for identifying the goals, policies, and procedures for training programs. Further, various ad hoc committees are likely to be responsible for specific issues or problems. In addition, union appointees, management designees, and/or externally hired professionals may serve as full- or part-time staff for one or more training programs. In some cases, external consultants or educational institutions will be under contract to provide various training services. Beyond the level of the plant and the local union, there may be an additional mix of joint committees, appointees, and external professionals at regional levels or at the corporatewide or international union level. In the case of a handful of large firms and unions, special national training centers are being established with separate facilities and full-time staff.

The Crafting Process

The key factor influencing success in an advanced joint initiative of the type being developed for worker education and training is the nature, quality, and "fit" of its governance system. Such a fit does not happen on its own. The parties must craft it. Further, there is no simple pattern. The particular form of governance must be compatible with the governance of the parties' overall relationship, even though they are different. Thus, achieving a good fit involves a curious kind of discussion. Since the parties are still engaged in a mixed motive relationship, the design process will not be some idealized, antiseptic exercise. Rather it will be a process of give and take as the parties engage in what can be termed bargaining over how to bargain (Cutcher-Gershenfeld, McKersie, and Walton 1989).

When restructuring or bargaining over how to bargain occurs in our political system, we rely on a series of checks and balances. The same is true of labor-management relations, only the checks and balances arise from collective bargaining and from the internal union structure and the internal management hierarchy. The agreement to build a local training facility or a national training complex, for example, brings to the fore a wide range of interest groups within the union and the employer, as well as core issues such as centralization. Thus, although crafting a governance structure opens up fundamental questions about how the parties will interact, it must still remain grounded in existing union-management arrangements.

Experience and analysis indicate unequivocally that joint education programs, like other joint processes, must be embedded in the collective bargaining agreement. They are a product of bargaining and operate in a labor-management atmosphere. At the same time, they must have their own indigenous structures and mechanisms. This duality requires that leaders pay close attention, first, to their own growing styles of interaction and to the degree of support they provide and, second, to the people they assign to these programs. The people assigned must have insight, a predisposition to working together to achieve results that cannot be obtained by unilateral action, and the ability to plan rather than merely respond. They must also be capable of learning, persuading, and celebrating individual and group achievements.

The strongest institutional arrangement is usually one in which the first-tier program leaders are leading members of their labor and management constituencies. These individuals are most able to attend fully to the mixed motive aspects of the relationship. Education and support professionals, while absolutely essential, usually fill positions in the next tier. When program content is paramount or is entirely new, it may be preferable to have professionals hold the chief governing positions and key union and company designees entrusted to see that the parties maintain a healthy mixed motive relationship. In any case, the most critical ingredient is shared ownership. All the parties must firmly believe and act on the simple principle that "this is ours."

In the short term, the union may take more "political heat" than management for proclaiming the virtues of joint ownership. After members start utilizing the programs, however, the union may reap great political benefits from the services its members receive. The difference in the time frame occurs largely because union officers are elected—a unique dimension of the collective bargaining system that has implications for joint training.

Related to the mixed motive management of a joint initiative is the question of the extent to which successful joint initiatives can lead to improvements in the overall labor-management relationship. For many union and management leaders, this benefit is an important reason for undertaking a joint initiative in the first place.

There has, indeed, been important research on many employers and unions that were propelled to transform their labor-management relationship by the wrenching economic, technological, and social developments of the 1980s. Kochan, Katz, and McKersie (1986) trace some of this willingness to work in new ways to positive experiences with joint processes. Without doubt, improvement in the overall labor-management relationship occurred in a significant number of instances as a result of the positive joint experiences. But that is only part of the picture; a good deal of collective bargaining in the United States has been hardly touched by these developments. Further, in some cases in which the parties installed joint processes, they did so only half-heartedly. A clear conclusion of the Kochan, Katz, and McKersie study is that joint initiatives can thrive and contribute to the overall union-management relationship only if the parties are willing to redefine some of their overarching, long-standing institutional assumptions. Joint processes are not an exogenous, independent activity. They can affect the overall relationship, but only if the parties allow them to.

Indeed, some mutual efforts seem to be undertaken as no more than a tactical tool to buy time or to further one's own exclusive aims. Used in this way, they can exacerbate the very distrust that is causing problems in the first place. The long-term effects of failure will most likely be more negativism, cynicism, mediocrity, and a weakening of the union-management relationship. Such failures often entail setbacks and penalties for individuals and can cause significant damage to unions, businesses, and the institution of collective bargaining. "Better never to have started" is the common wisdom in this case.

In other situations, paradoxically, joint processes can be so successful that they are "held hostage" to one party's broader aims. In these cases, either the company or the union suspends (or threatens to suspend) a joint effort, knowing that the other party values it highly. The idea is to obtain an advantage on some other seemingly unrelated issue. Such instances can generate accusations of broken faith and can affect the enthusiasm and dedication of those assigned to the joint endeavor. Given the potential to hold joint efforts hostage, leaders must assume responsibility for managing the governance of joint processes. This is a particularly vivid example of our larger point, that the task of crafting governance presents great opportunities but calls for uncommon abilities and insight.

Ultimately, labor and management should not take any set of institutional arrangements as given. Rather, the task is to examine the extent to which these structures are enabling or constraining joint activities to take place and then modify them as appropriate.

Jointness as an Emergent Strategy

The joint education and training initiatives of the 1980s evolved originally from broad, negotiated statements of goals and general concepts. But unlike so many other bargained programs, they did not appear with fully fleshed-out provisions. As a result, there was an evolution over the years characterized by what Henry Mintzberg (1987) calls an "emergent" (as opposed to a "planned") strategy. As Mintzberg implies, operating via an emergent strategy requires a unique mind set.

A planned strategy is characterized by a deliberate attempt to itemize future explicit actions based on predictable sequences, specific timetables, and detailed controls. It is assumed that a clear way is known to achieve desired goals and that a good deal can be thought through and set out in advance. Clearly, there are situations in which this is so, particularly when one is following a trail blazed by someone else or when institutional relationships are long established. During the 1970s in the U.S. auto industry, for example, the internal operations of management, labor, and even the collective bargaining process were all based largely on planned strategies.

In contrast, an emergent strategy is one in which activities are formulated and implemented around a general concept or vision. Actions are shaped in a fluid process of pattern recognition, learning, and input from participating members, who then help create particular programs. Because there is no single, ultimate design, programs appear at various times to be piecemeal, scattered, and out of sequence. Some observers, including labor and management sponsors, may therefore worry about the appropriateness of resource expenditures, timing, and even whether the parties know what they are doing or where they are going.

There is no such thing, of course, as a purely planned strategy or a purely emergent one. The tendency in joint worker education initiatives, however, has been toward the emergent model, at least to date. Whether this was serendipitous, a manifestation of a high degree of earned trust, dictated by the nature of the issue, or the result of a combination of all of these conditions, the outcome has been a formula that the parties have found extremely valuable.

An emergent strategy is especially useful in situations in which there is some ambiguity of purpose, many parties are involved, priorities are not clear, and grass-roots or senior-level support must be solicited. Everything cannot be done at once, of course. Choices are always necessary. For example, should the parties put more emphasis on displaced workers in their early efforts or on active workers? In the automobile industry, the answer was dictated by the extensive dislocations that took place in the early 1980s. But even then, there were hard choices to make: What kind of programs should be initiated? At what cost? In what locations? What percentage of job skills training and personal development education should there be? Will those who are not served immediately wait patiently? And for what, since no one knows what services will be offered in the future? In the auto industry, as in other places, the principles of the joint training program state that educational services and upgrading should be available to everybody regardless of age, skills, or gender, but is that always possible? Local committees and local groups should be asked for their ideas, and the good ideas supported, but with how much support and in what form? An emergent strategy allows these questions to be addressed gradually, through pilot programs and experiments, followed by broad participation when appropriate.

Such a strategy is well suited to handling changes that cannot be foreseen, particularly in a fast-paced, competitive environment. It permits adaptation on the part of key institutions and allows changes in direction as well as quantum leaps when necessary to address new needs or opportunities. In other words, in addition to incremental changes, there can be spurts or even shifts in the paradigm (Kuhn 1970). We stated earlier that a joint training initiative is characterized by a series of pivotal events. It is at these pivotal moments that the emerging strategy takes form and is most evident.

Key ingredients in the emergent approach are an "open" charter, discretion to initiate programs in between negotiations, and the availability of funding. Carrying out an emergent strategy requires the parties to develop a unique mind-set that can be thought of as entrepreneurial. The idea is to cause change, not just respond to it; to interact frequently; to exercise a direct hands-on involvement; to communicate widely with all constituents; to achieve success; to take risks; to improve continuously; and to anticipate and manage pivotal events. The process creates something entirely new and highly valued by virtually all the participants, while at the same time generating a new set of organizational learnings and relationships.

The beneficial results of an emergent approach can include the generation of wide support nationally and locally among both labor and management; greater ease in ironing out difficulties; openness to testing and judging alternatives; creativity in selecting the best providers; and, ultimately, higher-quality programs that have consistency and momentum. Indeed, emergent strategies may be the key to the survival of both employers and unions in the years to come.

Strategies in the Years to Come

What is the future of joint endeavors? Will they maintain their fervor as they mature? What about those in which the companies and unions are asked to negotiate programs developed by others, instead of initiating their own using an emergent strategy?

We should not expect mature programs to maintain the full spirit and vitality of their youth. As a program grows, as major educational needs are satisfied and difficulties are ironed out, we are likely to see a transition into a more controlled and orderly system. This process is simply a manifestation of the well-known stages of growth in any organization, from entrepreneurship to maturity, then possibly to decline or renewal (Kilmann, Covin, and Associates 1988). A few of the first large-scale initiatives in the automobile and communications industries already are exhibiting these changes. Staff are beginning to see evidence of more bureaucracy, the leaders do not come around as much anymore, and staff are making fewer visits to the field. In short, some of these programs are in a maintenance phase. Field staff know how to run the programs, often as well or better than central staff. A hands-on role for central leadership is less necessary.

The maintenance stage in the evolution of the joint endeavor calls for new leadership thrusts, especially efforts aimed at renewal and revitalization. Such activities are required to maintain "health," just as it is necessary to paint one's house every few years, tune up a car, and exercise. Parties who make maintenance activities a regular part of their programs should be able to make a healthy transition into so-called maturity with no loss of effectiveness.

Even if all needs were theoretically met, however, new, unforeseen needs would undoubtedly emerge. The needs of new entrants to the work force will have to be addressed, for example, and they may be different from those of the present work force. In assessing new needs, the parties must strive to avoid the bureaucratic tendency to "make work" (i.e., to direct resources to extremely marginal needs). This could be seen as a self-serving effort to preserve staff, and misadministration of time and money could weaken support for the total program.

Whether to install someone else's program is a more difficult question. Already we are seeing examples of one party pressuring the other to adopt all or many features of a program that was worked out by another employer and union. For the most part, this approach is ill suited to the concept, nature, and purpose of joint worker education programs. Needs, skills, and occupations differ by company and industry, as do, among other matters, the parties' resources and form of bargaining. The structure of training will depend, for example, on whether there is industrywide bargaining and whether there are several unions in one company, decentralized small operations, or differing corporate authority structures. A forced-initiation approach is asynchronous with the conditions necessary for successful joint undertakings: the creation of shared interests, prior periods of trust-building, crafted governance, and development by an emergent rather than a planned strategy.

The true benefits of jointism are in the development, the learning, and the cementing. Forced initiation mistakes the product for the process. Undue force or patterning could result in weak program implementation and utilization and in a hardening of adversarial attitudes, all of which are clearly antithetical to mutual interest undertakings. Parties would be well served, before "forcing" negotiations, to start with an agreement to conduct lengthy study, visits, and assessment, and then—if they go ahead—to allow considerable room for tailoring and normal growth over time. If a particular mind-set is required for an emergent strategy to work, its development most likely requires an investment of time and emotional resources.

Need for Dynamic Leadership

Because joint undertakings involve a fluid set of relationships and a constant balancing of resources and priorities, dynamic leadership is critical to their success. National and local leaders, either union or management, cannot simply make a one-time agreement, walk away, and leave it to others. In the best programs, senior leaders on boards and committees make field visits, appear at conferences and training events, give speeches, and, more important, provide one-on-one encouragement to key people. Activities such as addressing plantwide meetings, attending graduation ceremonies, and dedicating local centers provide both management and union leaders with opportunities to reach audiences they would never have reached otherwise in new settings and with new messages.

Leaders are aware of the need to pass on the baton—to educate new members and new leaders, who may have different job experiences and different personal values. Leaders in the most vital programs share stories, stay close to the members, communicate widely and frequently, and use campaigns, surveys, logos, awards, mementos, celebrations, dedications, and even perhaps a few myths as leadership-building activities. Leaders use funding and grants purposefully and creatively. They understand and maintain balance among competing forces. They help surmount barriers and restraining attitudes.

It is particularly during pivotal events that the leadership at all levels can determine whether a joint training initiative will be undercut or reinforced. Over time, this series of leadership decisions becomes a process of crafting governance, and ultimately it is those leaders who can capitalize on emergent strategies who will succeed in fostering joint training initiatives.

Leadership Dilemmas

There are a number of dilemmas associated with the leadership of joint training initiatives. First, there is the classic mixed motive dilemma, which involves balancing the integrative process of expanding the pie with the distributive process of dividing it. If leaders are not engaged in both integrative and distributive activities, they will not fully serve their respective constituencies. Nonetheless, choices have to be made about when to expand and when to claim the benefits of expansion.

A second dilemma is how to maintain independence while taking on joint administrative responsibilities. This was discussed earlier but cannot be overstated. Leaders have to educate their constituencies sufficiently so that the joint activities are viewed as furthering constituents' interests.

A third dilemma is how to balance the importance of operating via an emergent strategy while many other union and management operations (e.g., formal negotiations) still function on the basis of traditional, planned strategies. This dilemma often surfaces, for example, in the context of developing a budget for an organization, which is typically premised on the use of a planned strategy. This dissonance may be reduced somewhat in two ways. First, lessons from the emergent approach may be filtered down to other operations (such as development of the budget). Second, over time, training programs may take on somewhat more stable, planned characteristics. Nonetheless, leaders will feel the complexities of shifting from one mind-set to another more acutely than others.

A fourth dilemma of leadership involves how to balance the importance of stability with the importance of change. On the one hand, leaders are often the ones who initially define roles and norms. On the other hand, leaders must also recognize when constructive changes are called for.

A final dilemma of leadership is what might be called the participative dilemma. It is the leaders at national and local levels who create visions, but visions will not take form unless constituents become part of the process of shaping them. Ultimately, the task of leadership becomes one of empowering leaders and followers at other levels.

Jointism is relationship-intensive. When one partner will not make the effort to work with the other, the relationship comes apart. It takes time and effort to build skills and develop commitment. It takes patience and goodwill to deal with delays, frustrations, and unevenness. Each party must work to hold up its part of the bargain. To build up the relationship capital of organizations, the leaders must pay attention to the quality of the people they assign to joint work.

The concepts of joint worker education programs are not difficult to understand, and features and mechanisms can be replicated. Joint undertakings are not easily grasped with words and readings, however. They need to be experienced. Excellence is demonstrated in the execution. Leaders must want excellence if excellence is to result.

Summary

The record indicates that when they are carefully crafted and used ingeniously, joint union-management endeavors can be a valuable part of a collective bargaining relationship. They can contribute to accomplishing specific ends that might not otherwise be attained, and they can benefit the parties' overall relationship. Joint initiatives can help surmount traditional attitudes and barriers to change; they can be sources of improvement and innovation. Joint approaches are especially useful in the area of education because job markets—internal and external—are unpredictable and change quickly in our increasingly uncertain world.

The story of joint initiatives and joint worker training programs is a collective bargaining success story of the 1980s. Research on these initiatives is in its infancy and understandably highly descriptive. We have tried to isolate broad factors that are fundamental to the successful formulation and growth of such endeavors. These elements can provide a framework for analyzing the development of specific initiatives, and we encourage investigators and participants to use the framework for such analyses. Tracing pivotal events, milestones in the development of an emergent strategy, leadership activities, and the restraints or contributions of the mixed motive relationship should provide useful data for improving or constructing other joint training programs.

12 · PUBLIC POLICY AND RESEARCH IMPLICATIONS OF JOINT TRAINING PROGRAMS

Joel Cutcher-Gershenfeld and Michele Hoyman

This chapter summarizes the conclusions reached in this volume. Emphasis is placed on key reseach findings, recommendations for future research projects, and the implications of the research for public policy. The chapter should be of value to anyone considering or currently conducting research on joint training programs, to policy makers looking for an overview of the implications of this research, and to other government and education professionals eager for comprehensive information on the state of current thinking surrounding joint training.

What is the significance of joint training programs? Are they just a passing fad, or are they changing industrial relations and the field of training? How are these programs distinct from other public and private training? How are they distinct from other aspects of labor-management relations? To a certain extent, an assessment of the impact of an innovation cannot be made without the passage of time. Our conclusions, therefore, are based on preliminary evidence. That said, we feel labor-management training programs have immediate implications and pose immediate challenges for both scholars and policy makers.

229

One caveat is important at the outset. Each person's (and institution's) assessment of the usefulness of joint labor-management training programs will inevitably vary depending on the person's position, background, and values. Thus practitioners who have fashioned these programs may be overly optimistic (and not entirely objective) in their assessment of achievements and potential. Unions and unionized companies that do not have joint training programs may cling to an adversarial approach to labor relations because they think joint programs are nonsense, window dressing, evidence of "selling out," or a waste of valuable dollars. Scholars may wonder whether the programs will create a new loyalty among employees that will replace their primary loyalty to the company or the union or their loyalty to both. Scholars may also wonder whether the programs ease workers' alienation. Those who are enthusiastic about joint efforts may see the programs as an inevitable and positive next step in labor-management relations. Those who are cynical may see them as pernicious, rather than positive. Policy makers may be quizzical about how such efforts compare to government programs and other means of delivering training.

For both scholars and policy makers, these concerns highlight a fundamental challenge facing joint training programs: they span the fields of *both* training and industrial relations but do not fit neatly into either category. As a result, some subtle (and not so subtle) adjustments are required for any research or policy making that encompasses the programs. Ultimately, however, joint training programs provide both policy makers and scholars with unique opportunities and dilemmas. These opportunities and dilemmas are the focus of this chapter. We have organized the chapter around eight key findings from this volume (table 12.1).

Research and Policy Implications of Key Findings

Key Finding 1
Joint training programs involve many employers and unions. *In a survey of more than 160 union-management pairs involved in some form of joint activities, 42 percent had joint training programs. These programs were available to nearly 1 million bargaining unit members.*

Table 12.1   Key Findings Regarding Joint Programs for the Training and
Personal Development of Workers

---

1. Joint training programs involve many employers and unions.
2. Joint training programs are diverse in focus and structure.
3. Joint training programs have advantages over unilateral programs.
4. Joint training programs often involve partnerships with government.
5. Education professionals bring distinct skills and interests to joint training.
6. Joint training programs involve a continuous process of joint governance, in contrast to the more discrete interactions associated with collective bargaining.
7. Many methods can be used to study joint training.
8. Programs do not emerge randomly; there are correlates to their existence.

Research Implications

Given the large number of joint training programs identified in the survey conducted by Hoyman and Ferman (see chapter 2), it appears that joint training represents an important development in labor-management relations. Enough bargaining units now feature joint training programs to have firmly established the phenomenon as worthy of further study. But, although the data presented in chapter 2 represent the most comprehensive information available on the scope and extent of joint training programs, more information is needed. No data are available, for example, on the total number of unions and companies involved in joint activities.

The first research challenge is to extend the Hoyman and Ferman study to the state or national level, ideally in the form of a full census or random sample of joint training programs. There are, of course, many challenges associated with collecting such data. First, there is no one list of unionized firms from which the population could be identified or a sample constructed.[1] Second, the range of joint activities that involve some form of training is quite broad, from training in basic reading skills to preparation for new technologies to training in the skills associated with employee participation to safety training. Third, the depth and scope of each joint training initiative can also vary considerably, from one-day sessions to a nearly continuous process of learning. Fourth, there is the potential

---

1. Besides the Department of Labor list, many have been developed for slightly different purposes and may be somewhat incomplete. These include Ichiniowski, Delaney, and Lewin 1989; Cooke 1990; and ongoing research by Harry Katz of Cornell University and Jeffrey Keefe of Rutgers University.

232 · Cutcher-Gershenfeld and Hoyman

for great variation in the degree to which training is linked to the strategic directions of the employer or union. Fifth, there are a range of governance arrangements by which training initiatives become joint. Each of these aspects of joint training programs raises conceptual, definitional, and methodological challenges, many of which are discussed later in this chapter.

It is instructive to contrast research on joint training to controlled evaluation studies such as those of the Comprehensive Employment and Training Act (CETA), the Job Training and Partnership Act (JTPA), and other government programs. In addition to the absence of a comprehensive data base, these limits include the relatively early stage in development reached by most joint training programs, particularly considering that training is a long-term process, and the extent to which access to information is limited because of the jointness itself.

Any evaluation of a program just now being set up is probably being conducted prematurely. It is simply too soon to assess the full effects. Further, some joint training is ongoing, such as basic education, which may span several years, and personal development, which emphasizes self-actualization and empowerment. Empowerment in such cases may be a long-term process and therefore subtle and hard to measure. Typical ways by which the success of training is measured, such as rates of placement and percentage of former earnings, are not applicable.

Vocational training is an exception; the effects are discrete, measurable, and often achieved in a short time. Because such training is aimed at helping a displaced person find a new job, measures of success (the dependent variable), such as placement rates and comparisons with previous earnings, are fairly reliable and valid.

Obtaining access to data presents other challenges. Allowing an outsider to study a program may entail political costs and few perceived benefits to either the company or the union. If the scholar or other outsider finds fault with the program, it may damage the "house that labor and management have built." Thus, if access is granted, it is often with the assumption that the results of the study will be positive. Moreover, the union and company literally control and usually gather the data. Finally, the union and company tend to gather participation data more often than outcome data, which are commonly needed for evaluation studies.

Public Policy Implications

Given the scope and extent of joint training that has been documented, we feel safe in concluding that joint training programs are expanding the human resource capabilities of U.S. society. At the same time, the evidence is not in yet on whether these programs are the most effective way to achieve this goal. Without more complete information, it is difficult to assess how policy initiatives could reinforce and extend joint training. In addition, it is difficult to assess whether joint training programs effectively supplant public initiatives and hence possibly free public resources.

Additional data are clearly needed on the scope and extent of joint training programs, not just for research purposes but so as to establish a base line for the development of public policy. The federal government is uniquely capable of and responsible for taking the lead in generating and maintaining such data (Levine and Strauss 1989; Kochan, Cutcher-Gershenfeld, and MacDuffie 1989), but in addition to federal initiatives, state-level policies regarding training in the workplace must be informed by data on joint training activities. State policy makers in Michigan and Ohio, for example, have already shown an interest in learning more about the scope and impact of joint training activities, and we would strongly endorse other state-level efforts at data collection. The link between training and economic development, which is becoming better established, was the inspiration for these efforts. States have also discovered the link between improved or solid labor-management relations and joint training programs. In fact, twelve states have agencies to encourage labor-management cooperation with the development of joint training programs the ultimate goal (Howitt, Wells, and Marx 1989).

Key Finding 2

Joint training programs are diverse in focus and structure. *The focus of joint training programs can be quite broad and serve both active and displaced workers. Training can be in basic reading and math skills, new technology, principles of economic and strategic planning, and planning for retirement (see chapters 3, 4, 5, 7, and 8). A wide range of structural arrangements can be employed, including joint committees and distinct training centers at various levels (national, regional, industry, and plant) (see chapters 10 and 11).*

Research Implications

The diversity in focus and structure of joint training programs makes them interesting from a research perspective yet difficult to study. The diversity in focus, for example, allows for the study of workers' preferences for various forms of training; the types of training that are or are not well suited to joint administration; the resource requirements of different types of training; and other comparative questions. The diversity in structures allows for the study of differences in joint training in small versus large firms; variations across industries; the relative advantages and disadvantages of different structural arrangements; and other analysis focused on the causes or consequences of the structural diversity. Although some of the chapters in this volume touched on these issues, much more research is needed.

A key challenge involves developing a taxonomy or other classification for joint training programs. A more subtle challenge involves distinguishing functional explanations for the variation from institutional explanations. For example, do joint training programs have centralized administrative structures that match the degree of centralization in their given industries? Or do they copy their structures from successful high-profile programs in other industries?

Public Policy Implications

Variation in the focus and structure of joint training programs derives from the origins of the programs in the private sector. This diversity is an advantage. It indicates to some extent that programs have been crafted to meet the needs of the parties involved. This variation in the range of activity exceeds that typically found in government-run programs.

Perhaps the strongest policy implication associated with the variation in the scope and structure of joint programs is that they serve as a natural laboratory for innovation. Federal, state, and local government can play a central role in the diffusion of successful models, such as the use of Life Education Advisors in the UAW-Ford programs (see chapter 9) or the curriculum of the UAW-GM Paid Education Leave program (see chapter 5). For example, the Strategic Education Program under development by the state of Michigan is an effort to redesign the UAW-GM PEL program to make it useful to smaller employer-union pairs. Further, certain principles from

the private sector, such as employee participation in program design, can be directly imported into government programs, as in the
case of the Michigan initiatives aimed at worker dislocation, described in chapter 8.

Another implication deriving from the variation in joint programs
is that government agencies must not force joint programs into a
single mold. Programs associated with new technology, for example,
may be highly centralized in one firm or industry but highly decentralized in others, reflecting differences in the nature of the new
technologies. At the same time, it may be advantageous to foster
links between programs. Such arrangements may, for instance, facilitate cross-site learning about new technology training.

A final policy implication involves the distinction between large
employers and bargaining units and smaller ones. Smaller workplaces typically lack supportive institutional arrangements, such as
separate personnel or labor relations staff and time off the job for
union appointees. It may become appropriate for policy makers to
consider the extent to which government can facilitate the establishment of institutional arrangements that meet the needs of the
parties in smaller firms and bargaining units. For example, state
and local officials may be well situated to convene meetings of union
and management leaders from smaller workplaces in a given community, region, or industry who are interested or involved in joint
training programs.

Key Finding 3

**Joint training programs have distinct advantages over unilateral
training programs initiated just by employers, government, unions,
or other organizations.** *The advantages include enhanced program credibility for workers and formal mechanisms for input by multiple interests (see
chapters 7, 8, and 10). It is significant that AFL-CIO and government officials find joint programs the preferred approach for addressing certain
problems such as worker dislocation.*

Research Implications

This volume presents strong case study evidence to suggest that key
measures of success, such as participation rates, are enhanced when
joint governance structures are in place. The evidence merely sets
the stage, however, for more formal evaluation since a case study

cannot fully address whether the outcomes would have occurred in the absence of a joint structure.

Further evaluation of the advantages of joint training would have to include the following more focused research questions: To what extent does union involvement in what would otherwise have been a unilateral employer-run program enhance workers' perceptions of training programs, and to what extent do these enhanced perceptions lead to higher participation rates? To what extent does employer involvement in what would otherwise have been a unilateral program enhance the links between training and other workplace operations, especially strategic planning, in the firm? To what extent does a joint structure for training benefit other aspects of labor-management relations?

The standard way to answer research questions about what would have happened in the absence of a particular event or intervention is to use experimental designs, or what Cook and Campbell (1979) term quasi-experimental designs. A key dilemma with such designs, however, involves the ethics of having to deny services to individuals in the control group. Furthermore, U.S. labor law (the duty of fair representation) prohibits a union from treating some members differently vis-à-vis benefits. Because of the overriding importance to an employer and a union of providing training to as many individuals as possible, we urge an alternative strategy whereby researchers work with the parties to discover "natural experiments." Situations may arise, for example, in which some individuals are selected for training on a random basis and others receive training offered unilaterally by the employer or the union. It would then be possible to assess and compare training outcomes for these two populations. Similarly, in large corporations, it is possible to initiate joint training at a few work sites ahead of others. To the extent that selecting which sites will receive support is done without regard to expected success (a not insignificant caveat), it is possible to compare the range of training programs established, the extent of worker participation, and the application of new skills. Chapter 9 describes a particularly strong example of a naturally occurring situation in which a quasi-experimental design was used. We urge others to seek out similar opportunities but note that the research design described in that chapter rested on a foundation in which there was a high level of institutional knowledge of joint training.

Beyond the dilemmas associated with developing experimental or quasi-experimental designs to assess joint training initiatives, there are also research challenges associated with the specification of training outcome measures. In the discussion above, four outcome measures were alluded to: (1) the mix of training programs offered; (2) participation levels in the programs; (3) use of the new skills; and (4) impact of the program on the labor-management relationship.

Each of these potential training outcomes raises a wide range of conceptual and operational challenges. For example, is the mix of programs to be assessed on the basis of the breadth of its offerings or on how well it matches the priorities of workers and the firm? In measuring participation, should we count total enrollment in all courses or the number of unique individuals exposed to training (a smaller number since some individuals take more than one course)? Participation, however it is measured, is a throughput measure, in contrast to an outcome measure associated with impact. There is, however, ambiguity associated with impact measures as well. Measures of the use of new skills may represent overall postprogram work placement rates, only placements in positions where workers use what they learned, long-term career impact, links between training and strategic planning in the firm, broader links between training and organizational performance, and net gains or losses in skills in the community or state. Even more complex to assess, of course, is the impact of a program on the labor-management relationship. Outcome measures for joint training are clearly important, and given the complexity associated with them, they represent a fruitful area for further inquiry.

A final research issue associated with studying the advantages of joint training programs involves the political forces that work against conducting evaluations. Both the employer and the union have taken political risks choosing to work together on training. Each side may legitimately fear that the other will claim that it should be running the program.

The evidence from some of the chapters in this volume suggests that many employers and unions have overcome these challenges, but anecdotal evidence also suggests that even in the most established programs the company and union have concerns about the political ramifications of evaluation research. Researchers have to remain true to professional standards yet be savvy enough to avoid unwittingly becoming a vehicle for efforts to undercut joint training. A key component in resolving this dilemma is the presence of senior individuals in one or both parties who understand the research process and are committed to obtaining data. Without such a commitment, the research study is unlikely to survive the complex and sometimes competing pressures imposed by union and management.

Public Policy Implications

Proper documentation of the advantages of joint structures is critical for policy makers contemplating supporting joint initiatives directly or channeling program-specific public monies through joint governance structures. Moreover, given the parties' priorities about delivering services and their political concerns about formal evaluation, government may be justified in insisting on evaluation if the parties are using public monies. The advantages of this policy are multifold. First, accountability is provided for the use of public funds. Second, parties who are sympathetic to such evaluation are able to support it while minimizing their internal risks. Third, a relatively high standard of review is established, which may spill over into the parties' adoption of a more open learning approach in their own assessment of their joint efforts.

Key Finding 4

Joint training programs often involve partnerships with government. *Local, state, and federal governments may all be involved in partnership arrangements with employers and unions administering joint training programs.*

Research Implications

Research on training typically focuses on either government or private programs. To research the links between government and joint training programs is challenging. First, traditional methods of program evaluation usually assume consistency in service delivery, yet joint programs are idiosyncratic in their relationship to government support. Second, the range of government initiatives that can be linked to joint programs is quite broad, including local, state, and federal efforts and programs focused on everything from new technology to economic development to worker dislocation. Classifying the range of possible links between the array of government programs and training programs is a critical challenge.

Development of a classification scheme must precede other questions, including, What are the costs and benefits to employers, unions, or the government of public-private links for joint training, and what would have happened in the absence of such links? These are difficult yet essential research questions.

There is another deeper set of research issues. While models of industrial relations typically include government as an actor (Dunlop 1958), few theories fully explain the role of the state in the context of U.S. industrial relations (Cohen 1961; Goldfield 1989). Since U.S. labor-management relations has traditionally been relatively decentralized and private, there has not been an urgent need for such theories. The tighter public-private links being forged in the area of joint training heighten the need for such a theory, however. Bilateral relationships between labor and management, management and government, and labor and government now blend into a single set of multilateral relationships. These relationships should provide researchers with a particularly vivid context for examining the theoretical implications of involving the government more directly in labor-management relations.

Public Policy Implications
Government officials administering training programs face many concerns. There is the institutional challenge of dealing with the overlapping yet distinct priorities of an employer and a union. Government programs oriented toward training individual workers may risk not fully addressing the interests of employers, while government programs oriented toward training as a vehicle to improve economic competitiveness may risk not fully addressing the interests of unions and workers.

Beyond broad institutional issues, there are a number of pragmatic concerns, including, for example, the need to communicate jointly with the parties involved. Further, the employer and the union will follow different procedures when making decisions. If there is a particular administrative problem, management may have to take it to higher levels, while the union may have to take it to the members at a meeting. Finally, individuals responsible for government programs often must educate both the employer and the union about the structure and constraints imposed by the government.

Key Finding 5
Education professionals bring distinct skills and interests to joint training. *Education professionals, such as the life education advisors in the UAW-Ford program, can play critical roles in the operation of joint training programs (see chapter 9). At the same time, the distinct interests of these professionals pose challenges regarding governance for both the employer and the union (see chapter 11).*

Research Implications
Joint training initiatives can often result in the forging of new links between education professionals and labor and management. These links include (1) the subcontracting of specific training programs to professionals in the public schools (such as training in basic reading skills), in community colleges (such as blueprint reading), and in universities (such as the UAW-GM PEL program); (2) the hiring of education professionals as staff at work sites (such as the Life Education Advisors in the UAW-Ford program) or on joint committees and at national training centers; and (3) interaction with local schools and education officials regarding the quality of high school graduates.

All of these links may also occur in unilateral programs, but they are especially interesting in the context of joint training for two reasons. First, there is some evidence that education professionals take on more central and more permanent roles in joint training programs. Sometimes management sees the professionals as playing a needed role by improving the productive capacity of the work force, and sometimes the union sees the educators as expanding the capabilities and opportunities of union members. If one side questions the work of the educators, the other side may defend their efforts. In effect, there are checks and balances under a joint structure that assure the educators greater stability in the workplace. Since the evidence on this point is still highly anecdotal, the issue is a key area for further research.

A second is whether including educators in joint training programs helps to expand the traditional bilateral relationship between labor and management toward one that is more multilateral. There are hints that education professionals are often cast as junior partners in joint training programs, but that may change over time, especially as training becomes more tightly integrated into organizational operations. At issue, however, are the core bilateral assumptions that underlie much research in industrial relations. For example, human capital outcomes and internal labor market operations have always been of interest to industrial relations scholars, but what happens when continuous learning is a central activity of a majority of the members of an organization? The status of education professionals in the workplace is a timely issue in settings with and without joint programs, but their role is particularly noteworthy (and hence worth studying) in the context of joint programs.

Public Policy Implications

Fundamental policy questions are being raised in U.S. society regarding the education and capabilities of our work force. The questions begin with the extent to which public schools are preparing students for the workplace challenges ahead, including the competitive challenges of a world economy and new technologies. Many joint training initiatives serve as models as the education and training community strives to help address these pressing challenges. Innovations such as the Life Education Advisors or the Paid Education Leave program are already being studied for their applications to other settings.

Based on the experiences highlighted in this volume, we would caution policy makers in education and training against importing an innovation without attending to the contextual aspects of labor-management relations that may be integral to its success. For example, since most joint training programs are established by an agreement at the collective bargaining table, they are often preceded by a period of exploration and debate during which each side pays attention to what it hopes to gain and expects to risk by moving ahead with the idea. This process is usually quite different from the process of packaging and disseminating the program. The result of a bargained agreement is more likely to meet the parties' interests directly, but it requires a relatively high tolerance for variation across locations.

Key Finding 6

Joint training programs involve a continuous process of joint governance, in contrast to the more discrete interactions associated with collective bargaining. *Joint training is best approached as a process of governance in which the sorting out of multiple interests depends on effective leadership, institutional flexibility, mechanisms to pursue common concerns, and mechanisms to resolve conflicts (see chapter 11).*

Research Implications

Much of the academic literature on training is concerned, from either a psychological or an economic perspective, with the individual level of analysis. Measures are taken of individual characteristics, specific program content, and individual learning or placement outcomes. Such research is valuable, but the findings in this volume make a strong case for examining the larger institutional context within which the training takes place. That is, a worker dislocation program run just by government, an employer, or a union is different from one administered jointly. In other words, governance seriously affects service delivery and outcomes.

Chapter 11 in this volume represents one of the first attempts by a scholar and a practitioner to highlight governance issues and thus set the stage for future research. For example, it is argued that unions and employers must conceive of themselves as "crafting governance" so that their joint programs will satisfy their respective interests and be adapted so as to meet changing circumstances. More data are needed, however, on the process by which such crafting occurs. When is formal restructuring called for, and when is informal adjustment sufficient? What if one side sees the need for a shift in the governance arrangement but the other side does not? And, even more basic, what is the impact of change on the governance of joint programs?

One intriguing aspect of the governance question involves the analysis of joint governance structures by political scientists, anthropologists, and sociologists. Individuals from these disciplines are already experienced in examining governance by the state, within communities, and in other contexts and are concerned with issues such as the extent to which governance structures provide checks and balances on different collectivities, protect the interests of minorities, provide individuals with ways of adding meaning to their lives, contribute to a democratic society, and reflect a particular set of social or economic organizing principles. Fresh insights might come from extending the analysis of such matters to joint governance arrangements in the workplace. One particularly challenging governance dilemma that might be of interest to scholars concerns the presence of factions within a union or employer who are opposed to participation in the joint program. What is the status of such individuals who are opposed to the governance arrangement yet part of it?

Given that a relatively small percentage of the U.S. work force is organized, an important but controversial governance issue involves the implications of joint training initiatives for nonunion settings. One would imagine that the implications would be very limited since there are no readily identifiable partners. Anecdotal evidence suggests, however, that a number of nonunion employers are emphasizing employee participation in the design and administration of training programs, including the election of employee representatives to work with management. These developments raise legal questions, such as whether these company-dominated organizations are in violation of the National Labor Relations Act. They also pose complex governance questions: Is the administration of a union-management joint program comparable to the administration of a nonunion program that features extensive employee involvement? And, more controverisal, are the benefits of the two arrangements comparable?

We expect there will be a high degree of variance in the degree of jointness or participation in union-management training initiatives and participative nonunion training initiatives. We do not expect, however, that nonunion settings will be able to replicate the independent representative structure that a union brings to the training process. If they could, joint training would, by implication, have to attend to issues concerning institutional security and the status of unions. It may be unsettling for some to consider that nonunion initiatives can be similar to joint union-management training. It may be unsettling for others to consider that effective training requires bolstering the institutions of unionism. We see these issues as going to the heart of current changes taking place in U.S. industrial relations and hence requiring closer attention.

Public Policy Implications

The governance structures associated with joint training initiatives raise a host of practical, legal, and normative policy issues. On the practical level, government agencies that directly support joint efforts or that provide "pass-through" funds for specific programs may legitimately raise questions about their status. Government has an interest, for example, in seeing that worker training focuses on building general skills that are transferable to other work sites, since an increase in general skills means an increase in the human resource base in the community, state, and nation. In contrast, employers may prefer training that is more job-specific, because they see it as more directly applicable to the given work site and because it encourages employee attachment to the organization. Issues of governance center on both the structures and the choices involved in sorting out competing public and private priorities.

A broad question associated with governance structures concerns the extent to which joint or participative arrangements (unionized or nonunionized) are viewed under the law as employee-dominated labor organizations and thus in violation of the National Labor Relations Act. We find little evidence for concern about such issues in unionized settings, but serious questions arise regarding highly participative nonunionized arrangements. More technical legal questions arise in the process of establishing a distinct nonprofit center for union-management training activities, including bylaws, tax status determinations, and the like.

The most significant policy implication stemming from the governance findings in this volume may well center on the legitimacy and viability of unions in our society. If independent, democratic unions are a necessary component of joint governance structures, then discussion of joint training cannot be separated from issues of labor law reform and other policy matters that affect U.S. unions.

Key Finding 7

Many methods can be used to study joint training. *Multiple methods and approaches can be employed in the study of joint training programs: reports by participants that include survey-based tabulations of program activities; behavioral measurements of program participation; attitudinal assessments of program impact; econometrically oriented assessments of program impact; quasi-experimental program evaluation designs; and insti-*

tutionally oriented research that places training in the context of union-manangement relations.

Research Implications

This volume has presented a broad range of potential research methods for increasing understanding of joint training programs. Each has distinct advantages and limitations. For example, some of the chapters in this volume are by individuals in leadership positions who report on training initiatives in which they have been involved. Such reports are an excellent source of primary data. The disadvantage is that the material heavily emphasizes the most positive features of the programs, rather than the mistakes made or lessons learned the hard way.

The findings presented in chapter 9 are based on a fairly rigorous quasi-experimental design that allows a high degree of confidence in the findings, but the focus is limited to one particular component—the Life Education Advisor—of a much larger range of joint training initiatives.

The survey-based findings in chapter 2 help generalize our knowledge beyond a few vivid cases, but the data merely whet our appetites for more information about each of the locations surveyed.

One key limitation of such research concerns the proximity of the researcher to the joint training activities and thus his or her candor. Closer ties bring greater access to more detailed information, but they also bring greater constraints on what can be put in print. It is likely that every contributor to this volume had to modify certain research methods and temper certain phrases because of a concern about the message that might be conveyed to labor or management leaders. Whether their conclusions are utilitarian (for example, a continuing research relationship is desirable) or motivated by other ethical principles, all the contributors share a commitment to leaving their joint training programs in no worse condition as a result of the research effort. Such commitment to some degree threatens the independence of scholars. Where a social phenomenom is relatively new and fragile, as joint training initiatives are, such trade-offs are inevitable.

In addition to broad choices about methodological approach, a wide range of micro-level methodological concerns have surfaced. For example, there was great ambiguity associated with everything from measures of the scope and structure of training programs to the construction of outcome measures. To address these dilemmas, scholars need a fairly deep institutional understanding of the nature of joint programs and, of course, conceptual clarity about the guiding research questions. In that joint training programs change over time, it may be necessary to use a longitudinal research design to achieve deep institutional understanding. We strongly feel that the diversity of methods used by the contributors to this volume has strengthened the research. No one research method should be imposed. As an emergent phenomenon, joint training is particularly well suited to study using the methodological principle of triangulation—a full picture emerges when the object under study is viewed from multiple vantage points and with different lenses.

Public Policy Implications

Government funds are likely to underwrite, at least in part, many of the evaluation studies and other research centered on joint training programs. Public interest in evaluating this phenomenon can and should be addressed through multiple methods. For example, the use of quasi-experimental designs for cost-benefit analysis could be very helpful in examining the justification for channeling public funds through joint training programs. At the same time, institutionally oriented case studies could offer insight into how to strengthen the links between public and private programs.

Key Finding 8

Programs do not emerge randomly; there are correlates to their existence. *The preliminary data presented in chapter 2 support this contention. Joint programs tend to occur in large firms, in the Midwest, and in industries that are in decline or changing. There is a related correlate: a commitment to jointism is the chief driving force behind the programs. Leadership, the needs of displaced workers and other special populations, technology, and the role of schools and community colleges are also important.*

Research Implications

Because of the limited size of the survey described in chapter 2, the findings are only a beginning. Future research should be done on a larger sample. In this way one could control for all possible variables simultaneously and find out, relatively speaking, the most important factor in helping to establish these programs. Through further research, we could perhaps discover whether joint training programs emerge because of change in general, technological change in particular, change in ownership (through mergers and acquisitions), foreign competition, or changes in the market.

Public Policy Implications

The fact that diffusion of any innovation occurs at different rates may help inform the design of sound public policy for joint training programs. For example, the government may want to encourage training of a generic sort, including joint training, in industries where the technology is changing at a rapid rate. Likewise, it may want to use both current government policies such as EDWAA and WARN, plant closing policies, and the research and policy findings from this volume to justify early intervention in industries forced to lay off workers because of foreign competition. Such intervention would take the form of a joint labor-management training committee where there was a union and an employer who were amenable to such an effort. In either case, the infrastructure would be in place to save the plant before a crisis deepened to the point where adversarial issues dominated. Even two to three months lead time is a very short time period in which to retool workers for new employment.

Conclusions

Joint training is a fascinating and increasingly robust development in industrial relations and worker training. It also has deep implications for research and public policy. It is not, however, a panacea for all problems in industrial relations or for all challenges in training.

Overall Public Policy Implications

The findings presented in this volume argue for active roles for federal, state, and local governments in joint training initiatives. These policy findings can be summarized as follows:

• State and federal governments can play key roles in facilitating the collection of data on the number and scope of joint training programs in the United States.
• The diversity in the scope and content of joint training provides a valuable source of innovations that may be of interest to policy makers.

• The diversity across joint training initiatives makes public-private links more complex, but it also points to an important policy role regarding the facilitation of cross-site learning and diffusion.

• Preliminary evidence suggests that joint training programs may be a preferable mode of service than unilaterally sponsored programs. If so, government policies ought to provide appropriate incentives to encourage joint initiatives.

• Policy makers can facilitate the evaluation of joint training initiatives via quasi-experimental designs and other methods by giving priority to such assessment where public-private links occur.

• Policy makers need to be sensitive in working with joint training programs to the distinct and often opposing interests of labor and management, as well as to the norms associated with joint activities.

• Policy makers concerned with future directions in education policy would be well advised to examine joint training programs, which can provide the education community with a rich source of innovative methods for service delivery, program content, and subject mix.

• The education community can learn from joint training programs only if the educators are sensitive to the collective bargaining context within which joint training occurs.

• Joint training programs raise key policy implications regarding the transferability to nonunion settings of the lessons learned from such programs and suggest that joint training programs depend on there being a strong labor movement in society.

Given that every contributor to this volume reported positive outcomes associated with joint training activities, increasing the government's role vis-à-vis joint training raises a core question: if private joint activities are achieving great gains, is this then an area in which government presence is not needed? Our answer is no; the development of joint training programs is at a juncture where government activities are critical.

While the many successes reported in this volume can be taken as evidence of what can occur in the context of joint governance arrangements, joint training is still occurring in only a small proportion of unionized relationships and therefore represents only a fraction of all employment relationships. (It should be noted that the number is larger if we use the number of bargaining unit members covered rather than the number of bargaining units/firms since joint relationships are disproportionately found in larger firms.) It is our contention that further diffusion—especially to smaller and medium-sized firms and bargaining units—will not take place without government encouragement. The barriers to establishing strong joint programs (cost, time, and the history of the relationship) are just too great otherwise. In addition, certain information-gathering activities are best handled by government.

Research Implications
The following section summarizes the overall research implications of the eight key findings in the volume. They point out both the complexities and the importance of research on joint training.

• More complete data are needed on the number and scope of joint training programs in the United States.
• Developing such data requires clarification of how best to measure the intensity of training, the range of subjects to be measured, the degree of jointness, and other factors.
• The diversity in the scope and content of training offered under joint structures allows for the investigation of a broad range of comparative research questions, but to conduct such work requires a full taxonomy for organizing the range of training activity.
• It is critical to determine the benefits of joint training compared to those of unilateral training. This is best done using quasi-experimental designs. Such research requires high trust with the parties, naturally occurring experimental situations, and strong examples of case studies that highlight the institutional operations of joint programs.
• While the preliminary data presented in chapter 2 suggest that certain conditions—size, amount of change and amount of decline in an industry, economic situation in the region, and experience with jointism—foster the establishment of joint labor-management training programs, there is clearly a need for a national data base that could be used in assessing more fully the relative importance of these factors.

• Further conceptual understanding is required regarding the outcome measures associated with assessments of joint training initiatives.

• Caution and sensitivity are required to overcome the political risks to both labor and management that accompany research on joint training initiatives.

• Traditional methods of program evaluation developed for public training programs such as CETA programs in the 1970s may not be useful in the context of joint training since there is such a diversity of structures and such variation in the anticipated outcomes.

• Links between joint training programs and government (at various levels) and education professionals raise questions about industrial relations theories that begin with assumptions about the bilateral nature of labor and management. The new links urge the development of frameworks that favor a more multilateral approach.

• Additional research is required to understand the evolving roles of education professionals in the workplace, particularly in settings where joint training programs are part of a larger movement that stresses continuous learning and there are direct links between training and strategic planning in the firm.

• Joint training initiatives raise a broad range of governance issues that argue for an institutional perspective rather than the traditional, individually focused psychological and economic perspective on training.

• Consideration of governance aspects of joint training would be greatly enhanced by cross-disciplinary analysis by sociologists, anthropologists, and political scientists.

• The emergence of highly participative structures for training in nonunion settings are not, on their face, equivalent to joint training structures that feature an independent union. Still, key questions must be addressed regarding the similarities and differences in operation and outcomes.

• Multiple methods can and should be used to study joint training initiatives.

One additional issue is the relative importance of joint training in the context of current U.S. industrial relations. It has been argued that the field is in the midst of a transformation (Kochan, Katz, and McKersie 1989). If this is so, then to what extent are joint training programs an integral component of this transformation? More broadly, what is the larger significance of joint training for the field? It is our conviction that joint training initiatives represent a unique opportunity to address simultaneously management concerns with competitiveness and flexibility, labor concerns with employment security and career opportunities, and government concerns with human resource capabilities. We hope further research will bear this out.

REFERENCES

Abelson, Philip H. 1987. "Continuing Education for Blue-Collar Workers." *Science*, November 13, 875.

Abt Associates. 1983. *Displaced Worker Demonstration Program: Interim Status.* Cambridge, Mass.: Abt Associates.

Adams, Avril V. 1978. "The Stock of Human Capital and Differences in Post-School Formal Occupational Training for Middle-Aged." *Southern Economic Journal* 44 (April):929–38.

Adams, Avril V., Stephen L. Mangum, and Philip W. Wirtz. 1987. "Postschool Education and Training Accessible to All?" *Review of Black Political Economy* 15 (Winter):68–86.

Anderson, James G. 1978. "Causal Models in Educational Research: Nonrecursive Models." *American Educational Research* 15:81–97.

Ashenfelter, Orley, and David Card. 1985. "Using the Longitudinal Structure of Earnings to Estimate the Effect of Training Programs." *Review of Economics and Statistics* 67 (November): 648–60.

Baltes, Paul B., and John R. Nesselroade. 1970. "Multivariate Longitudinal and Cross-Sectional Sequences for Analyzing Ontogenetic and Generational Change." *Development Psychology* 2:163–68.

Bassi, Laurie J. 1983. "The Effect of CETA on the Postprogram Earnings of Participants." *Journal of Human Resources* 18:539–56.

Becker, Gary Stanley. 1964. *Human Capital.* New York: National Bureau of Economics.

Bednarzik, Robert W. 1986. "Facilitating Worker Adjustment: Canada's IAS Program." *Entrepreneurial Economy* 4 (May):6-8.

Bellush, Jewel, and Bernard Bellush. 1984. *Union Power and New York: Victor Gotbaum and District Council 37.* New York: Praeger.

Benjamin, Gerald, and T. Norman Heard, eds. 1985. *Making Experience Count: Managing New York in the Carey Era.* Albany, N.Y.: Nelson A. Rockefeller Institute of Government.

Bishop, John H. 1982. *The Social Payoff for Occupationally Specific Training: The Employers' Point of View.* Columbus: National Center for Research in Vocational Education, Ohio State University.

Bloom, Howard S., and Maurren A. McLaughlin. 1982. *CETA Training Programs—Do They Work for Adults?* Washington, D.C.: Joint Congressional Budget Office, National Commission for Employment Policy.

Bluestone, Barry. 1984. "Is De-Industrialization a Myth?" *Annals of the American Academy of Political and Social Science* 475 (September):39–51.

Bluestone, Barry, and Bennett Harrison. 1986. *The Great American Job Machine.* Washington D.C.: U.S. Joint Economic Committee. December.

————. 1988. *De-industrialization of America: Plant Closings, Community Abandonment, and the Dismantling of Basic Industry.* New York: Basic Books.

Bowman, William R. 1986. *Do Displaced Worker Programs "Work"? Final Report.* Annapolis, Md.: Annapolis Economic Research.

Branst, Lee, and Agnes Dubberly. 1988. "Labor/Management Participation: The Nummi Experience." *Quality Progress* (April):30–34.

Brock, William E. 1987. "Future Shock—The American Work Force in the Year 2000." *Community, Technical and Junior College Journal* (February/March):25–26.

Brody, David. 1980. *Workers in Industrial America: Essays on the Twentieth Century Struggle.* New York: Oxford University Press.

Brookfield, Stephen. 1986. *Understanding and Facilitating Adult Learning.* San Francisco: Jossey-Bass.

Brown, Warren. 1988. "General Motors Steps on the Gas." *Washington Post,* April 4–10.

Burstein, Karen S. 1986. *Report to Governor Mario M. Cuomo on Civil Service Revitalization.* Albany: Department of Civil Service. January.

Campbell, Donald T., and Julian Stanley. 1963. *Experimental and Quasi-Experimental Designs for Research.* Chicago: Rand McNally.

Campbell, Paul B., Jack Elliot, Suzanne Laughlin, and Ellen Seusy. 1987. *The Dynamics of Vocational Education Effects on Labor Market Outcomes.* Columbus: National Center for Research in Vocational Education, Ohio State University.

Carmines, Edward G., and John P. McIver. 1981. "Analyzing Models with Unobserved Variables: Analysis of Covariance Structures." In *Social Measurement: Current Issues,* edited by George W. Bohrnstedt and Edgar F. Borgatta, pp. 65–115. Beverly Hills, Calif.: Sage.

Carnevale, Anthony, and Harold Goldstein. 1990. "Schooling and Training for Work in America: An Overview." In *New Developments in Worker Training: A Legacy for the 1990s,* edited by Louis A. Ferman, Michele Hoyman, Joel Cutcher-Gershenfeld, and Ernest J. Savoie, pp. 25–54. Madison, Wisc.: Industrial Relations Research Association.

Castle, C. Hilmon, and Patrick B. Storey. 1968. "Physicians' Needs and Interests in Continuing Medical Education." *Journal of the American Medical Association* 206:611–14.

Charner, Ivan, and Bryna Fraser. 1986. *Different Strokes for Different Folks.* Washington, D.C.: National Institute of Work and Learning.

Cherns, Albert. 1976. "The Principles of Socio-Technical Design." *Human Relations* 29: 783–92.

Cohen, Sanford. 1961. "An Analytical Framework for Labor Relations Law." *Industrial and Labor Relations Review* 14 (April):350–62.

Cohen-Rosenthal, Edward, and Cynthia Burton. 1987. *Mutual Gains: A Guide to Labor-Management Cooperation.* New York: Praeger.

Congressional Budget Office. 1982. *Dislocated Workers: Issues and Federal Options.* Washington, D.C.: GAO.

Cook, Thomas D., and Donald T. Campbell. 1979. *Quasi-Experimentation: Design and Analysis Issues for Field Settings.* Chicago: Rand McNally.

Cooke, William N. 1989. *Cooperative Efforts to Solve Employment Problems.* Washington, D.C.: U.S. Department of Labor, Commission on Workplace Quality and Labor Market Efficiency.

———. 1990. *Labor-Management Cooperation: New Partnerships or Going in Circles.* Kalamazoo, Mich.: W. E. Upjohn Institute.

Cooke, William N., and David G. Meyer. 1990. "Structural and Market Predictors of Corporate Labor Relations Strategies." *Industrial and Labor Relations Review* 43 (January):280–93.

Corson, W., S. Long, and R. Maynard. 1985. *An Impact Evaluation of the Buffalo Dislocated Worker Demonstration Program.* Princeton: Mathematica Policy Research.

Cross, Patricia. 1979. "Adult Learners: Characteristics, Needs, and Interests." In *Lifelong Learning in America,* edited by Richard E. Peterson and Associates, pp. 75–141. San Francisco: Jossey-Bass.

———. 1981. *Adults as Learners.* San Francisco: Jossey-Bass.

Cutcher-Gershenfeld, Joel. 1988. *Tracing a Transformation in Industrial Relations: The Case of the Xerox Corporation and the Amalgamated Clothing and Textile Workers Union.* BLMR 123. Washington, D.C.: Bureau of Labor-Management Relations and Cooperative Programs.

———. 1990. "Constructing a New Social Contract: The Role of State-Level Initiatives in the Transformation of U.S. Industrial Relations." In *Transforming U.S. Industrial Relations,* edited by Franco Ageli, pp. 162–202. Milan, Italy: ISVET-MIT Industrial Relations Section.

Cutcher-Gershenfeld, Joel, Robert B. McKersie, and Richard E. Walton. 1989. "Negotiating Transformation: Negotiation Lesson from Current Developments in Industrial Relations." Paper presented at the Academy of Management meetings.

Cutcher-Gershenfeld, Joel, Robert B. McKersie, and Kirsten R. Wever. 1988. *The Changing Role of Union Leaders.* BLMR 127. Washington, D.C.: Bureau of Labor-Management Relations and Cooperative Programs.

Cutcher-Gershenfeld, Joel, Richard Walton, and Robert McKersie. 1990. "Negotiating Transformation: Bargaining Lessons Learned from the Transformation of Employment Relations." In *Best Papers Proceedings,* edited by Frank Hoy, pp. 366–70. Washington, D.C.: Academy of Management.

Darkenwald, Gordon G., and Sharon Merriam. 1982. *Adult Education: Foundations of Practice.* New York: Harper and Row.

Denker, Joel. *Unions and Universities.* 1981. Montclair, N.J.: Allenheld, Osmun.

"Denver Program in Place Months before Layoff; Uses Some EDWAA Components." 1988. *Employment and Training Reporter,* November 16.

Donahue, Thomas R. 1982. "Labor Looks at Quality of Worklife Programs." Speech, University of Massachusetts, Amherst, January 7.

Dunlop, John. 1958. *Industrial Relations Systems.* New York: Henry Holt.

Employment and Immigration, Canada. 1985. *The Industrial Adjustment Service: Answers for Employers and Workers.*

Ephlin, Donald F. 1986. "United Auto Workers: Pioneers in Labor-Management Partnership." In *Teamwork: Joint Labor-Management Programs in America,* edited by Jerome M. Rosow, pp. 133–45. New York: Pergamon Press.

Fedrau, Ruth. 1984. "Responses to Plant Closures and Major Reductions in Force: Private Sector and Community-Based Models." *Annals of the American Academy of Political and Social Science* 475 (September):80–95.

Ferman, Louis A., and Michele Hoyman. 1988. "Report on the UAW-Ford Joint Training Program" (unpublished).

Flaim, Paul O., and Ellen Sehgal. 1985. "Displaced Workers of 1979–1983: How Have They Fared?" *Monthly Labor Review* 108 (June):3–16.

Foerman, Sue R., Robert E. Quinn, and Michael P. Thompson. 1987. "Bridging Management Practice and Theory: New York State's Public Service Training Program." *Public Administration Review* (July/Aug.): 310–19.

Fornell, Claes. 1982. "A Second Generation of Multivariate Analysis: An Overview." In *A Second Generation of Multivariate Analysis,* edited by Claes Fornell, pp. 1–21. New York: Praeger.

Fossum, John. 1990. "New Dimensions in the Design and Delivery of Corporate Training Programs." In *New Developments in Worker Training: A Legacy for the 1990s,* edited by Louis A. Ferman, Michele Hoyman, Joel Cutcher-Gershenfeld, and Ernest J. Savoie, pp. 129–56. Madison, Wisc.: Industrial Relations Research Association.

Fraser, Bryan S. 1980. *The Structure of Adult Learning, Education and Training Opportunity in the United States.* Washington, D.C.: National Institute for Work and Learning.

Fuchs, Victor R. 1983. *How We Live.* Cambridge: Harvard University Press.

General Accounting Office. 1986. *Dislocated Workers: Extent of Business Closures, Layoffs and the Public and Private Response.* HRD 86–4. Washington, D.C.: GAO. July.

———. 1987a. *Dislocated Workers: Local Programs and Outcomes under the Job Training Partnership Act.* HRD 87–41. Washington, D.C.: GAO. March.

———. 1987b. *Dislocated Workers: Exemplary Local Projects under the Job Training Partnership Act.* HRD 87–70BR. Washington, D.C.: GAO. April.

———. 1987c. *Plant Closings: Information on Advance Notice and Assistance to Dislocated Workers*. Washington, D.C.: GAO. April.

Goldfield, Michael. 1989. "Worker Insurgency: Radical Organization and-New Deal Labor Legislation." *American Political Science Review* 83 (December):1257–84.

Goldstein, Howard. 1981. *Social Learning and Change*. London: Tavistock.

Gordus, Jeanne P. 1987. *A Status Report on the UAW-Ford Life Education Planning Program*. Center Report 6. Ann Arbor: Institute of Science and Technology, University of Michigan.

Gordus, Jeanne P., Cheng Kuo, and Karen Yamakawa. 1987. "An Analysis of Participation in Adult Education: Evidence from a Quasi-Experiment." Institute of Science and Technology, University of Michigan (unpublished).

Grasso, John T., and John R. Shea. 1979. *Vocational Education and Training: Impact on Youth*. Berkeley, Calif.: Carnegie Council on Policy Studies in Higher Education.

Gray, Lois, and Joyce Kornbluh. 1990. "New Directions in Labor Education." In *New Developments in Worker Training: A Legacy for the 1990s*, edited by Louis A. Ferman, Michele Hoyman, Joel Cutcher-Gershenfeld, and Ernest J. Savoie, pp. 91–128. Madison, Wisc.: Industrial Relations Research Association.

Green, Thomas F. 1969. "The Concept of Teaching." In *Teaching and Learning*, edited by Donald Vandenberg, pp. 5–14. Urbana: University of Illinois Press.

Greenberg, Jonathan. 1988. "Sold Short." *Mother Jones*, May.

Gustman, Alan L., and Steinmeier, Thomas L. 1982. "The Relation between Vocational Training in High School and Economic Outcomes." *Industrial and Labor Relations Review* 36 (October):73–87.

Hansen, Gary B. 1984a. "Ford and the UAW Have a Better Idea: A Joint Labor-Management Approach to Plant Closings and Worker Retraining." *Annals of the American Academy of Political Science* 475 (September):158–74.

———. 1984b. *The San Jose Assembly Plant: UAW-Ford Approaches to Retraining and Job Assistance for Dislocated Employees*. Report 4. Dearborn, Mich.: UAW-Ford National Development and Training Center. November.

———. 1985. "An Assessment of the UAW-Ford Joint Approach to the Training and Retraining of Workers." In *Proceedings of the 1985 Spring Meeting of the Industrial Relations Research Association*, pp. 548–52. Madison, Wisc.: Industrial Relations Research Association.

———. 1986. *Two Years Later: A Followup Survey of Labor Market Status and Adjustment of Workers Displaced by the San Jose Assembly Plant Closure*. Logan: Business and Economic Development Services, Utah State University.

———. 1987. "A Follow-up Survey of Workers Displaced by the Ford San Jose Assembly Plant Closure." In *Proceedings of the Fortieth Annual Meeting of the Industrial Relations Research Association*, pp. 125–34. Madison, Wisc.: Industrial Relations Research Association.

Hill, Martha S., Sue Augustyniak, Greg J. Duncan, Gerald Gurin, Patricia Gurin, Jeffrey K. Liker, James N. Morgan, and Michael Ponza. 1985.

Motivation and Economic Mobility. Ann Arbor: Institute for Social Research, University of Michigan.

Horvath, Francis W. 1987. "The Pulse of Economic Change: Displaced Workers of 1981–1985." *Monthly Labor Review* 110 (June): 3–12.

House, James S. 1981. *Work Stress and Social Support*. Reading, Mass.: Addison Wesley.

Howitt, Arnold, John Wells, and Stacey Marx. 1989. "A National Overview of State Labor-Management Cooperation Programs." Paper presented at the Forty-second Annual Meeting of the Industrial Relations Research Association, Atlanta, December 28–30.

Hugentobler, Margrit, and Susan J. Schurman. 1988. *Local Paid Educational Leave Program: Assessment of Changes in Participant Perspectives*. Technical Report. Ann Arbor: University of Michigan. November.

Ichiniowski, Casey, John Delaney, and David Lewin. 1989. "The New Human Resource Management in the U.S. Workplace: Is It Really New or Is It Nonunion?" *Relations Industrielles* 44 (1):97–123.

Israel, Barbara A., Susan J. Schurman, and James S. House. 1989. "Action Research on Occupational Stress: Involving Workers as Researchers." *International Journal of Health Services* 19 (Winter):135–55.

Janis, Irving L. 1983. "The Role of Social Support in Adherence to Stressful Decisions." *American Psychologist* 38:143–60.

Joreskog, K. G., and D. Sorbom. 1984. *LISREL VI: User's Guide*. 3rd ed. Mooresville, Ind.: Scientific Software.

Kantor, Rosabeth. 1984. *The Change Masters*. New York: Touchstone Books.

Kassalow, Everett M. 1987. "Employee Training and Development: A Joint Union-Management Response to Structural and Technological Change." In *Proceedings of the Fortieth Annual Meeting of the Industrial Relations Research Association*, pp. 107–17. Madison, Wisc.: Industrial Relations Research Association.

Katz, Harry C., and Charles F. Sable. 1985. "The Future of Automaking: What Role for Unions?" *Technology Review* (October):54–61.

Katz, Harry C., Thomas Kochan, and Kenneth Gobeille. 1983. "Industrial Relations Performance, Economic Performance, and QWL Programs: An Interplant Analysis." *Industrial and Labor Relations Review* 37 (October): 3–17.

Kay, Evelyn R. 1982. *Participation in Adult Education, 1981*. ERIC Document Reproduction Service no. ED 221 751. Washington, D.C.: National Center for Education Statistics.

Keller, M. 1989. *Rude Awakening: The Rise, Fall, and Struggle for Recovery of General Motors*. New York: William Morrow.

Kilmann, Ralph H., Teresa Joyce Covin, and Associates. 1988. *Corporate Transformation: Revitalizing Organizations for a Competitive World*. San Francisco: Jossey-Bass.

Kochan, Thomas, Joel Cutcher-Gershenfeld, and John Paul MacDuffie. 1989. "Employee Participation, Work Redesign, and New Technology:

Implications for Public Policy in the 1990s." Report prepared for U.S. Department of Labor Commission on Workforce Quality and Labor Market Efficiency.

Kochan, Thomas, Harry C. Katz, and Robert B. McKersie. 1986. *The Transformation of American Industrial Relations.* New York: Basic Books.

Kochan, Thomas A., Harry C. Katz, and Nancy R. Mower. 1984. *Worker Participation and American Unions: Threat or Opportunity.* Kalamazoo, Mich.: W. E. Upjohn Institute.

Kornbluh, Hyman, Richard Pipan, and Susan J. Schurman. 1987. "Empowerment Learning in Workplaces." *Journal of Socialization Research and Educational Sociology* 4:253–68.

Kornbluh, Joyce. 1987. *A New Deal for Workers' Education.* Urbana: University of Illinois Press.

Kuhn, Thomas. 1970. *The Structure of Scientific Revolutions.* 2d ed. Chicago: University of Chicago Press.

Kulik, Jane. 1986. *UAW/Ford Employee Development and Training: A Case Study of Two Program Approaches.* Cambridge, Mass.: Abt Associates.

Kulik, Jane, and Howard Bloom. 1986. *The Worker Adjustment Demonstration Evaluation: Preliminary Impact Report.* Cambridge, Mass.: Abt Associates.

Kulik, Jane, and Linda Sharpe. 1985. *The Worker Adjustment Demonstration Projects: A Comparative Evaluation Report.* Cambridge, Mass.: Abt Associates.

Kulik, Jane, Dalton Smith, and Ernst Stromsdorfer. 1984. *The Downriver Community Conference Economic Adjustment Program: Final Evaluation Report.* Cambridge, Mass.: Abt Associates.

Levine, David, and George Strauss. 1989. "Employee Participation and Involvement." Report prepared for U.S. Department of Labor Commission on Workforce Quality and Labor Market Efficiency.

Levitan, Sar, and Frank Gallo. 1990. "Uncle Sam's Helping Hand: Educating, Training, and Employing the Disadvantaged." In *New Developments in Worker Training: A Legacy for the 1990s,* edited by Louis A. Ferman, Michele Hoyman, Joel Cutcher-Gershenfeld, and Ernest J. Savoie, pp. 225–56. Madison, Wisc.: Industrial Relations Research Association.

Liang, Jersey, and Kenneth A. Bollen. 1985. "Sex Differences in the Structure of the Philadelphia Geriatric Center Morale Scale." *Journal of Gerontology* 40:468–77.

Lilliard, Lee A., and Hong Tan. 1986. *Private Sector Training: Who Gets It and What Are Its Effects?* Santa Monica, Calif.: Rand Corp.

Mangum, Stephen, and Avril Adams. 1987. "The Labor Market Impacts Transferability of Post-School Occupational Training for Young Men." *Growth and Change* 18 (Fall):57–73.

Mangum, Stephen, and David E. Ball. 1989. "The Transferability of Military-Provided Occupational Training in the Post-Draft Era." *Industrial and Labor Relations Review* 42 (January):230–45.

Mangum, Stephen, Garth Mangum, and Gary Hansen. 1990. "Assessing the Returns to Training." In *New Developments in Worker Training: A Legacy for* the 1990s, edited by Louis A. Ferman, Michele Hoyman, Joel Cutcher-Gershenfeld, and Ernest J. Savoie, pp. 55–89. Madison, Wisc.: Industrial Relations and Research Association.

Maruyama, Geoffrey, and Bill McGarvey. 1980. "Evaluating Causal Models: An Application of Maximum-Likelihood Analysis of Structural Equations." *Psychological Bulletin* 87:502–12.

Meyer, Richard. 1982. "Job Training in the Schools." In *Job Training for Youth*, edited by Robert Taylor, Howard Rosen, and Frank C. Pratzener. Columbus: National Center for Research in Vocational Education, Ohio State University.

Mintzberg, Henry. 1987. "Crafting Strategy." *Harvard Business Review* (July/August):66–77.

Monat, Jacques, and Hedva Sarfati, eds. 1986. *Workers' Participation: A Voice in Decisions, 1981–1985.* Geneva: International Labour Office.

National Alliance of Business. 1988. *Back to Work—The States and Dislocated Workers.* Washington, D.C.: National Alliance of Business.

National Governors' Association. 1988. "The Emerging Role of States in Labor-Management Cooperation." *Labor Notes,* August 29.

Nordhuag, O. 1987. "Adult Education and Social Science: A Theoretical Framework." *Adult Education Quarterly* 38:1–13.

Novak, Joseph. 1977. *A Theory of Education.* Ithaca, N.Y.: Cornell University Press.

Parker, Mike, and Jane Slaughter. 1988. *Choosing Sides: Unions and the Team Concept.* Boston: South End Press.

People and Productivity: A Challenge to Corporate America. New York: New York Stock Exchange, Office of Economic Research.

Pestillo, Peter J. 1983. "Employee Development Enables Ford to Lead Change, Not Be Led by It." *Financier* 3(9):34–38.

Petersen, Donald E. 1987. "The UAW-Ford EDTP." *Community, Technical and Junior College Journal* (August/September):25–27.

Piore, Michael, and Charles Sabel. 1984. *The Second Industrial Divide: Possibilities for Prosperity.* New York: Basic Books.

Podgursky, Michael, and Paul Swaim. 1987. "Job Displacement and Earnings Loss: Evidence from the Displaced Worker Survey." *Industrial and Labor Relations Review* 41 (October):17–29.

Poling, Harold A. 1988. Speech at Friends of the Labor Department Seventy-fifth Anniversary Dinner, Washington, D.C., March 10.

Puetz, B. E. 1980. "Differences between Indiana Registered Nurse Attenders and Non-Attenders in Continuing Education in Nursing Activities." *Journal of Continuing Education in Nursing* 11(2):19–26.

Reilly, John. 1987. "Once Mighty GM Battles to Recover." *Ann Arbor News,* September 20.

"Report to the National Center." 1987. Report prepared for the National Center for Employee Development.

Root, Kenneth. 1984. "The Human Response to Plant Closures." *Annals of the American Academy of Political and Social Science* 475 (September): 52–65.

Rosow, Jerome M., and Robert Zager. 1988. *Training—The Competitive Edge.* San Francisco: Jossey-Bass.

Rubenson, K. 1977. *Participation in Recurrent Education.* Paris: Center for Educational Research and Innovations, Organization for Economic Cooperation and Development.

Ruttenburg, Ruth. 1990. *The Role of Labor-Management Committees in Safeguarding Worker Safety and Health.* BLMR 121. Washington, D.C.: Bureau of Labor-Management Relations and Cooperative Programs.

Savoie, Ernest J. 1985. "Current Developments and Future Agenda in Union-Management Cooperation in Training and Retraining of Workers." In *Proceedings of the 1985 Spring Meeting of the Industrial Relations Research Association*, pp. 535-47. Madison, Wisc.: Industrial Relations Research Association.

———. 1986. "Creating the Workforce of the Future: The Ford Focus." Statement submitted to the President's Advisory Committee on Mediation and Conciliation. September 16.

Scanlan, C. L. 1986. *Deterrents to Participation: An Adult Education Dilemma.* Information Series no. 308. Columbus: National Center for Research in Vocational Education, Ohio State University.

Schultz, Theodore W. 1961. "Investment in Human Capital." *American Economic Review* 52:1–17.

Schurman, Susan J. 1989. "Reuniting Labor and Learning: Toward a Holistic Theory of Work." In *Socialization and Learning at Work: A New Approach to the Learning Process*, edited by Heinz Leyman and Hyman Kornbluh, pp. 42–68. Aldershot, Eng.: Gower Press.

Schuster, Michael H. 1984. *Union-Management Cooperation.* Kalamazoo, Mich.: W. E. Upjohn Institute.

Secretary of Labor's Task Force on Economic Adjustment and Worker Dislocation. 1986. "Adjustment Assistance in a Competitive Society: Partners in Progress." Report. December 11.

Serrin, William. 1973. *The Company and the Union.* New York: Knopf.

Siegel, Irving H., and Edgar Weinberg. 1982. *Labor-Management Cooperation: The American Experience.* Kalamazoo, Mich.: W. E. Upjohn Institute.

Sultan, Paul. 1989. "Literacy in the Workplace." Paper presented at meetings of the Industrial Relations Research Association, Southern Illinois University, Edwardsville, May 19.

Sutton, Robert I. and Susan J. Schurman. 1985. "On Studying Emotionally Hot Topics: Lessons from an Investigation of Organizational Death." In *Exploring Clinical Methods for Social Research*, edited by David N. Berg and Kenwyn K. Smith, pp. 333–49. Beverly Hills, Calif.: Sage.

Task Force on the New York State Public Workforce in the Twenty-first Century. 1989. *Public Service through the State Government Workforce: Meeting the Challenge of Change.* Albany, N.Y.: Nelson A. Rockefeller Institute of Government. February.

Taylor, E. B. 1967. "Relationship between the Career Changes of Lawyers and Their Participation in Continuing Legal Education." Ph.D. dissertation, University of Nebraska.

Tomsho, Robert. 1987. "The Big Squeeze." *Dallas Life,* October 11.

Treinen, Donald, and Kenneth Ross. 1989. "The Alliance." Presentation to the Facilitating Worker Adjustment through Labor-Management Cooperation Conference, January 5.

U.S. Department of Education. Office of Post-Secondary Education. 1988. *Comprehensive Program Information and Application Procedures, Fiscal Year 1989.* Washington, D.C.: Department of Education.

U.S. Department of Labor. 1986. *Economic Adjustment and Worker Dislocation in a Competitive Society.* Washington, D.C.: Department of Labor. December.

————. Commission of Workforce Quality and Labor Market Efficiency. 1989. *Work Re-Design and New Technology: Implications for Public Policy in the 1990s.* Washington, D.C.: Department of Labor.

United Steelworkers of America. 1988a. *Responding to Steelworkers' Needs in a Changing Economic Environment.* Pittsburgh: United Steelworkers of America.

————. 1988b. Policy statement, Basic Steel Industry Conference. December.

Walton, Richard E., and Robert B. McKersie. 1965. *A Behavioral Theory of Labor Negotiations: An Analysis of a Social Interaction System.* New York: McGraw-Hill.

Warren, Alfred S. 1986. "Quality of Work Life at General Motors." In *Teamwork: Joint Labor-Management Programs in America,* edited by Jerome M. Rosow, pp. 119-32. New York: Pergamon Press.

Weinstein, Steve. 1987. "The New Safeway." *Progressive Grocer.* November.

Welch, Finis. 1975. "Human Capital Theory: Education, Discrimination, and Life Cycles." *American Economic Review* 65:65–73.

Westat, Inc. 1982. "Net Impact No. 1, the Impact of CETA on 1978 Earnings: Participants in Selected Program Activities Who Entered CETA during FY 1976." Report prepared for the U.S. Department of Labor under contract 23–25–75–07.

Wiegand, R. 1966. "Factors Related to Participation in Continuing Education among a Selected Group of Graduate Engineers." Ph.D. dissertation, Florida State University.

ABOUT THE AUTHORS

Richard Baker is an industrial adjustment consultant with the Governor's Office for Job Training in Michigan, where he organizes joint labor-management committees at work sites that are closing or experiencing permanent layoffs. He has also assisted communities in developing economic strategies after plant closings and massive layoffs.

Joel Cutcher-Gershenfeld is an assistant professor at Michigan State University with appointments in the School of Labor and Industrial Relations and the Social Science Research Bureau. He has written extensively in the area of labor-management relations and is the co-editor of *New Developments in Worker Training: A Legacy for the 1990's*. He holds a Ph.D. in industrial relations from the Massachusetts Institute of Technology.

Kenneth K. Dickinson is the Ford co-executive director of the UAW-Ford National Education, Development and Training Center, where he is responsible with the UAW co-executive director for developing and administering a wide range of education and training programs for UAW-represented Ford employees. He has held various industrial relations positions with Ford at plant, division, and corporate levels.

Louis A. Ferman is a professor of social work and the director of research in industrial relations at the University of Michigan. He has published extensively on coping with unemployment, plant shutdowns, economic/job development, and the informal economy. As a consultant, he has worked with AT&T, the Ford Motor Company, and General Motors, as well as the United Automobile Workers and the Communications Workers of America. He has also conducted numerous workshops on union-management training.

Jeanne Prial Gordus was the director of the Employment Transition Program at the University of Michigan School of Social Work from 1982 until her death in 1990. She directed several projects that helped unemployed workers rejoin the labor force and studied the social and psychological effects of unemployment, plant shutdowns, and early retirement. She was the author of six books and monographs and about forty articles and reports on unemployment.

Lois Gray is the Jean McKelvey–Alice Grant Professor of Labor-Management Relations in the New York State School of Industrial and Labor Relations at Cornell University. She was the associate dean and director of extension and public service for the school for twelve years, during which she oversaw educational and technical services to unions, management, and government in New York State. She is the author of numerous publications dealing with training and education and chairs the New York State Apprenticeship and Training Council.

Michele Hoyman is an associate professor of political science at the University of Missouri–St. Louis and a fellow at the Centers for Public Policy Research. She is also a professional arbitrator. Hoyman's research focuses on the impact of law on the behavior of labor unions and on union democracy. A regular contributor to leading law and policy journals, she holds a Ph.D. in political science from the University of Michigan.

Margrit K. Hugentobler is an assistant research scientist at the Labor Studies Center and the School of Public Health at the University of Michigan. She is currently involved in teaching, evaluation, and research activities in a variety of joint labor-management projects in the areas of worker education, workplace health and safety, and worker participation.

Cheng Kuo is an assistant professor at Central Connecticut State University. Among her research interests are participation by adults in education.

Michael G. McMillan is the executive director of the AFL-CIO Human Resources Development Institute, a position he has held since 1985. Before becoming director, he served as assistant director and as national building trades coordinator for HRDI's national office. He has also been coordinator of building trades organizing in the Gulf Coast area for the AFL-CIO Department of Organization and Field Services.

Thomas B. Quimby is a management specialist and district director of the Capital District for the Extension Division of the New York State School of Industrial and Labor Relations at Cornell University. He works with public and private sector employers in such areas as human resources management, labor relations, and conflict resolution. He has been on the staff of the New York State Civil Service Employees Association and president of the Albany Dispute Mediation Program.

Kenneth Ross is a co-founder and the co-executive director of the Alliance for Employee Growth and Development. Before joining the Alliance, he was division staff manager of labor relations for AT&T and a manager with Northwestern Bell. Known for his expertise in work force empowerment through labor-management programs, Ross lectures frequently to management and union groups.

Ernest J. Savoie is director of employee development at the Ford Motor Company, where he is responsible for planning, designing, and installing a wide range of human resource development programs for represented and nonrepresented hourly and salaried employees. He has served in a variety of professional, supervisory, and managerial human resource positions at Ford and has been a member of the Ford National Negotiating Committee since 1976.

Kathy Schrier is the administrator of the District Council 37 Education Fund of AFSCME, which develops and implements training programs for union members. She has also served as the associate administrator of the education fund and as the coordinator of the union's steward, leadership, and staff development programs.

Susan J. Schurman is director of the Labor Studies Center at the University of Michigan. She is also a research investigator for the University of Michigan School of Public Health. She has published extensively on worker participation in decision making.

Hal Stack is director of the Labor Studies Center at Wayne State University. He worked closely with the UAW-GM Human Resource Center during the development of both national and local paid educational leave programs.

Elizabeth S. Tomasko is an international representative to the UAW National Ford Department. She is responsible for administering the joint

UAW-Ford Health and Safety Program. A member of the UAW since 1966, she has held a variety of positions with the union.

Donald Treinen is the co-executive director of the Alliance for Employee Growth and Development. A full-time representative of the Communications Workers of America, he began his union career as the shop steward for his AT&T work location and since then has served as chief steward, vice-president, and president of his local and as assistant to the vice-president of the CWA.

Karen Yamakawa is a senior research associate in the Employment Transition Program at the University of Michigan School of Social Work. Her work has focused on the economic and noneconomic effects of job loss on workers. Her work on retraining and workplace education has resulted in more than a dozen articles and reports.

INDEX

United Steelworkers of America,
125–26
United University Professions (UUP),
99, 106–8
University of Michigan, 61, 65, 77,
144, 156, 166
Upgrading workers' skills, 18

Value of education, perception of,
172, 173, 179
Vendored services, in-house vs., 193,
201, 210
Viani, Al, 99
Vocational training, 232

Wages of reemployed displaced workers, 141–44

Wagner-Peyser Act, 118
Wayne State University, 77
West, programs in the, 24
Western Electric, 33
White Consolidated Industries, 144
Williams, Lynn, 125
Williams, Raymond, 40, 41
Worker Adjustment and Retraining
Notification Act (WARN), 150
Worker Literacy Consortium (NYC),
102–3

Xerox Corporation, 213

Yamakawa, Karen, 9, 167